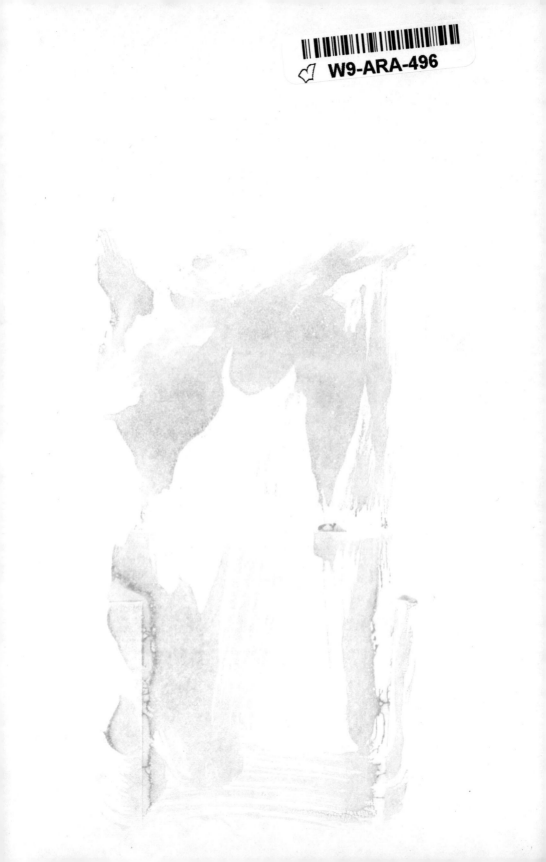

DIVORCE TALK

Divorce Talk

WOMEN AND MEN MAKE SENSE OF PERSONAL RELATIONSHIPS

Catherine Kohler Riessman

RUTGERS UNIVERSITY PRESS
New Brunswick and London

Excerpts from *The Cocktail Party*, copyright 1950 by T. S. Eliot and renewed 1978 by Esme Valerie Eliot, and from *Four Quartets*, copyright 1943 by T. S. Eliot and renewed 1971 by Esme Valerie Eliot, reprinted by permission of Harcourt Brace Jovanovich, Inc., and Faber and Faber Ltd.
Excerpt from *Diving into the Wreck*, copyright 1973 by Adrienne Rich, reprinted by permission of W. W. Norton & Co. and Adrienne Rich.
The author wishes to thank the editors of *Gender & Society, Social Science and Medicine*, and *Smith College Studies in Social Work* for permission to reprint material that appeared in different form in these journals.

Library of Congress Cataloging-in-Publication Data
Riessman, Catherine Kohler, 1939–
    Divorce talk : women and men make sense of personal relationships
/ Catherine Kohler Riessman.
        p.   cm.
    Bibliography: p.
    Includes index.
    ISBN 0-8135-1502-5 (cloth)   ISBN 0-8135-1503-3 (pbk.)
    1. Divorced people—United States—Psychology.   2. Interpersonal
relations.   I. Title.
HQ834.R54   1990
306.89—dc20   89–36065
                                                                    CIP

British Cataloging-in-Publication information available

To the memory of my mother
Mary Conway Kohler

CONTENTS

PREFACE

How do women and men make sense of getting divorced? Like other events that we experience during the course of our lives—job loss, a move we don't want to make, the death of a family member or a friend—divorce challenges the stability and continuity of the world we take for granted. To cope with events that jar our illusions of permanency, we usually talk about them. We reflect on what has happened, assign motives, and characterize the situation in the context of a general scheme of meaning, which includes explanations provided by our cultures. Through interpretation, we not only render events meaningful but also empower ourselves to go on, despite loss and change.

I studied a group of divorced or divorcing women and men to see how they went about making sense of divorce and how they went on with their lives after they had separated from their spouses. I learned from them that although divorce is difficult, interpretative work is the way through the hardship. The healing and empowering effects of talking about the process of reconstructing themselves allow the divorced to develop positive outlooks on their lives. In contrast to other students of the topic, I do not conclude that divorce has a generally negative impact on the partners.

Although women and men go through much that is the same when they divorce, they also have experiences that are distinct to their gender. The sexes make different sense of divorce. Women, more than men, find much to praise in their divorced state, even though they often experience considerable personal trauma and financial hardship. Women and men remember their marriages quite differently, which suggests that what they are looking for when they marry again may not be the same. Both women and men go through a process of defining the marriage as moribund, but they seem to be mourning different dreams of what marriage ought to provide. When marriages end, women and men construct different lives, distinguished by gender-linked pressures and opportunities, and both groups claim to discover new aspects of themselves. In a word, the divorced say it isn't all bad.

I came to these findings because I used an approach that allowed me to enter into the points of view of those I studied. What began as a survey of the adaptation patterns of women and men became a more intensive study of the ways women and men talked and made sense of their experiences. The research process provided an opportunity for the divorced to go through a thoughtful assessment of their lives, and these assessments, in turn, became categories for analysis and interpretation. There are numerous approaches that rely on inter-pretative methodology, of course, including symbolic interaction, hermeneutics, psychoanalytic investigation, and qualitative sociol-ogy. My approach probably comes closest to symbolic interaction, though I do not in every case refer specifically to this tradition. Like it, however, I focus on process, language, and the definition of the situation—member's views of social reality.

I should add that although I am a sociologist, this work does not fit neatly into any single theoretical or methodological tradition of that discipline. It is an effort at "blurred genres," as Clifford Geertz so eloquently described in *Local Knowledge*—reaching into a variety of disciplines for insights and methods to study social life. Through at-tention to the interpretation of meaning as an issue, increasing num-bers of social scientists are trying to forge links between sociology and the humanities. I also take inspiration from Henry Glassie, whose words in the preface of his book, *Passing the Time in Ballymenone*, articu-late what "blurred genres" can mean:

> We have one enterprise. We could call it historical ethnography or local history or folklore in context or the sociology of the creative act or the ecology of consciousness—the potential for flashy neologism seems boundless—but whatever its name, study is distorted and reality is mangled when disciplines harden into ideology, categories freeze into

facts, and the sweet, terrible wholeness of life is dismembered for burial . . . if work is good old categories will slip and shift, and then melt away as we find the place where social science joins the humanities, where art and culture and history, time and space, connect, where theoretical and empirical studies fuse.

To set the stage for what follows, I begin with the historical and cultural context of divorce in Chapter 1. In the next four chapters I analyze "divorce talk" in several different ways, comparing how women and men explain why they divorced and how they felt afterward.

Chapter 2 examines divorce accounts—what people say to explain why they are no longer married. I treat these accounts as templates, into which women and men have poured their visions and passions for marriage. The approach here is on the content more than on the form of the talk, that is, *what* they say rather than *how* they say it. Chapter 3 shows how personal meanings and narrative form are related, and how the interview context enters into each narrative because of the "teller's problem"; the interviewer and interviewee together produce a text, making sense together. The *how* of the telling is important in understanding *what* it is that is significant for the teller. It is becoming common for investigators to refer to, and sometimes to recount, the "stories" subjects tell in interviews. Here I go one step further and analyze how narratives are told, how divorcing individuals reconstruct their shattered selves through the language of autobiography and heal parts that only narrative can bind.

Chapters 4 and 5 are mirror images of each other, one analyzing how women as opposed to men express and interpret the personal trauma of divorce, and the other analyzing how women as opposed to men make positive sense out of it. I also use both quantitative and qualitative findings in Chapter 4 to discuss what may be termed the feminization of psychological distress, through which traditional mental health research has considerably underestimated distress in men. In Chapter 5 I examine the considerable innovation that divorce brings in its stead, as individuals construct new structures of meaning to replace what they have lost. Instead of considering only pathology (as most studies of divorce have done), this work looks at benefits, too. There may be clues here to understanding why so many people are getting divorced and what the positive side of the trend is. The book ends with reflections on divorce, remarriage, and alternatives to remarriage.

In sum, this book concerns the divorcing process, as veterans of the experience understand it. The analytic approach emphasizes the relationship between personal experience and historical, social, and cultural contexts—the link between people and settings, self and society. The detailed analysis of personal narratives knits these themes together and shows more precisely how the divorced create themselves and their social worlds through language and interpretation. The contrast throughout is between women and men—how gender shapes the experience and meaning of divorce.

CONTEXTS have been important for my interpretive work, just as they were for those I studied. The research project was originally designed and the data collected with Naomi Gerstel. As my interests shifted to the interpretative process and to language, we eventually decided to pursue independent projects. Yet ideas we developed together infuse this book.

I have been in the fortunate position of working in two settings, Smith College School for Social Work and the Department of Psychiatry of Harvard Medical School, that have greatly facilitated this project. As a sociologist and social worker in a school of social work, I have not had to attend to some of the disciplinary imperatives that sociologists face in traditional departments, and this fact has indirectly made this book possible. I thank two deans of the School for Social Work, Katherine Gabel and Ann Hartman, who have each been supportive of my research in very different ways. I also received a Brown Foundation Award from the Clinical Research Institute at Smith, which supported the research for Chapter 5. Peg Whalen did much of the computer work, always with care, and Debbie Katz assisted immeasurably with tracking down references. The clerical support at Smith was extraordinary, especially from Muriel Poulin, who always came through, and provided badly needed humor, as well.

An individual postdoctoral fellowship from the National Institute of Mental Health (5F32MH09206) enabled me to take a leave from

Smith and go to the Department of Psychiatry at Harvard Medical School to study qualitative methods, which, in turn, transformed the study. Elliot Mishler in the Laboratory of Social Psychiatry at the Massachusetts Mental Health Center was my mentor while at Harvard, and his thoughtful criticism of my work did not end with the conclusion of my fellowship. He taught me about narrative approaches, supported me through my "paradigm shift," and was an attentive (but uncontrolling) midwife for the project. My debt to him is very deep. The weekly research seminar he led at Harvard, and the exciting discussions all the fellows had in it about alternative methods, also provided a critical context for my work.

Friends, many of whom also happen to be first-rate social scientists, were another important source of support and help. Rosanna Hertz and Patricia Rieker read the entire manuscript and gave much thoughtful criticism. Gail Hornstein read several drafts of the whole work with a particularly critical eye, picking up (among many other things) my changing epistemologies as the book progressed — which helped me not only to construct a more coherent book but also to think about and write the Appendix in the way I did. Elliot Mishler patiently read draft after draft and always helped me to clarify my ideas and tighten my prose. I am also grateful for the support of Susan Bell, Jack Clark, Uta Gerhardt, Joy Newmann, Cynthia Shilkret, and Alexandra Todd, some of whom also commented on draft chapters. Others who gave good suggestions for revision at various points were Kathy Davis, Sue Fisher, Joan Laird, Charles Lemert, and Dennie Wolf. Sandy Jencks may not be aware how helpful our conversation was (sitting on the banks of Long Pond), but he helped me think through how to handle social class in the book. Lyn Harrod gave me many insights on our long walks together through the woods of Cape Cod, and her warm friendship made my final work on the manuscript much easier. Finally, the members of my two study groups provided important feedback and support: my philosophical friends from schools of social work in the Boston area, and the narrative group from the Massachusetts Inter-disciplinary Discourse Analysis Seminar (MIDAS).

Marlie Wasserman at Rutgers University Press understood and valued the approach of the book from the very start. The readers she obtained for the manuscript, Arlene Kaplan Daniels and Deborah

Tannen, were of immeasurable help in revisions; I thank them both. Elizabeth Gretz's editing of the final manuscript was superb.

The study could not have been done without the cooperation of the women and men who agreed to be interviewed and who talked so fully and so frankly about their lives. Although they cannot be identified by name, I am deeply grateful to them. My three children— Robin, Janet, and Jeff—continue to be an important context for my life and my work. They have taught me, among many other things, that children of divorce can grow into happy and productive adults. Finally, I thank my mother, who made this book possible in more ways than one.

Wellfleet, Massachusetts

DIVORCE TALK

CHAPTER 1

Making Sense of Divorce

Personal Meaning in a Social Context

For there is no creature whose inward being is so strong that it is not greatly determined by what lies outside it.

—GEORGE ELIOT, Middlemarch

Divorce has touched the lives of more individuals today than ever before in history. The marital bonds that in earlier generations (and in many parts of the world to this day) were broken most often by death are in many Western societies now most often broken by divorce. As a relatively common response to marital unhappiness, divorce is a recent phenomenon, characteristic of the past century only.[1] Yet because of it, the world is changing for the large numbers of people whose lives are uprooted by the experience.

Like death, divorce can be traumatic, because our lives are organized around particular relationships that are crucial to how we find meaning in our lives. When we lose an important relationship, whole structures of meaning disintegrate, as do the routines of everyday life organized around the relationship, and these losses often lead to distress, anxiety, and grief. We search for a compass, a new structure to give us bearing, as we try to separate emotionally both from the person and from our own previous identity associated with the relationship. Eventually, we reconstitute a new identity so that we can live and act. Central in this process is the development of an account—what happened and why. Because divorce assaults the world we and others take for granted, it requires explanation.[2]

We usually think of this process of making sense of a stressful event as a private matter. People go through it on their own, in isolation, perhaps with family and friends, but out of public view. Similarly, we often think of divorce as an individual problem, having to do with someone's character, relationships, or milieu. In the words of C. Wright Mills, it is a "private trouble"—values cherished by the *individual* are threatened. But as Mills argues, private troubles can become *social* issues when they transcend local environments and people's inner lives. Divorce is a social issue because it suggests there may be structural trouble in the institution of marriage, in relationships between husbands and wives in general. Divorce is a *public* issue, as well, because it involves institutions outside the family, notably the state, and raises a variety of policy questions.[3]

In its frequency alone, divorce can no longer be viewed only as a personal matter. Particularly for Americans born after World War II, it has become commonplace. Between 1963 and 1975 the divorce rate in the United States increased 100 percent, and it continued to increase each year until it reached its all-time high in 1981, when 1.21 million people divorced. Although there is debate over the reasons for this trend, it is clear that as a consequence of the liberalization of divorce laws, divorce became possible for countless individuals who would never previously have considered this means of ending marital unhappiness. Had the spiraling rate of increase of the late 1960s and 1970s continued, by the end of the century nearly every American would have ended a marriage through divorce. As it is, demographer Andrew Cherlin estimates that if recent trends persist, about half of the people getting married today will eventually get divorced. Historian Lawrence Stone estimates that in England over a third of current marriages "will end in the divorce court rather than the funeral parlor." (England and the United States have the highest divorce rates in the Western world, apart from Scandinavia.) The enduring married couple has become somewhat of an endangered species, and couples in which one or both members have been married before are increasingly the norm.[4]

It is paradoxical that individuals must take pains to make sense of divorce—to interpret it to themselves and to others—given that so many people end marriages and that it is so easy to do. Legally, the event is handled "with conveyer-belt speed and impersonality," suggesting that it has become an administrative action and is no longer a moral or judicial action.[5] Yet divorce, while statistically normal, is not normative in a sociological sense: marriage remains the desired state for adults. Witness the rituals and symbolism that surround weddings, and the absence of these for divorce. Rituals carry powerful messages about the kinds of women and men we are expected to be, just as they perpetuate beliefs necessary to maintaining a particular social order. The custom of elaborate weddings persists from one generation to the next, with the bride usually wearing white, and the language of the ceremony reflects the belief that the union will be permanent—"until death do us part." Even in weddings of "modern" couples, who construct their own rituals and write their own vows, or even for couples who themselves were raised with divorce, there is still the expectation of "forever."

Although the belief in living happily ever after may have been replaced by the idea that marriage is "work," commitment nonetheless is the rule of the day. Marriage continues to be something that people take very seriously, despite massive changes in other aspects of family life. Divorce challenges this cultural value. It is not surprising that in spite of all the rhetoric of liberalization (and the fact that Americans broke the divorce barrier and elected Ronald Reagan, who had been divorced and remarried, as President), divorcing individuals still consider themselves somewhat deviant, at least while they are going through the process. Feeling like "damaged goods," they perceive that others view them as stigmatized.[6] They seem to continue to carry in their heads past notions of matrimonial fault, despite the no-fault ethic of contemporary legal practice. Societal expectations help explain why divorce is so stressful, and why individuals must go to such great lengths to explain why they are divorced.

In contrast, another major change in family life—married women working outside the home—has become both statistically normal and sociologically normative. In the not too distant past it was thought that something was wrong with a man if his wife had a job; perhaps he was not a good provider.[7] Although these beliefs may still persist in some pockets of American society, especially if the wife's job is not in a traditionally "female" sector, in general families are not stigmatized and women do not need to give elaborate explanations for their decision to work outside the house. Women's earnings are now usually necessary for families to maintain the way of life they desire. Employed wives may experience considerable distress because of their multiple roles, but typically this strain is not tied to feelings of being deviant or outside the normative order.[8]

Thus the ideology of women's proper place has changed, but the ideology of marriage as forever, in contrast, has not changed to nearly the same degree. There has been little breakdown of the ideology of marriage as a lifelong state, despite the reality of a high rate of divorce that contradicts it.

Divorce also constitutes a public issue because of the poverty of families affected by it. Children of divorce, along with their mothers, are disproportionately poor, and have come to depend increasingly on social services from the state. Whereas 13 percent of the children in two-parent families lived below the poverty line in 1983, the figure for female-headed households was 56 percent, the majority made poor by divorce. Sixty-six percent of children living with only one parent do so because of marital dissolution; only 27 percent are children whose parents never married.[9] Mothers turn to welfare and/or to jobs in low-paying sectors of the economy because they lack sufficient economic support from their ex-husbands or receive no support at all, and because they often have few marketable skills. Divorce has created a national crisis, exemplified by the question posed frequently in the media, "Who will care for the children?" In the absence of a collective answer, individuals devise their own solutions, making do in private ways.

Divorce is a public problem in at least one other arena: health care. Research has shown that divorce is associated with a variety of physical and mental health problems, both for women and for men. Divorced men are more likely than their married counterparts to die, for example, and they are also more likely to enter hospitals of all types, including psychiatric ones. Divorced women are at risk for acute illnesses and for depression, for which they visit physicians more than married women do. Admittedly, the direction of the causal link between divorce and illness is not entirely clear; does the stress of divorce compromise health, or is divorce more common among those with health problems? What is clear, however, is that the problem affects the medical care system: it must respond proportionally more to the divorced than to the married and, as one conservative critic recently speculated, the "flight from marriage" may be a source of rising medical costs.[10]

This study links the social and public issues of divorce with the personal and private experience of divorce. Specifically, the book concerns the interpretive process through which individuals make sense of their former marriages and their current lives—a process that can be studied by focusing on how people talk about their experiences. Though seemingly private, their stories of "what happened" are socially patterned in various ways, and women's accounts are distinctive in certain respects from men's. Embedded in an individual's account of a divorce, too, is a social discourse and often a set of public issues that need collective solutions.

The "talk" that I analyze comes from interviews with fifty-two women and fifty-two men who had been separated and/or divorced for no more than three years—the period most salient in making sense of the past marriage and the current self. (Throughout this book, I use the terms "separated," "divorced," and "divorcing" interchangeably; "separated" is *not* used in its more restricted sense, indicating individuals who have not yet obtained a legal divorce, but rather refers to anyone living apart from his or her former spouse.) The women and men were located both through court records and through referrals from individuals already contacted through the court sample. Referrals were used to allow the inclusion of some who were recently separated and less likely to be involved yet in court proceedings; otherwise, there were no significant demographic differences between the two groups of interviewees.

The sample was chosen with care to be representative of the general population of individuals going through the process of marital dissolution, and ultimately the group included individuals with a range of incomes, educational backgrounds, and occupations. All were between the ages of twenty-five and forty-eight. All but a handful had been married only once, for at least a year; twenty individuals had been married to someone else in the sample (but their responses are not treated any differently from the others', as explained in the Appendix). Some had children, some did not. The Appendix contains a detailed description of the characteristics of the sample and the methods of the study, and a discussion of how it began and the unexpected ways in which it evolved. I will return at the end of this chapter to a description of the study's general approach.

PREVIOUS RESEARCH

Two empirical traditions are relevant here—studies of stress and of divorce. In neither has the process of interpretation that divorcing individuals undergo been a central focus of inquiry, nor have the positive effects of this process been studied in any detail. In the stress tradition, there is a large literature linking disruptive events with a variety of physical and mental health problems. Over the last decade, Leonard Pearlin and his colleagues have empirically demonstrated how particular events and chronic strains combine to produce stress. In this theory, individuals are not seen as passive in the face of stressors (such as divorce); rather, the perspective is that in an effort to master difficult situations, individuals confront stress-provoking conditions, and their behaviors and perceptions (often referred to as social supports and coping) can alter the conditions and/or moderate their impact. One such activity, according to these investigators, is the alteration of the meaning of a situation so that the aspects of it that arouse stress are reduced. People may trivialize problematic situations, for example, or define them as normal and to be expected.[11]

Although they acknowledge the importance of meaning, investigators of stress have not studied *how* people engage in the process of making cognitive and emotional sense of events that happen to them; the kind of detailed accounts that would allow this process to come to the fore have not been sought. Instead, researchers have adopted measurement approaches that rely on sets of items or appraisal scales that classify generalized patterns of coping. These measures describe the range of discrete efforts individuals employ to solve a problem, but they are not meaningfully related to individuals' particular understanding of that problem. Aaron Antonovksy's approach has a similar difficulty. Although he makes a strong theoretical case for the importance of how individuals make sense of life events, he subsequently argues that this is a reasonably stable trait, a dispositional orientation that can be measured with a global sense of coherence scale. Bypassed entirely in these inquiries is the process through which individuals actually go about constructing meaning—the interpretive practices and the contexts in which these occur. This is somewhat ironic, for Pearlin and his colleagues have been acutely sensitive to stress as a process that incorporates both emotional and cognitive features.[12]

Stress research, furthermore, has focused exclusively on the "dark side" of life events. As their indicators, investigators have used physical and mental health symptoms—outcomes that are, by definition, negative and "private." As Antonovsky argues, research has been dominated by a concern with pathology and has focused solely on negative states of mind, to the neglect of what he calls "salutogenesis," or positive adaptation. The assumption is that stressors are only bad for health. Yet early work in physiology, in contrast, shows that stress can mobilize an organism and may potentially be beneficial. Even recent work on health fails to acknowledge the possibility that in the wake of difficult experiences, individuals can display both positive and negative emotions.[13]

In divorce research, too, there is silence about divorce's positive aspects, though there is an increasing trend away from viewing divorce as a private experience, unrelated to political and economic issues. Like investigators in the stress tradition, divorce researchers have mainly studied symptomatology and distress, though they have occasionally noted respondents' "relief" at being out of difficult marriages. There are two notable exceptions to this trend, both qualitative studies of small samples of women, that document some of the benefits, along with the hardships, of divorce. The major in-depth studies, however, either minimize the positives or view them with suspicion. Robert Weiss notes the "euphoria" and new confidence that the divorced speak of, but he dismisses this as "inherently fragile" and says that the divorced "often displayed tension and anxiety without being aware of it." The euphoria is seen as a defense, with the "true" emotion being despair and depression. In a later book Weiss also emphasizes hardship, though he notes in passing that "women, particularly, seem sometimes to emerge [from divorce] with enhanced self-esteem."[14] No investigator to date has paid systematic attention to gender differences in the occurrence of positive and negative affects after divorce, or to the contexts in which each emerges for women or for men.

The most recent study in the divorce-as-unmitigated-disaster tradition is Judith Wallerstein and Sandra Blakeslee's clinical study, which focuses mostly on children. It is unclear whether their sample is representative of the divorced in general, but the authors' conclusions point to severe difficulties in "psychosocial adjustment" ten years later, and these problems are attributed directly to divorce. Even this study, however, finds that two-thirds of the women (versus one-half of the men) are more content with their lives after divorce, despite the fact that they also face considerable financial hardship and loneliness.[15]

Methodological questions aside, why the lack of detailed attention in all these studies to the bright side of divorce and to detailed gender comparisons? Given the high value placed on marriage, it stands to reason that the dark side of marital disruption is emphasized. More than thirty years ago, William Goode noted the tendency of investigators to view divorce as a kind of bereavement. Through the 1970s, some family sociologists saw divorce as an indicator of the demise of the nuclear family, and others argued that, despite the severing of ties to an individual spouse, marriage was here to stay. In the 1980s, conservative politicians and social critics used the high rates of divorce as evidence of a "breakdown" in the family and of the social fabric more generally. It appears that the ideal of lifelong marriage is embedded in public consciousness, just as the model of the conjugal family has, until very recently, remained the prototype of the family for researchers. So, too, has been the assumption that the well-being of women is inevitably tied to men and to marriage. These attitudes and values have shaped research and led investigators to neglect to ask about and analyze positive dimensions of alternative family forms, including divorce, for women in comparison with men.[16]

Despite their lack of attention to potential benefits, divorce researchers have attended to the question of what ending a marriage means to people, though like stress researchers, they have not explored in sufficient detail how individuals actually go about making sense of loss. Weiss observes that individuals construct accounts, "a history of marital failure, a story of what their spouse did and what they did and what happened in consequence." He argues that accounts serve important psychological functions, allocating blame and imposing an order on an otherwise disordered phenomenon. (Stress researchers might call this a form of cognitive coping.) Attribution theorists who have studied divorce show that individuals assign causality in an effort to reestablish a sense of control in the wake of a relationship's end. [17]

The complaints that individuals cite to explain their failed marriages are a major topic in divorce research. There are a number of problems with this approach. Researchers assume that individuals mean the same thing when they identify a particular complaint— such as emotional unavailability, drinking, or an extramarital affair. Further, investigators assume that it is the sum of these perceived complaints that "causes" individuals to leave marriages. Although Goode was careful to say that not everyone would divorce for the reasons given by his sample, he and others in the "complaint" tradition have assumed a direct correspondence between what people offer as their reasons for separation and the causes of divorce. Based on this assumption, some investigators have analyzed divorce by aggregating different types of complaints, comparing the frequency with which contrasting groups mention the same complaint, and correlating types of complaints with various outcomes, such as mental health. The "complaint" approach tends to decontextualize people's experience of marriage and divorce, ignoring the personal meanings divorce has for each individual and the social contexts in which people make decisions about divorce. [18]

This study builds on past work in the stress tradition and in divorce research by analyzing the vocabularies that individuals themselves use to make sense of and survive difficult experiences and by examining how these understandings are embedded in particular historical and cultural contexts. To do this, I ask several basic questions: How do individuals actually go about constructing meaning out of divorce? How do the understandings of women and men differ? What social understandings do individuals draw on to interpret their personal experiences?

THEORETICAL FRAMEWORK

I have also drawn on several theoretical traditions—frameworks not usually applied to divorce or to stress—in analyzing my data. These traditions all share the presupposition that reality is, in large part, socially constructed, though each approaches differently the problem of how we know this constructed reality.

The first—which I call the personal meaning tradition—is exemplified by the work of Peter Marris, a British sociologist, though other sociologists, psychologists, and psychoanalysts have also contributed to it in major ways. Marris argues that with any loss—of a specific person through death or of a community through urban renewal, for example—there is a crisis of discontinuity for the self. Customary structures are lost, and the individual must reinterpret the world to find new structures of meaning. According to his theory, our need for meaning evolves from two innate human predispositions—to conceptualize or render sensible our worlds and to become attached to others. These two predispositions interact with experience as we form habits of feeling and behavior in our relationships. We depend on interpretive structures of meaning to act, and a life event like divorce profoundly disrupts them.

> When people can no longer find meaning in their situation—whether because some crucial attachment which gave purpose to life has been lost, or because the interpretive structure has been overwhelmed by events it cannot grasp or contradictions it cannot resolve—the loss of any basis for action causes intense anxiety and searching, from which new meanings have to evolve.[19]

These ideas suggest that individuals will construct accounts of what went wrong in their marriage and interpretive explanations for the turbulent emotions that follow. They are also likely to innovate, as they construct new lives after loss. These actions are essential steps in the process of reconstituting a self.

The personal meaning tradition gives prominence to the fact that accounts are always versions, rather than objective and impartial descriptions, of reality. As sociologists argue, individuals act on the basis of a *definition* of a situation, for they constantly interpret what they perceive. Tamotsu Shibutani summarizes the perspective of a long tradition of sociological inquiry: "The way people define a situation is reality for them, even if others regard them as mistaken, and scientists could prove that they are wrong." At the core is the philosophical assumption Bertram Cohler articulates, that "there are no events or facts regarding lives which are independent of interpretations which are made of them." "Fact-making" in an account of an event may undergo a process of simplification and deletion over time. Just as scientists present streamlined findings and delete facts and anomalous cases that do not fit, people in general pare down their explanations for events and feelings and make the complicated upheaval of their world appear, at least in part, orderly, predictable, and bounded. [20]

Scholars from the psychoanalytic tradition argue further that reworking memories is an ongoing process that occurs at every phase of the life cycle. Events are remembered as elements in a narrative, the function of which is to provide coherence to an often disjunctive life course. Meaning or coherence is not static, but is constantly reworked as new events and discontinuities are integrated into the story of one's life. Meaning is constructed in context: the same event can take on different meanings depending on the conditions under which it is remembered. Again, in the context of divorce, individuals are likely to engage in the creation of reality in their tellings and retellings, constructing their worlds and themselves through interpretation. [21]

Yet individuals do not create biographical accounts of their marriages or their separations in a social vacuum. As Marris notes, meanings are not only a private construction—the property of individuals—but have a collective counterpart, representing history and cultural understandings. Or, as Shibutani puts it, "What we call reality actually consists of meanings that enjoy a high degree of consensus." [22]

This social side is elaborated in a second theoretical tradition, exemplified in the work of a variety of sociologists and others who, for the purposes of this discussion, I will refer to as social context theorists. These scholars elaborate the broader contexts and social roots of motives that individuals invoke to explain their actions, and they explore the functions served—both for the individual and for the society—by particular explanatory schema. [23]

From Max Weber on, sociologists have noted that motives—such as reasons for leaving a marriage—must be perceived as "adequate grounds" for the conduct. Individuals resort to definitions of a situation that are part of their cultural lexicon and that enjoy a high degree of consensus. Motives for leaving a marriage are thus not intrinsic to individuals and their particular psychodynamics, but vary in content and character with particular historical periods and social structures.[24]

This tradition alerts us to the fact that the process of making sense of divorce may be socially situated in a variety of ways. It is important to note at the outset that the accounts of divorce I analyze occurred in a particular cultural and historical climate—the northeastern United States in the 1980s—and evidence of this context might be anticipated in interpretations of self and spouse and in interpretations of what marriage "ought" to provide. The accounts were also related in a specific situation—a research interview—that has its own constraints and dynamics. In these conversations "tellers" (interviewees) tried to persuade listeners (interviewers) of the validity of their claims, and a social identity was presented and negotiated in the process of the interaction. This perspective prompts us to look for the ways in which individuals compose impressions of themselves and project definitions of their divorcing situations—making choices about how to present their stories in order to draw listeners into their point of view.[25]

Some sociologists suggest that making sense is contextual in yet another way: lengthy explanations are brought into play when deviance occurs, for it is only in untoward situations that behavior needs to be "accounted for." As I argued earlier, getting divorced is such an instance, because of the ideology of marriage as forever. Accounts are called into play to manage a "spoiled identity"—that of a divorced person in the context of a culture that values the conjugal family. We might therefore expect to see individuals portray divorce as not so bad. Accounts may be face-saving devices in social interaction that deflect blame and restore the individual to a place in the moral order. In these ways, actors develop personally meaningful explanations that, at the same time, "take account" of culture.[26]

The third theoretical tradition on which I draw is scholarship on the family. I will discuss it only briefly here because I refer to it often below. Feminists have taken issue with Talcott Parsons's functional analysis of the nuclear family, held together and made stable, he argued, because of men's instrumental roles in the public arena and women's expressive ones in the home (learned through a complex process of gender socialization). These scholars have pointed to the personal strains wives experience in this traditional division of labor and have argued that the marital dyad is a form of social control, imposing unnecessary and excessive constraints, especially on women. Traditional marriage is a gendered institution—not just because women and men participate in it but because the gender-based division of labor in it in turn creates inequality between women and men. Going further, feminist scholars have analyzed the asymmetrical relations of power built into the structure of traditional marriage, a system of dominance and subordination that is obscured by terms like "gender roles."[27]

An analysis of this kind suggests that we look for evidence of structural strains in the marriages women and men describe. Women and men do not experience the family in the same way and, consequently, after divorce, are likely to differ in how they interpret what went wrong. Just as there is a "his" and "her" marriage, we might also expect to find a "his" and "her" divorce, in mirror image of marriage itself.[28]

These three theoretical traditions—personal meanings, social context, and gender relations in the family—emphasize quite different features of social life. Together they provide a broad framework for interpreting how making sense of divorce is not solely a psychological or cognitive process even though, as the personal meaning tradition makes clear, it has important psychological aspects. Although to individuals themselves, coming to terms with loss and reconstructing meaning seem intensely personal and private, and indeed are often done in isolation, at another level this process is both social and public in a number of ways.

First, it is impossible to conceive of accounts of divorce and the emotions that follow divorce apart from social experience. As Russell Jacoby puts it, "the social does not 'influence' the private; it dwells within it."[29] Individuals use the resources that their cultures provide to define and make sense of difficult experiences. As the feminist tradition makes clear, each of us constructs explanations using taken-for-granted definitions of what it means to be a woman as opposed to a man as well as ideologies about contemporary marriage and gender relations in it.

Second and more specifically, individuals develop their accounts of marital breakdown in interaction with others, both "real" and imaginary: in particular social contexts, often public ones, such as courts of law, but also in therapy offices and, as we shall see, in the research interview itself. As a consequence, such accounts are typically coauthored. They are also coauthored in a more general sense because they depend on consensual meanings, just as they rely on historically situated motives. As scholars in the social context tradition argue, people do not construct accounts of divorce out of whole cloth; they use culturally specific reasons to explain their behavior. Without such reasons, they would surely be considered deviant, and their accounts, moreover, would not make sense to us. To construct and sustain a valued social identity, individuals explain their divorces by citing a cause—some antecedent event or condition is deemed responsible—yet these causes themselves are socially constructed.[30]

GENERAL APPROACH

Divorce and the situations it creates are ambiguous, and it is only through interpretation—by divorcing individuals themselves, and here also by an investigator—that the ambiguity can be rendered meaningful and orderly. In analyzing interviews with divorcing women and men, this study combines several different approaches—both narrative and qualitative analysis, supplemented by quantitative analysis of symptoms of psychological distress (see Appendix). Each way of examining the phenomenon of divorce tells us something different, but all contribute to the interpretive approach needed to study how people make sense of their former marriages and their current emotions.

An interpretive approach requires a stance toward those studied that is somewhat different from what is customary in much of social research. Paulo Friere makes a distinction between persons as subjects who know and act, and persons as objects who are known and acted upon. Similarly, Arlie Hochschild makes a distinction between the sentient actor—who is both conscious and feeling—and the social actors that sociologists typically portray. Because I am concerned here with people's own definitions and understandings, I approach those I study as active subjects and as self-interpreting beings, both conscious and feeling, who have the ability to represent their social worlds through language. Yet, as a sociologist, I assume, as does Jeff Adams, that it is "a highly structured social world that is being represented." Thus at the same time that I focus on individuals' own accounts of their experience, I have also looked for patterns across the experiences of many individuals to see what can be learned more generally about the process of making sense of divorce. Just as the individuals I study are interpreting their worlds, so too do I interpret their interpretations.[31]

To see how individuals actually go about making sense, it is necessary to take language seriously, for in large part it is through language that we create our realities. Rather than bypassing the messy stuff of "talk," it needs to come to the center of the analysis, so that we can examine what people mean by what they say.[32]

The need to attend more closely to talk was stressed by C. Wright Mills, a sociologist not usually linked to the study of conversation: "The only source for a terminology of motives is the vocabularies of motive *actually and usually verbalized by actors in specific situations.*" Mills was arguing for taking speech seriously, with simultaneous attention to the social contexts in which it is produced. Similarly, Kenneth Burke argued for the contextual basis of motives: when we try to find an explanation for our attitudes, we employ the vocabulary of our group, "for what are [our] language and thought if not a socialized product?" Both Mills and Burke are saying that we interpret with the only vocabulary of motives that we know, and they draw attention to how discourse is rooted in historical and social contexts.[33]

In the analysis that follows, talk is treated as text; it is closely analyzed in order to "unpack" it. I have been influenced by the constructionist and the deconstructionist perspectives, and I approach language, especially in Chapter 3, not as a "static reference to objects in the world," but, as Gary Peller describes, with an interest in how meaning is being constructed and how it might be constructed differently. There are many ways to say things, and the particular way a person chooses tells us something important about her. Close attention to talk—its structure and the images it invokes, as well as its content—yields insights that cannot be gained in any other way about how people make sense of problematic experiences. As Clifford Geertz puts it, there is no meaning to what is said independent of the *way* it is said; the *way* of saying—form, structure, organization—illuminates the *what* of saying. (Some might even add that it *is* the what of saying.)[34]

People's accounts of divorce are a distillation and interpretation of events. The significance of events is not self-evident: it depends on what Harold Garfinkel calls "background expectancies," including the meanings and contexts in which the events are embedded for members of a culture and, in turn, the meanings and contexts investigators use to interpret them.[35] Interviewees often provide context in their tellings, including the information necessary to read their texts in the ways that are most appropriate. Rather than treating language merely as a means—a vehicle to get to content—I will explore the interdependence of form and meaning. Analysis of both is necessary if we are to attend, more fully and deeply, to what our subjects are trying to tell us, and what we are able to hear, about their divorces and about themselves.

The next four chapters present the findings of the research. To preserve the anonymity of those interviewed, I have changed all identifying information. Each person interviewed has an identification number that is used with each quotation from his or her interview, however, so it is possible to track and relate the responses of particular individuals. In addition, I have given those who are quoted most frequently names and described something of their life circumstances (appropriately disguised), to help the reader get to know them as real people who have something to say about the topics of concern in this study. In the identification codes, the letters N, C, and L indicate which interviewer conducted the interview. I decided not to ignore the context of production of each quotation, that is, the participation of the particular interviewer (N and C are women; L is a man); in a study of gender and divorce, it seemed inappropriate to act as if the gender of the interviewer were not important. This form of representation is not typical (it may even make some social scientist readers uncomfortable by implying that interviewers are not interchangeable). But some feel, and I agree, that it is more "objective" to take into account the dialectic between speaker and listener in analyzing speech. [36]

I wondered how to identify interviewees' social class, and ultimately decided not to attempt this for several reasons. In particular, I do not have a measure of how the individuals see themselves in the class hierarchy. I do have measures of the indicators of social class that sociologists traditionally use, such as years of education, occupation, and income, but these indicators are very problematic for studying the divorced, especially women, who quickly become declassé when marriage ends. [37] Some of the women in this study have very little money and have taken working-class jobs, but they may consider themselves to be middle class and they may possess some of the symbols of that style of life, including homes in distinctly middle-class neighborhoods. I interviewed one woman, for example, who had been reasonably well-off while married, but whose former husband now paid child support to the welfare department and who received public assistance herself—facts that would place her squarely in the lower class. Yet other facts belied this easy categorization: she had a master's degree and her school-aged children attended private school (their father paid the tuition). As a result of contradictions like these, I have not assigned class labels to individuals and have chosen instead to use the categories of everyday life to identify individuals' social location (such as job type or welfare status) and to reserve the concept of class for the analysis and interpretation.

Because of the nature of my sample, social class is the primary axis of social diversity; I did not study non-Western women and blacks do not appear (the counties from which I sampled court records have few black residents but some Hispanic ones). Readers should bear in mind that this is a white sample as they interpret my interpretations; I do not make this limitation explicit in every case, particularly when I make use of psychological theories about gender and when I generalize across cases in order to contrast the divorce experiences of women and men. The issues of social class and race are especially important, because research on gender (and feminist thought, more generally) has been criticized for "essentialist" assumptions, that is, the belief that all women contain an essential "womanness," irrespective of social class, racial, ethnic, cultural, and religious differences. When examined closely, the seeming essential core of this belief is, in

fact, the experience of white, middle-class women in Western societies.[38] Here I have tried to avoid typification about white women
in general, and about white men, as well, and to argue for complex
variation in what divorce means to the individuals involved, despite
the commonalities of class and gender they may reveal.

CHAPTER 2

Mourning Different Dreams

Gender and the Companionate Marriage

How is it possible to bring order out of memory?

—BERYL MARKHAM, West with the Night

Jennifer is a graphic artist who has been separated for a few months. She has two small children. The large house that has been her marital residence is up for sale, and her living room is cluttered with boxes as she packs; she is moving into a small apartment. As she tries to make sense of her divorce, she uncovers a contradiction—a personal myth about what the "good" life is that is at odds with the reality of her experience:

> That there's a daddy and a mommy and the children and the house. And I know that that myth, for me anyway, was terrible. And the life that I've created beyond that myth is a million times better. But there's still . . . this longing for the completion of the original unit. (C004)

Other divorcing women and men describe similar myths and similar longings for this "original unit." Gloria—an educational consultant separated a year longer than Jennifer—mused about the specifics of this notion of marriage:

> We really had a lot of things going for us. We were professionally interested in the same field . . . and the dream was to have a very satisfying couple life and a professional life where . . . he would be . . . working more than I am, but I would be working and I would enjoy that. But I would maintain my home as a first priority. And we could do a lot of things together . . . work things together, fun together, travel together. . . . I felt Keith and I were very close friends when we married. Very close friends. (C012)

In this "dream," Gloria tells us a great deal about what individuals expect from modern marriage—an exclusive "couple life" in which to realize emotional intimacy, companionship, and, as she says elsewhere in the interview, sexual fulfillment. She links these core components to a set of institutionalized roles: her primary commitment is to the domestic sphere and her husband's is to work outside the home. At the same time that marital roles are different, her choice of the metaphor of friendship suggests she expects equality with her husband and mutual respect.

Both Gloria and Jennifer were sorely disappointed. Jennifer's husband was incapable of the kind of emotional intimacy she wanted, and Gloria's husband was sexually unfaithful. To explain what went wrong and to make sense of her separation, each constructs a lengthy account, legitimating the divorce by noting how the dream had been betrayed. Gloria describes the repeated infidelities of her husband, a minister:

> That's where the most pain is. I guess that's where the dream ended. . . . We'd been married about eight years . . . and we were in the parish and Keith began having an affair with a former parishioner—twenty-five years his junior—who he claimed to be a counseling case for six months. Until I got wise and asked him and he said yes, he was having an affair, but he was trying desperately to end it. Two years later he was still having it. And that nearly drove me literally nuts. . . . And when we left that parish and he decided to go to Greenville, I thought, Oh, good, maybe this will all end. . . . And I remember when we

bought our first house—we'd lived in . . . parsonages before—he was still seeing Bea and I said, "Damn it, if you take that black mud pot of a relationship into our new home it will kill me." And he took it, for the first four or five months. And it was very difficult but I kept thinking, Maybe, maybe with Greenville and [if] he gets into something he really likes, maybe that'll take care of it. Except that [when] he went to Greenville he started up another one. And that's still going on. I have become aware of two or three others, all of whom I know. I know all these people. (C012)

Gloria's husband not only betrayed her dream of what marriage ought to be but personally betrayed and humiliated her by having affairs with people she knew. Gloria continues her account by saying she went into therapy where, over a period of time, she came to define the problem and decided to leave the marriage. Like others, she took charge of her divorce by reconstituting the meaning of what had occurred, and an important step in this process of understanding was the construction of an account, an interpretation of what happened and why.

CONSTRUCTING AN ACCOUNT:
THE IDEOLOGY OF THE COMPANIONATE MARRIAGE

In making sense of divorce, individuals recall and reinterpret the events of their marriages, bringing "order out of memory." They construct accounts that make sense, both to themselves and to others, out of nonsense—images, memories, random happenings. Accounts develop in particular historical and cultural contexts: for example, there are socially acceptable reasons for ending a marriage in the 1980s that might have been unacceptable in past decades or are still unacceptable today in some parts of the world. There is a link between these private and social understandings, particularly concerning gender. The divorce accounts reveal an essential paradox: women and men construct heavily gendered definitions of what marriage ought to be, but at the same time they mourn these gender tensions and blame their divorces on them.

The major cultural theme that both women and men use to create divorce accounts is the ideology of the companionate marriage—the belief that husband and wife should be each other's closest companion at the same time that they are expected to retain gender-specific roles. This belief, whose roots I will discuss below, is an essential piece of each individual's "tool kit" in accounting for divorce. Although this ideal vision of marriage—the "dream" that Jennifer and Gloria refer to—has failed them, women and men nevertheless affirm it by justifying their divorces on the grounds that particular core elements of the companionate ideal—emotional intimacy, primacy and companionship, and sexual fulfillment—were missing from their marriages. They find fault with their spouses' performance of the institutionalized roles that are part of the companionate ideal. They describe how the preconditions for the companionate marriage—role differentiation and yet equality—have not been met in their particular cases. Women and men differ in the aspects of this ideal vision they select as justification for divorce, however, and there are social class variants in themes within gender groups, as well. Even when they identify the same missing elements, on closer examination women and men seem to mean different things by them.

WOMEN'S CONSTRUCTIONS OF EMOTIONAL INTIMACY

To explain why they divorced, individuals often use the phrase "lack of communication," and in doing so they are making sense of private experience by drawing on an ethic and vocabulary of love that is particular to contemporary American culture.[1] Women, more than men, identify this interpersonal aspect as missing in marriage. Nearly two-thirds say they did not get the kind of emotional intimacy they expected from their husbands. Closer examination of their talk suggests women are referring to a special kind of emotional intimacy: "feeling really in touch, communicating deeply and closely" (C002), "inner connectedness" (N025), "warmth and sharing" (C042), "getting down to gut feelings" (C033).

Deep Talk and Small Talk

Talk with a spouse is how women think emotional intimacy ought to be realized. At the same time that they want to talk about both "deep" topics and everyday events, they also want communication that goes beyond words, and that is reciprocal. As women construct it, a spouse should "know them" in some all-encompassing way. This ideal of romantic love, however, is tempered by the twentieth-century American belief in the value of "struggle" in relationships.[2] Women want to talk with husbands about negative feelings as well as positive ones. A salesclerk says:

> We never fought. If I became angry, I could scream and yell and even throw things and get no feedback. None. Nothing. (L008)

Yet, though women want complete communication with a spouse, they appear to hold somewhat contradictory ideas about how it should be displayed. On the one hand, women expect intuitive understanding—to be understood without a lot of words. A clerical worker expresses this expectation:

> If you love me, you should know where I'm coming from, why and how I reacted to such and such . . . different things he should pick up on, what I had to say before the incident occurred, and give way sometimes and recognize what my need was. I think that when there is love, you do that. (N025)

On the other hand, women want talk. They constantly complain that husbands were silent about their feelings, both positive and negative, as this proofreader describes:

> I had, for so many years, beaten my head against the wall and cried and screamed and said, "Talk to me. Tell me how you feel." And he'd go upstairs and read a book and leave me sitting down here with a bottle and nine million cigarettes, snuffling. (L013)

Not only do women want to talk about emotions, they also want "small talk"—about mundane things that happen during the day at the job or at home. They especially want verbal interaction about work—their own as well as their husbands'—but, as they construct it, their husbands are at fault because they will not talk about these topics, at least with them. Women typically do not understand that the problem may have to do with the different kinds of work women and men do, and resultant absence of similar activities to talk about.

Instead, as they see it, the problem is in husbands' characters. One women, whose husband was a factory foreman, defines the issue:

> I remember I would ask Nick questions when he would come home from work. . . . He was tired a lot so we would have deadening conversations where I'd say, "Well, tell me what happened today?" And he'd say, "Nothing much." And I'd talk about what happened to me and then I'd wonder if he could tell me anything 'cause I felt so out of his life. Maybe he didn't think I wanted to really know. I don't know. I think it was difficult because I had the college education and he (voice trails off). I think I'm a competitive person, very competitive and this may have been hard for him, maybe he just didn't want to compete at all. But we gradually had nothing to say to each other. (C014)

She constructs the problem psychologically—his lack of "competition" in comparison with hers. Yet she also notes that she has a college education (and a middle-class job), whereas he works in a factory—two very different contexts to come home and discuss at night. We know from other research that working-class men are more likely to talk to their buddies than to their wives about their daily lives at work.[3] Women like Lynn, a clerical worker, lament this gender division:

> I would talk but I don't think he ever listened. I think actually I bored him. And I would ask him, "What did you do today?" and he'd say, "Oh, nothing." Somebody else would walk in and he would say, "Oh, you wouldn't believe what I saw today." (C022)

A particularly vivid example of the importance of talk for women and the conflict it creates in marriage is given by Betty, who took extreme action in order to get her husband to talk to her:

> George was not the greatest conversationalist. I used to do things to bug the guy and the thing is, I did it on purpose. If I felt like he was not paying enough attention. You see, he was not playful at all. I mean, most people can put a smile on their face sometimes and he very seldom did. . . . There was no child in him at all and there's a lot in me. You know, I like to play.

She continues by telling a story about a particular incident:

Well, one time he was sitting here reading his newspaper (points to chair in living room). I just wanted to talk, walk over and say, "Hi, I remember you," you know, anything. I set his newspaper on fire to get attention. I did that once and boy did he get mad. See, playing is so important to me, you don't know how important, especially after being married to someone who was not playful. Yeah, there was a lot of times when I felt like I was being crazy and I was being crazy all by myself. (C013)

It is significant that Betty—a full-time homemaker during her marriage who became a construction worker after her separation—explicitly states that she wanted "attention," in the form of talk with her husband. Her rather dramatic action—setting his newspaper on fire as he was reading it—is an effort to get him to talk to her. The imagery she selects to elaborate her values (liking to "play"; there was no "child" in him) is rooted in female culture and maternal thought.[4] Her closing statements express how it felt to try to be "crazy" and "playful" in the context of a companionless marriage, where emotional intimacy, as she defines it, could not be realized.

The Expectation of Reciprocity

Women expect reciprocity in verbal exchanges but, as they look back on their marriages, too often they see "one-way love." A clerical worker describes the norm of reciprocity:

I guess it's called "give and take." Just recently I was thinking about it . . . and I thought what a cliché, give and take. I was wondering what it really meant and I've come to the conclusion that it should mean that there is one person that is supposed to take first, and the other then gives, and then the other person takes and then you give. It's like giving way to what their need is. And there was none of this that occurred either by me or him. I consider that love. There was no love. (N025)

Others also spoke about reciprocity as love, calling it by other names: "giving and getting" (N013) or "emotional exchange" (C008).

Although women are more alike than different in referring to the absence of talk and reciprocity in marriage, women in contrasting economic circumstances use distinctive vocabularies to describe the emotional barrenness of their situations. Poor women use imagery that is rooted in the material conditions of their lives, specifically the metaphor of money:

> I felt like I was talking to a bank president, you know, who was telling me about a loan I was defaulting on. I was just so discouraged. There was no compassion. There was no hug. And it reminded me of other times I had cried and how he always turned to stone. (C042)

These women invoke images of bank presidents, wallets, and loans to signify the emotional distance of husbands. The language that women in middle-class occupations use, in contrast, is more abstract, reflecting psychological understandings. A physician says:

> There was a deadness [in the marriage], there was no life. All we could talk about were impersonal things and there was no ability to deal with what was behind things. We couldn't talk about things at an emotional level. (C010)

Women of all social classes often make reference to friendship in explaining what emotional intimacy ought to be like. An academic puts it this way:

> There wasn't such a strong bond [in my marriage]. I mean, I didn't see it then, but I see it in contrast to my relationship with Tim [current boyfriend], like the person was your friend in a way. . . . There just wasn't that tie. (N004)

A woman on welfare looks back on her marriage and invokes the same image, saying, "My husband was never a friend to me, we were like bedmates" (C017). Friendship, women of all backgrounds suggest, entails talking and listening, giving and getting, equality not hierarchy.

PRIMACY AND COMPANIONSHIP FOR WOMEN

A common explanation for divorce in the accounts of both women and men is that they had "nothing in common" with their spouses. This reflects the belief about modern marriage that the conjugal relationship is the primary relationship, one that takes priority over all others. Joint activities and shared leisure are expected, because they vivify the bond between the spouses. More than half of those in the sample make sense of their divorces in the context of problems with companionship and its corollary complaint—that the commitment to the marital tie was not primary enough. Women interpret the relationship between primacy and companionship differently than men do, and women in different social circumstances see the issues in contrasting ways, as well.

Women do not expect husbands to relinquish ties to kin and friends nearly to the extent that men expect this from women. Women usually do not fulfill this expectation. Repeatedly, women note that their husbands were resentful when they wanted to spend time with close friends. Often, but not always, conflicts arose when women were needed by friends or family members in crisis, as this salesclerk describes:

> My mom was going to have a mastectomy. And I told him I was going home. And he never wanted anything to do with my family. I was his and no one else's. As soon as he found out I wanted to go home, [he said], "No, you are not going," to which I replied, "I am going, she is my mother, if you don't like it, too bad." And I went. (C024)

"I was his and no one else's"—this lament is echoed implicitly or explicitly by many women. As women construct it, they do not expect this exclusivity from husbands. They do not define the marital relationship as emotionally exclusive, relegating kin and friends to a marginal position. Certainly, they resent some of the types of friends and the "male" activities husbands pursue with them—drinking and gambling, for example. One solution women see to these problems, however, is to incorporate men's friendships into the family, perhaps in an effort to control their husbands' behavior. A case in point is this clerical worker:

> Well, on the one hand, some of his friends I really couldn't accept. They were mainly interested in going out and having a good time, drinking and gambling. Things like that. From my point of view it was a men's thing to do and the women were not included. . . . We didn't have friends that were family. Like husband and wife and children,

let's get together and do something. Most of his friends were men. They were married, but we never associated on that level. They would come over for a brief period and have a drink, leave, and I always kept to myself, just extended whatever was the polite thing to do. Receive them at home and talk a little. . . . I tried many times to have his friends over, [asking], "Why doesn't he bring his wife over or children? We could do things together." (N025)

Rather than keeping husbands to themselves, women seek to integrate the family into a larger social world of kin and friends, and sometimes they even use these ties to buffer and preserve the troubled marriage.

Women do not expect primacy nearly to the extent men do, but they still expect companionship in marriage—to "do things together." Women's ideas of what these joint activities ought to be differ markedly from men's. An office manager describes one of the hopes she had when she married that was never realized:

We got married in April and the first Christmas, I mean, see, I always have these dreams and everything has to go with the way the dream is. . . . I wanted to go to midnight Mass with my husband, only he didn't want to go. . . . It used to bother me going to Christmas alone, church alone. (N023)

"Going to Christmas alone"—this woman's slip of the tongue reveals the loneliness of a companionless marriage.

As women construct it (especially women whose husbands had working-class occupations), "male" leisure pursuits get in the way of doing things together. A clerical worker interprets her resentment this way:

See, the type of recreations he had were, like I say, more male-oriented. Like, "Let's go to the bar, or Hialeah, or the dog races," things like that which I didn't care to attend. And he didn't want me to come anyway. It's like there were two worlds and there was no way of putting them together. (N025)

This woman makes explicit the link between gender and lack of companionship, for it is the "male-oriented" nature of her husband's recreational interests that excludes her, not his overt exclusionary behavior or his ties to male friends. In her mind, bars, Hialeah, and the dog races are "male" settings. According to her report, her husband invited her to join him in these places ("let's go"), but she wasn't interested ("I didn't care to attend"), interpreting his invitation as his lack of sincerity ("he didn't want we to come anyway"). In her mind, separate spheres pivot on tacit theories of "appropriate" settings and activities for women as opposed to men. These beliefs, in turn, produce tension in marriage, where companionship is expected.

Women in professional occupations complain less than do poorer women about the lack of shared leisure (almost half of poorer women saw it as a problem). Professional couples expect and do take time together, but even here some women recall "two worlds" of sex-typed leisure. A physical therapist highlights the differences:

> I enjoyed going to plays and theater and things like that, where he hated it. If we went, I could see him doing it, just *doing* it, maybe falling asleep. (C016)

Her husband, like many others, had a major interest in sports and was what she called "a TV freak." For many wives this was a bone of contention, particularly as they began to develop interests on their own, as the college administrator did:

> We stopped sharing daily lives. First our friendship started to sort of split apart and I found I didn't want to watch the Bruins and I didn't want to go to softball. I began to assert what I wanted to do rather than saying, It's all right, I'll join Nick in what he likes to do. . . . He also watched a lot of TV and I . . . dislike TV and what it did to conversation. (C014)

Women's accounts suggest that they have strong feelings about where and how joint leisure ought to occur in marriage that, in turn, reflect gender divisions. Women, particularly those in working-class occupations, speak over and over again of wanting to "go out," intimating that the home is no place to spend time that is not focused on household chores and child care. A woman who has children and is on welfare puts it this way:

He did not mind dedicating a lot of time toward sports, his friends, the softball league, and things like that. If I asked just like to go to a movie with the children or go out to dinner at a restaurant—just one day—he couldn't understand why I wanted to do that when I could do it at home, just sitting down and watching TV. Or just have a family dinner, which [he thought] would be the same as going to a restaurant. (N013)

As this woman goes on to explain, one difference between having dinner in a restaurant and at home is that "you don't do the dishes afterwards."[5] Women want to "go out" and "be sociable" because their workplace is the private sphere of the home; men, in contrast, are "out" all day at their jobs. Even if wives are also employed outside the house, they do not define the home as a space for leisure because it is associated with chores, demands, and responsibilities—a "prison" rather than the "haven" it is for men.[6] In women's minds, there is no "free" time for them at home.

WOMEN'S VIEWS ABOUT SEX IN MARRIAGE

Sexual gratification for both wives and husbands is a core aspect of modern marriage, something taken for granted. It is closely related to the other expectations, because in addition to providing physical release, marital sex may be a way to realize emotional intimacy, primacy, and companionship. Given the high value placed on sex in American culture, it is not surprising that sexual issues figure in nearly 60 percent of the divorce accounts. Women and men interpret sexual events in distinctive ways, however.

Sexual infidelity was mentioned in 34 percent of the accounts.[7] Women take this action very seriously and interpret it as evidence of betrayal or as the catalyst for divorce. For Gloria, for example, whose account of her husband's repeated affairs with women she knew opened this chapter, discovering the affairs was significant to her because they were proof that her husband could not be trusted. In this construction (which other women share), it is not only the sexual behavior itself but what it signifies about the spouse's character that is disturbing to the wife. This deeper discovery—that the husband is not the person the wife thought he was—is especially troubling, because it compromises her ability to love in return, thereby contradicting her beliefs about reciprocity in emotional expression. Gloria makes this point clear:

> Although I still had the love, the freedom to love him just got absolutely slammed shut. Even though we had a relationship after that [discovery of the first affair]. Not with my heart in it. (C012)

For another group of women, affairs mean something different. Although these women still view affairs as very serious and as key turning points in the decision to divorce, they believe that the marriage was "over" in an emotional sense by the time that the affair occurred. In this construction, the affair is the catalyst for separation, but the web of explanation for the problem goes deeper. After a lengthy description of a series of marital problems, a news reporter concludes:

> We just sort of withdrew into our separate worlds. Then, as luck would have it, he met someone that he fell in love with and that was the catalyst. As soon as he met her and had real feelings about her, he wanted out. So the final ending was very sudden. (L003)

Not only do women see their husbands' infidelities as the catalyst; they define their own in this way as well. A recurrent plot exists in some women's accounts: their marriage existed "in name only," they then "met someone" and fell in love, and this provided the "push" needed to end the marriage. The academic speaks directly about the emotional logic, which was also implicit in several other women's explanations, behind this scenario:

> It really took meeting somebody else before I could leave. I might have left anyway, but I think it would have taken a lot longer. . . . I think it might have taken meeting somebody else because I'm so afraid of being alone. That's really a big, that's my big problem. . . . I was so terrified and I think, really, I think it's possible I wouldn't have done it unless I'd met somebody else. (N004)

The fear of being alone keeps these women in "empty" marriages, and they rationalize moving quickly to another relationship after they have an affair. A few women even define being "mentally un-faithful" as incompatible with marital vows. Several women described how they began to be attracted to someone else toward the end of their marriage. The proofreader says:

> I eventually started to feel like I liked Vince much better than I liked my husband. And if I was going to be mentally unfaithful, I might as well leave him. (L013)

By making sense of infidelity in these ways, women are drawing on a gendered belief that sex and emotional closeness go hand in hand—that sex and love cannot be separated.[8] In this belief system, women's sexual infidelity is justified in the absence of deep emotional ties to a spouse. Similarly, husbands' affairs are legitimate cause for ending a marriage because they mean that the husbands are giving away their love—to the women they are sleeping with, rather than to their wives. Even if it is also clear at some level to their wives that this is not the case, they cannot continue to give their love freely if their husbands betray them and thus challenge the expectation that sex and love are one. Women have deeply held beliefs about the rules that should govern the relationship between sexual and emotional intimacy, and these influence how they interpret sexual infidelity. (Interestingly, though the joining of sex and intimacy is a woman's theme, it is voiced by both women and men to explain marital failure. Several men in their accounts describe their wives' sense of betrayal when they—the men—were sexually unfaithful. Once discovered, they were never forgiven.)

In women's talk about sexual gratification there is additional evidence that women tend to link sex and intimacy. A number of women raise the issue of marital sex while talking about emotional closeness in their marriage. As closeness began to wane, so did sex. A factory worker talks explicitly about the connection between physical and emotional intimacy:

> To me, sex isn't just sex. It doesn't bother me not to have sex. To not have a relationship would bother me more than not having sex. In a close relationship, in a close feeling with someone, of sharing and confiding, and being together and cuddling, to me sex is a natural thing. Without that I don't want it. Consequently, there were many times we

had problems [and] he wanted to have sex and I wasn't interested. (C033)

In her view, sex is "natural" when it flows from emotional closeness. When this condition was lacking in her marriage, she withheld sex. As she later states, when her husband wanted sex, she'd say, "I'm sorry, if you can't give me what I need then I don't see why I should give you what you need" (C033). The giving and withholding of sex is an exercise of power—one of women's major weapons, it appears, in the face of husbands' failure to live up to wives' standards of intimacy. It is not surprising in this context that a number of women comment on the decline in frequency of sex as the marriage became emotionally strained. Paradoxically, the absence of sex then becomes a justification for ending the marriage. As a factory worker says, "What kind of a marriage is this when you don't sleep together?" (N026)

Other women talk about sexual problems interfering with gratification. Sometimes the problem seems to be his: "He was impotent and I couldn't take it anymore" (C008). More often, the problem appears to be hers. A clerical worker gives her understanding of the sexual issues in her marriage:

> I really didn't enjoy sex. I wondered sometimes if I were frigid because I just didn't get anything from sex and Alex is a very sexual person and had a great need for sex and I, it just bored me. . . . I think I convinced myself over the years that there was something wrong with me sexually and that nothing could be done about it at forty-four. (C006)

When the interviewer asks if she has continued to have this problem since her separation, she replies:

> No. I don't have that problem now at all. I'm capable of having—it's not a deep rooted thing. So it must have been some mental block, I suppose. (C006)

A teacher describes a similar discovery about her sexuality:

> An important thing [in the marriage] was sexual incompatibility, I mean to the point that he suggested to me that I might be frigid. And at

the time, not having other experiences, I believed him. Until I had an affair [after my separation] I then realized, wait a minute here, it isn't all me. (L015)

Whatever the truth might have been—a "mental block" or poor sexual technique—women tend to blame themselves in marriage for sexual incompatibility and sometimes explain difficult sex lives on the basis of lack of love or "low sex drive." In subsequent retellings, however, some women transform their understandings of their "frigidity."

For example, a woman with a different sexual issue tells how she accepted her husband's definition of the situation while she was married. After the formal interview was over, but while the tape recorder was still on, she takes the opportunity to talk more about it:

> I just thought you'd ask more questions about our married sex life. You didn't get into that at all. I never found it very fulfilling because my husband didn't seem to need as much sex as I did. He always made me feel, he once referred to me as a nymphomaniac because I wanted sex two nights in a row and I just, I wondered. A lot of my friends, we talk about sex, and I guess we're sexually liberated in some ways. (N010)

She then asked the interviewer whether she was "the only one [in the study] who felt that way." This question, coupled with her forthrightness about her strong sexual appetite in her marriage (and afterward), suggests that some women alter understandings about the inevitable linking of sex and love.

MEN'S CONSTRUCTIONS OF EMOTIONAL INTIMACY

Like women, some men blame divorce on "lack of communication"—a phrase that is commonly used to explain a flawed relationship. When men elaborate, saying "we weren't real close" (C003), there was a lack of "emotional support" (L009), or "I had love to give but wasn't getting it back" (C037), at first glance they sound like their female counterparts. But there is a difference. Only one-third of the men (as opposed to two-thirds of the women) say they did not get the emotional intimacy they expected from marriage. The comments men make about the topic tend to be brief in contrast to women, who go on at length about it. Closer examination of men's talk suggests they are defining "closeness" in distinctive ways.

In their accounts of their marriages, men blame themselves for not living up to women's standards of intimacy. As they construct it, they were the silent partners in marriage, not giving wives enough "love and understanding" (C021). When they talk about specifics, however, it is clear that their style involves less talk and more action. As a physical therapist says bluntly, "I'll act and she'll feel." At the same time he subtly considers himself at fault for his way of relating in the marriage:

> I'm a very private person. . . . I think that was the problem in the marriage, that my wife felt I didn't talk enough, I keep things very much to myself and I'll act and she'll feel, like, "Where in the hell is this coming from because there's never been any prelude to this, we never discussed this, we never talked about this and all of a sudden, he's done something." In my own mind, I've worked it out, just seemed like the best course of action or whatever at that time. But I'm not the type of person to sit down and discuss things with people at any length. (N036)

Although this man admits he is not "the type of person" to talk things out, he nevertheless believes that his style "was a problem in the marriage." He appears to accept women's view that shared introspection is a good thing. The modern cultural ethos of communication holds sway over both sexes, and this man feels the worse for it.

In men's definitions of emotional closeness, talk is not the centerpiece. Rather, men expect wives to be there for them in much fuller ways. Lillian Rubin argues that it is physical proximity that is desired, but the men in my sample suggest this is only one aspect.[9] Men want a variety of physical and other concrete demonstrations of intimacy. A factory worker vividly depicts what was missing in his marriage:

> When you come home from work at night . . . just to have somebody greet you at the door with open arms, you know, kiss and ask how you are, or how your day went. I never received that. (C037)

To be greeted at the door by a wife with open arms—this image recurred with remarkable regularity, particularly in the accounts of working-class men, just as the wish for reciprocal talk about emotions with a husband recurred in the accounts of women from all social backgrounds. As this man says, he wants talk to a certain extent—he wants his wife to ask about his day—but this is just one small part of what he expects. It is just as important that his wife be at the door, with "open arms" and a kiss—physical manifestations of caring. Note that his expectations for intimacy here are unidirectional. Like a number of other men, he complains that he did not "receive" love. In his view, marriage is a kind of haven, a place to retreat to, where he can be tended by a wife, away from the pressures of alienated work. In exchange for her emotional support of him, he expects to support her financially. This is reciprocity as many men understand it.

Other men voice similar understandings of the importance of physical, not verbal, manifestations of emotional intimacy. Joe, a corrections counselor with a master's degree, is one of four men who discuss the absence of intimacy in marriage at length. He says:

> I don't think I was ever as close to Jackie [former wife] as I am to Sue [current girlfriend]. . . . Part of it is, I tend to be somewhat of an emotional person. I grew up in a very close family, I grew up in an extended family. My grandmother and my aunts and uncles and cousins on the top floor. And summers, we had a summer house, it was a collective summer house with aunts and uncles, cousins, and so we spent every summer together. And then I'm a very affectionate person and Jackie's very cold, came from a very staunch New England family that didn't show emotion, you know. Her mother frowned on us holding hands together when we first met. . . . I show emotion. I think that was the hardest thing. Jackie never really felt that, you know . . . if I put my arm around her in public, she'd shun it or kissed her in public, she'd—even after we'd been married for ten years—she felt that someone might see it. I used to ask her, "Who cares? I really don't care." Sue is very affectionate and I like that. (N012)

Although emotional intimacy is a topic of obvious importance to Joe, he does not offer it as a reason for his separation. Instead, he discusses it in another context in the interview, after a question about how his relationships have changed since divorcing. When asked about the "main causes of his separation," he describes how he and his wife "grew in different directions" and how work stress undermined the marriage. Women who speak about the absence of emotional closeness, in contrast, tend to define it as causally related to the end of the marriage.

Joe's description of his emotional nature can also be seen as a type of justification.[10] He needs to account for his nature, because it is deviant in our culture for a man to be so affectionate; he explains that he got that way because of his early family experiences. No woman in the sample needed to justify the importance of emotional expression.

Most obviously, Joe defines emotional closeness as physical demonstrativeness. Talking about feelings and problems does not figure in his construction of what being "an emotional person" is. He wants to express his love physically, not talk about it. His understanding of emotional intimacy is markedly different from what women describe it to be.

PRIMACY AND COMPANIONSHIP FOR MEN

Men assume that they will have easy access to their wives when they marry. They expect that the marital tie will be the primary tie for them and for their wives—that the couple will be self-contained. Consequently, men count on spending considerable time with their wives—alone together, as a couple.

Men's central complaint (nearly half mention it) is that wives are not "there" for them because they are not emotionally exclusive. In their minds, their wives' other relationships limit the time the couple can spend alone together and undermine the primacy of the marriage. Continuing bonds and obligations to kin are often seen as the problem. One man recalls, "she would show more attention, you know, to her family than she would to me" (N017). Wives' involvements with relatives, and sometimes even with the couple's children, are seen as usurping time and energy that husbands want. Wives' friendships with other women are seen similarly. Women, as noted earlier, have their own language for this problem—"I was his and no one else's."

Men in middle-class occupations are more likely than those with working-class jobs to complain about wives' kin ties. Joe, though he has mentioned growing up in a large, close extended family, wanted a different sort of life with his wife. He described in a vivid way the variety of relationships that occupied his wife and, even more, took over their home:

> Jackie was like a little old lady in the woods who lives with sixty-four cats. Anytime something wandered to the back door that was injured, which is fine, I mean, if an animal is injured, I took it in too and I played doctor. But I didn't want to keep them and she ended up gradually building up to a whole house full of animals. We had five cats in a two-bedroom apartment. Plus her brother came to live with us and I felt that I was supporting him and putting him through school as well as putting myself and her through school. And he lived with us for three years. He lived in the other bedroom in a two-bedroom apartment, and I just felt the lack of privacy, even though he and I are friends. I felt that he wasn't contributing to the house—he never did any cleaning, I had to clean up after him as well as pay for the food, he never really contributed to the food and never paid us rent, so I didn't feel that obligation. Maybe she felt a strong obligation to him, but I didn't feel it and that was a source of arguments, that was one of the problems. (N012)

Cats, brothers, sisters, mothers and the obligations wives feel to them—men echo this lament over and over. As men see it, wives' overinvolvement in the lives of others interferes with marital "privacy," especially when wives respond to others' trouble by giving them a temporary home. They perceive, often correctly, that wives take care of others even when they don't want to, that obligations to others are a burden for women. Wives need to learn to say "no," to stop "overdoing it" (N012), and to tend to the immediate family instead.

When relatives get too involved, moreover, men feel a husband cannot fulfill his mission—to be a good provider for the family. Relatives use up scarce material goods that men have worked hard for, as this apartment superintendent describes:

> Her father was living with us, her brother just moved in with us, without any help. I mean, it's not that they were bad people, but they were

sponging off me, I felt. And, you know, I'd be working all day, they'd be eating all the groceries and stuff. (N017)

Beyond these concrete sources of resentment, wives' ties to others are also directly responsible for the demise of the marriage in some men's minds, because wives can turn to others for help in difficult times and are not solely dependent on their husbands or on themselves:

I have these strong feelings that if her mother didn't help her she would have been forced to try to make things work. She didn't have to just come home. (N039)

A handful of men resent the time and attention that children require from their wives. This is especially true if the children are from the wife's previous marriage, because they acutely compromise the primacy of the couple relationship. As one man says, "We were right off the bat a family." In his account (heavily influenced, one suspects, by the family therapy literature), this prevents the "formation of the spouse subsystem" (C041). Another man is more direct, calling his wife's children "an intrusion in the marriage" (C025).

Men want the home to be their haven from work. Children and relatives (particularly if they move in) severely diminish peace and quiet at home and interfere with easy access to emotional support. Husbands have a hard time enjoying their wives and getting what they need from them with so many others around. Under these conditions, men feel that they have to compete—that there is not enough attention to go around. They believe that the home should be *their* space, for they have worked hard to get it, and that they should not have to share it. (For some, having a wife and children is similarly their accomplishment, evidence of their lineage.) A lawyer speaks of his resentment of the collectivity of his wife's women friends, who, as members of a consciousness-raising group, invaded his home on a regular basis:

My own feeling is that it [the separation] was rather heavily influenced by the explosion of the women's movement and my wife's participation in it and her changing expectation. My inability to understand what was going on. . . . Women developed support groups which met often, in fact, they were meeting in *my* house and it became simply stated that I was not welcome to even be in *my* house at the time that these meetings were taking place. And I felt extremely resentful about that. In fact, angry. And so the whole notion of the support group became a very big conflict between us because I felt that there were other people who were discussing my own personal affairs. . . . And there was developing this movement among women that had very little . . . understanding about how this was all going to impact on males and as a male, I had no way of dealing with that. There were no male support groups and I wouldn't have participated in one even if there were because I didn't like the notion of them. And I think that it was very bothersome for me because I felt that all of the changes that were happening in my own house were coming from this whole movement over which I had no control. Or no input. And it was totally mystifying to me. (C027)

As this man formulates the problem, he lost the privacy of his relationship with his wife and the privacy of his home, as her ties to women and the women's movement usurped his place and changed the rules of marriage. (There may also be another issue here, one that may not be as gender-linked: is the marital home his, hers, or theirs? His account is reminiscent of the remarks of the woman quoted earlier who disappeared whenever her husband's friends came over to the house.) Bob, a factory foreman, constructs the problem that women's friendships pose to a marriage a bit differently, emphasizing his wife's time away from home:

When Lisa was going out a lot with her friends, you know, I felt lonely and I felt responsible for a lot of that, too. I could have made her stay home or whatever and just let her go out once in a while, but I let her have everything at once.
Int.: Sounds like you feel that was a mistake.
Bob: Yeah, I do. [If I had it to do over again] I'd let her go out maybe once a week with her girlfriends or whatever. I feel everybody should have at least one free night in a week. (C031)

Both men feel they lost control over their wives and link this loss to their wives' deep involvement in friendships.

But they are suggesting something more. We know from other research that men depend on a spouse for connection and emotional support much more than women do; wives are men's primary, often only, confidant.[11] If their spouse is not available, men feel they have nobody. It makes sense, then, that men expect the marital relationship to be primary, exclusive, private, and to take precedence over all other relationships.

Men do not always put marriage first, of course, and some tended to realize this in their retellings. A number of men spoke of their overinvolvement in work:

> Within our marriage, my job was more important than my family. That was one of the things that kind of, it wasn't *the* thing, but it was certainly one of the things that contributed to the breakup of the marriage. (N032)

> I used to spread myself really thin. I spent as much time with my social life and my friends in the Biology Department [his job] as I did with Cindy and that probably wasn't a good idea. (C035)

> I had a partner [in the insurance business], so I was spending most of my time with my partner. Not paying enough attention to my wife's needs. (L012)

> I got so wrapped up in some of those things [politics, work], I got lost in priority of what was important in my life. I didn't really pay that much attention to my wife, I guess. When I look back at it. (N019)

It is no coincidence that all these men have solidly middle-class occupations and thus jobs they can "lose themselves" in, to the exclusion of family. No man with a working-class job makes such a statement. But all these men, working and middle class, are making the same point in different ways: if they had the marriage to do over again, they would have made the relationship more central in their lives. In their accounts the marriage failed, at least in part, because they did not make it emotionally exclusive and primary.

A related ideal of modern marriage that both men and women prize is doing things together with a spouse, enjoying companionship when not working. Husbands expect easy access to their wives for leisure activities but, as they experience it, their wives are either too busy or do not want to do what they want to do. Tension over different leisure interests is especially characteristic of marriages that working-class men describe. Free time is especially important for these men, who have little control over their work, yet working-class marriages (more than middle-class ones) tend to be sex-segregated, and consequently, men's leisure interests are often different from women's. An x-ray technician complained that he and his wife "did not do things together" and expressed his sadness that she did not join him in doing things that were important to him:

> I don't think she ever rode my motorcycle. Which is no big deal, but I thought she should try it. It's not that big a thing, but enough things like this add up. (N034)

His words recall those of the woman office manager who spoke in a similar vein about having to go to midnight Mass alone. Company at midnight Mass or on a motorcycle—both speakers are remembering separate spheres of leisure in marriage; both exemplify how far apart women and men in working-class marriages are in the activities they value and want to share with a spouse. Although women and men can and do go to church and ride motorcycles, in practice both of these activities tend to be gender-linked. Attendance at church has a long tradition as part of a woman's sphere, and is associated with the wife's historic role as moral arbiter of the home. Motorcycle riding is firmly anchored in the world of male adventure and daring.[12]

Men remember and describe gender segregation and tension even in family outings. A highway foreman tells a story about a time when he, his wife, and their son and daughter went out together:

> She never liked to do the things that I liked doing. Once, we were going through the old town of Sturbridge and there's different things that I wanted my oldest son to see, different ways of life back in the past. I wanted to show him what they did back then. And my ex-wife would say, "Go ahead and take him." She would sit there waiting for us and then she'd send my youngest boy in. "Ma wants to go. Ma wants to go." When we were right in the middle of something, me explaining something to him. . . . Instead of her taking my daughter to a place where they made clothing or something that a woman would do, cooking, show them what the women did. No, she wanted all of them there so she could more or less have fun, instead of showing what happened in the past. (N020)

"Having fun" means very different things to this husband and wife. His account is permeated with commonsense understandings about what should interest boys, not girls, and women, not men. These tacit rules of thumb include the belief that his wife and daughter would be interested in clothing and cooking in colonial America. For reasons that are not clear in his account, his wife resists this definition, maybe because she wants the family to do things together. Whatever the reason, we see the link between gender and leisure being forged not only for the couple but for their children. At the same time, "his" and "her" recreation interests produce tension in marriage, clashing with the expectation for companionship.

Although men with professional occupations complain less about lack of shared leisure with wives, when they do it is almost as if the existence of contrasting interests constitutes "proof" that the marriage is not viable. These men reason that if a marriage does not provide companionship, it offers nothing at all. Leisure and planning for leisure occupy a large part of middle-class life, and men work hard in order to be able to provide for family recreation. "Doing things together" solidifies bonds, and if men cannot have good times with wives at these moments, they sense there is no basis for marriage. A physical therapist sums up his recollections of his marriage:

> I think we had a relationship that was a strong physical relationship, but I don't believe we really had a real commonality of interest. We kind of would make things do, that we could share, that neither one of us was terribly excited about. She might humor me by going to see a play or something that I wanted to see and I might see a ballet or something that she wanted to see. But there were no real common interests. Like I like to run, I like to play tennis, I like to be physically active and play golf. Judy would go out to play golf and walk through holes, sit down in the shade and say, "To hell with this." She took some tennis lessons, but she's never developed any interest or any aptitude for it. So you had two people who really cared a lot about each other but I don't think we really had the commonality of interest in the relationship. (N036)

MEN'S VIEWS ABOUT SEX IN MARRIAGE

As mentioned earlier, both women and men in the sample complained about sex in marriage but, as others have found, the men tended to be more dissatisfied with it than did the women. The men's responses suggest why this might be so. Instead of viewing sex as women tend to—as a way to express intimacy already established by talking and sharing—men expected to become intimate with their wives through sex. In their minds, if the sexual aspect of a marriage is working, that is proof that good communication is taking place.[13]

Because wives see sex so differently, it is no wonder that many men are dissatisfied with the sexual aspects of marriage and that the bedroom becomes a major battleground in the modern family. Some men describe conflict over the frequency of sexual intercourse and corroborate women's remarks cited earlier that indicate women exercise power in marriage by withholding sex. A high school teacher says:

> I was . . . sick of fighting about sex, and when to have sex. Having to, you know, almost beg for it at times. (C023)

Wives try to enforce their definitions to how sex ought to occur. Because men cannot feel intimate if they do not have sex, a consequence of the downward spiral in frequency of marital sex is extreme loneliness. Bill, a maintenance supervisor, portrays this vividly:

> In my bedroom, I felt really lonely. In my bedroom. I don't have to tell you about it, but when you get married, and the first night of your marriage and someone turns to the side and says goodnight, I mean, what the heck. (C046)

Because sex is a major way to achieve intimacy for men, the absence of sex creates a kind of loneliness for them that women never describe. As a way of managing their disappointment, some men blame their wives by defining the problem as "frigidity." (The women's accounts suggest that the problem may have been otherwise.) Several men, at the same time that they admitted that their sexual style was different from their wives', retrospectively understood that their wives wanted emotional intimacy before physical intimacy. An academic says:

> She would be much more desirous of tenderness, affection, you know, apart from a sexual relationship, and I'd be much less available, let alone initiating of that with her. (C041)

Another man, a pharmacist, talking about his difficulties in "communication" with his wife, describes his approach:

> I went in with the wrong point of view. I went in from the sexual point, I thought, tried more stimulating new approaches and stuff. That wasn't where she was coming from. That's where I thought things were. That's what was bothering me. I found out later that [other] things were bothering her and she just withdrew. (N019)

An extreme example of difference in sexual styles is expressed by an accountant:

> One of the reasons we separated, on my part and on my wife's part, was sexual incompatibility. I wanted to do lots of things, in experimental types of ways, group sex, bisexuality, swinging, and my wife does not like to do that. (N032)

Some men handle sexual issues in marriage by having affairs. As noted earlier, when women find out about them they often feel deeply betrayed—a reaction that men are acutely aware of. Joe, the corrections counselor, comments:

> Once I told her that I wasn't monogamous, she would never forgive me for that . . . that caused a slow degeneration, that was a snowball rolling down hill, gradually got worse and worse.
> *Int.:* She hadn't known?
> *Joe:* Well, I was honest with her. I mean, from the beginning I told her that if I couldn't get [enough of] it at home, I would get it someplace else . . . and that created problems. . . . There were times when I wasn't honest with her, but that was because I saw her reaction to my honesty. . . . But I always tried to be honest with her about the decisions I made, things I was doing. (N012)

Joe displays his awareness of his wife's values—for honesty and faithfulness—however insensitively he attempts to accommodate them. Another man—an attorney—is more considerate of his wife's values while at the same time he struggles with being gay:

> I think there was a time in there when I didn't know what I was, whether I was bisexual or whether it was a fantasy or whatever. I needed time to explore and what I really wanted from her was

permission to go out and do some exploring. And I didn't get that from her and I didn't feel that I could really carry on that kind of a relationship knowing how much she opposed it. . . . She thought that my being gay was just a phase and she thought that I was attracted to men and that I had never slept with men. And it was not until I admitted that I had had sexual relations with men that she said, "O.K., let's go see an attorney." Then she was very quick, when she realized that it just wasn't a fantasy of mine, a phase. She just refused to acknowledge it for a long time. And then once she knew for a fact, that was it. (N035)

Surprisingly, some men judge their wives' infidelity lightly, or not as harshly as wives tend to view their husbands'. A few men (but no women) define infidelity as a "nonissue" in the marriage and mention it in passing, their words suggesting that their wife's affair is not the critical factor in their calculus of why the marriage failed. A bank officer, who found out that his wife had had an affair at a convention, says:

I knew that she, at some important level, still loved me . . . but I realized that there were areas [where] our marriage wasn't working and so I felt if she needed to do that [have affairs] then that was all right. (N040)

Several months after this decision, his wife "decided it was time to leave."

That some men interpret wives' affairs less harshly than women do is surprising. Historically, a wife's adultery has nearly always been seen as a profound insult to a man's virility and punishable by divorce or worse, while men's adultery was accepted and condoned. More recently sexual scripts have been changing, and younger middle-class women and men, especially, are beginning to behave in ways more similar to each other, which perhaps influences some divorcing men's reactions to their wives' affairs.[14]

At the other extreme, there are men who are jealous of their wives' relationships with men, even when it is not altogether clear that the involvements were sexual. Five men (four of whom have working-class occupations) report that their wives "stayed out late" or went "out to coffee" with a man after work. For Neil, a truck driver, it is what his wife told him about her life before they married that he cannot forget:

Every now and then she would stay out late and she said she was out with some of her friends. It was always in the back of my mind. I didn't like to bring it up because we would start arguing.
Int.: What was in the back of your mind?
Neil: Well, knowing what she told me, what she was like before I met her. It's something you don't forget, it is something you don't talk about, but you don't forget it. (C011)

For a highway foreman, the sexual nature of his wife's occupation—she is a stripper—bothers him deeply, even though he goes along with it because the pay is good:

Her and I went out one night and she got up—they were having an amateur contest—she stood up and did it [danced] after my telling her no, I didn't want her doing it. She went and did it anyway. From then on, she advanced into it. At the time, the money was, you know, the money was good because we were behind on bills. . . . [I felt] degraded, jealous somewhat . . . the way she treated other men. (N020)

For other men, the spouse's infidelity is more than a suspicion; it is real. In these cases, a typical response—particularly for more affluent men—is to emphasize other problems in the marriage that led to the affair. Affairs may function as a catalyst, as husbands' affairs do for some women. The lawyer whose comments on his wife's support group were quoted earlier describes his wife's growing involvement in the women's movement, which in turn led to increasing activity outside the home in political and artistic activities:

As the children got somewhat older and she complained about not having any satisfaction outside the home, she became involved in a number of things. None of which brought in any money. So that became an issue. . . . Acting, . . . dance groups, she had something to do nearly every evening . . . do her own thing and find her own fulfillment. And, you know, that didn't leave me with very much. . . . [Then] through the theater group that she was in, her play husband became more than just a play husband. (C027)

This man situates his wife's affair in an unfolding series of events that take place overtime—the women's movement and the conflict it engenders over the household division of labor, his wife's need for "fulfillment" in activities outside the home, her community participation. In his account, these role changes "didn't leave him with very much" except sole responsibility for economic support, which he deeply resented. It is in the context of all these changes that the affair takes on meaning for him, becoming the "proximate cause" for the separation.

Although this sort of contextual reasoning is much more characteristic of more economically advantaged men, two less advantaged men use it as well. A particularly poignant example is given by an unemployed machinist. Nine years before his separation he had been diagnosed as having multiple sclerosis. His gradual loss of physical function led his wife to begin to drink heavily, according to him, and then to have an affair.

> She met this man at work and she wanted to go out with him. [I said] "Go ahead if you want to, it's your life. You don't have to stay here with me all the time." And she finally moved out and moved in with this man. And I mean I didn't want her still being married to me and going out with this man and so that is when I went ahead and filed for divorce. (C045)

From this statement it would appear that marital infidelity was the primary "cause" of marital failure. When we took at the account as a whole, however, such a conclusion is not warranted. In fact, shortly after making this statement, when the interviewer asked what were the main causes of the separation, he stated emphatically: "My disease. The main cause. She didn't accept it."[15] In other words, he—like a number of others—placed the affair in a web of other events that, taken together, eroded the marriage. Discovery of the affair brought things to a head, but in these men's interpretive schemas, things were troubled already and the affair merely served to resolve the situation.

Men sometimes interpret their own infidelity in the same way. One working-class man, after a lengthy description of the problems in his marriage, described how he had used marital infidelity to resolve the situation:

> I cheated on her. Yeah, I picked up a girl in a bar and I just said, If I'm not going to be faithful, I'm not going to be married. She never knew

about it, but that was it. I said, If I can't be true to her, obviously it is not going to work. (N017)

INSTITUTIONALIZED ROLES

Men and women make sense of their divorces by drawing on an ideal of what modern marriage is supposed to provide: intimacy, primacy and companionship, and sex. Although women and men are alike in noting these three aspects, they tend to define and value each somewhat differently, as we have seen, which suggests that women and men construct marriage in quite distinctive ways. The ideology of the companionate marriage is, in fact, *two* ideologies—his and hers—with specific visions forming the basis each gender uses to explain what went wrong.

But the companionate marriage is more than a set of gender-linked beliefs and expectations. It is also a set of gender-linked roles that, reciprocally, shape women's and men's beliefs about what it means to be a good spouse. Husbands (especially white men) are expected to provide economically for the family; wives may help with support if they are employed. Wives are expected to support husbands by tending the home and raising the children; men may help out around the house. (The word "help" is used advisedly to characterize these gender roles, because primary responsibility and not assistance is the issue here.) Although there has been some change in the content of expectations over the last decade and specific groups in American society have evolved different role structures, considerable research suggests nevertheless that the institutionalized roles of husband and wife continue to provide a general blueprint for marriage, situating men's work primarily in the public sphere and women's in the private.[16] Accounts of divorced women and men provide strong evidence for the continuing presence of traditional beliefs about gender in modern marriage.

Who Should Provide for the Family?

Both women and men expect husbands to support the family economically. To explain divorce, women criticize men, and men criticize themselves, for not fulfilling this expectation. Nearly one-fifth of the sample (20 percent of women and 16 percent of men) mention this issue in explaining why their marriages failed. Implicit in their explanations is a set of assumptions about paid work: men should be the primary ones doing it, and they should do it steadily; even if the wife does it, husbands should make more money; ideally, men should have "good" jobs, but in any case they should be committed to a work ethic and seek advancement; if they become unemployed, it is their own fault.

Although male employment is the ideal, the reality is often quite different. When husbands become unemployed, wives become breadwinners, and this causes considerable resentment, voiced in different ways by different women. This factory worker says:

> He sat home and I worked three jobs. . . . Stop and Shop [a grocery store], I was doing Tupperware, and I was working at Rush Chemical [a factory]. And it got to a point where I would come home and I was cranky and didn't know what time it was. At that point, my mother-in-law said you have got to stop this and make him go to work. (N026)

A physician is equally outraged by her husband's lack of commitment to the breadwinner role, even though her income amply provides for the family:

> Bob has not worked in the years of our marriage very much; the last seven years we've been here he's worked essentially one year. And he was able to be chairman of the board [of the temple] because I was working and I was supporting him. (C010)

The behavior of these husbands would not merit comment if "he" were a "she." For other women, it is not unemployment but the kind of work their husbands do. Middle-class women expect husbands to have careers, not just jobs, and they fault them for lack of ambition when men choose occupations that are "mindless" (L014), even if the pay is good.

When husbands do not work steadily and at jobs that are considered appropriate, wives define this as individual failure. A Hispanic woman's husband was chronically unemployed during their marriage. She says that he understood it as ethnic discrimination, but in her mind the explanation is different:

Several times we had to apply for state assistance. And for me I grew up in an environment where that was looked upon as being the wrong thing to do. I always felt that as long as you were healthy and capable you should work and earn your own living. And for him to accept defeat so easily was not something that I approved. (N024)

In her account, *his* responsibility for *their* situation is a dominant theme, and alternative sources of economic support, such as state aid, are unacceptable. She, like other wives, locates blame in the man rather than in the economic order, where discrimination and structural unemployment are central features. In using these explanatory schemas, women are drawing on widely held cultural beliefs about individualism, the work ethic, and how men's worth is determined.

Men speak poignantly of the effects of these beliefs on their self-esteem, remembering back to their marriages: "If I didn't have enough work, I was not a valid, existing person" (N030). The amount of money men bring into the home is a direct indication, in their minds as well as their wives', of their ability or worth. The burden of the role of breadwinner, coupled with the cultural ethic of individual responsibility for material failure, erodes men's sense of themselves and undermines their position in the family.

Although women frequently respond to tight budgets by seeking employment themselves, they often do so resentfully. This further exacerbates marital problems, as Ruby, an exotic dancer, recalls:

When he was working, he wasn't bringing in enough money and he would not go out and get a second job. A part-time job. He totally and absolutely refused to get another job. He was really mad that I was working, but like I told him, "If you don't want to make the money, I gotta. There are habits that are very hard to shed, like eating or having a roof over your head so you don't get wet in the rain and don't freeze your tail off in winter." (N018)

Women's employment is a source of friction in a number of the marriages.[17] Cynthia, an academic administrator, says that the "immediate precipitating event" of her separation was that "he insisted I leave my job," and she goes on to interpret this demand, saying, "My area of independence has to do with my work and he wants to take that away from me" (C026). Other women say that husbands did not

53

take their work outside the home seriously. For one, the issue was her graduate studies:

> He treated me rather paternalistically. If he were asked [about it, he'd say] going to school was nice, because it gave me something to do. I think he never took it very seriously. (C034)

For a psychotherapist, the lack of respect her husband showed toward her work chronically undermined her sense of herself as a worthwhile person:

> My work was a big thing that he devalued and just simplified. . . . He essentially thought I was holding hands, you know, kind of superficially kind of patting people on the back. . . . Everything will be O.K., that kind of thing. (C048)

Men's lack of enthusiasm for their wives' employment is understandable, because in many ways it does not serve their interests. As a general rule, women's employment results in their greater independence and power in the family. It may also increase the likelihood of divorce, because as women's earnings increase, so does the probability of marital dissolution.[18] Paid employment may lead to the loss of the wife's services in the home, and put pressure on husbands to do more around the house.

In a complaint reminiscent of wives' objections to what they saw as their husbands' overcommitment to work, husbands also find that their wives' employment takes time away from the primacy and companionship they expect. Bob, a professor, when asked what were the causes of his separation, said, "Her lack of concern for me, my lack of importance to her." He goes on to specify:

> She's a schoolteacher and five nights a week she would be locked away in the study doing homework, and very often Saturday and Sunday afternoons. (N006)

In some men's minds, the employment of their wives is linked to affairs. In the course of explaining why the marriage failed, men associate their wives' involvement with work outside the home with their actual or imagined sexual involvement with other men. A truck driver describes the sequence of events this way:

My wife never worked. She wanted to work and I didn't really want her to work. Finally I said, O.K., we can use the money. That is where she met the first person she wanted to be with. (N039)

When wives work outside the home, it relieves men of the pressure to be the sole economic providers, but at the same time it lessens their sphere of control in the family. To some men, it may imply they have failed as providers. It also undermines the primacy of the marriage and limits the time available for companionship from wives— expectations of marriage that men hold dear.

Who Should Care for the Home?

Just as women blame men for not being good providers, some men blame women for not being good housekeepers, with a quarter making negative comments about the quality of their wives' performance in the role of homemaker. A worker in a group home said:

She was not a very good housekeeper and was a pretty disorganized and sloppy person most of the time. When she wanted to be organized, she would do a very good job of it, but then she would let everything go to hell and she wouldn't pick up after herself. (L009)

Not unlike women, who locate responsibility for the family's economic problems in their husbands' deficient characters and not the economic system, men locate responsibility for poor housekeeping in their wives' characters, not in the system of roles in the family. Bill, the maintenance supervisor, who complained about "laundry piled up all over" and "mold growing in the refrigerator," suggests a solution that did not occur to him at the time:

Yeah, I could have done it myself, but that's another issue. . . . Maybe that's a chauvinistic thing, well, why didn't I always clean the house? I don't know, but I didn't. (C046)

In the role structure of modern marriage, wives are expected to care for the home, and even if employed, wives continue to do the vast majority of housework, tasks that are menial, repetitive, done in isolation, and carry no economic independence. As feminists have argued, this work is not only essential to maintaining the family but essential to maintaining a work force.[19]

Wives speak of feeling devalued when their labor is not respected. Many report they did not receive "recognition" for their responsibilities in the household—for example, "appreciation" for the care that went into food preparation. Tessa describes the resentment she came to feel:

> He was a pig. I had to scrub and wax floors just about every day and he'd come in with three inches of clay on his boots and I'd have to, I'd literally have to follow him from one end of the house to the other. And he was in the bedroom with greasy clothes, laid on my clean bed. It made me furious. He had so little respect and consideration for me. It's totally demeaning to have to do that every day. (C017)

In reinterpreting their marriages some men rethink their tendency to take their wives' labor for granted, as this truck driver comments:

> I think that was one of my greatest problems. I didn't really treat her as a person. She was the robot of the house, you know. (N039)

Wives press husbands to do their share, especially chores like fixing things and minor repairs that are usually the province of men in traditional marriages. Women try to exercise power by controlling husbands' behavior in the home, often unsuccessfully, as Steve, a highway foreman, describes:

> My wife, and this is something that led up to our divorce, was awfully demanding about things around the house that had to be done. I'm not enthused about stuff that has to be done around the house. . . . There was a lot of pressure put on me to be the perfect husband/father, who worked eight hours a day and came home at night, was out mowing the lawn or, Saturday, cutting the grass. (C040)

The home ceases being the haven men want and instead becomes the battleground for a war about seemingly trivial matters—who does what.

The institutionalized roles that form the basis of modern marriage cause conflict, in large part because they are not separate and equal. The role of breadwinner brings status, recognition, and economic reward in the larger world; the role of homemaker does not. The subordinate economic position women held perpetuates their dependence on men within families and further reinforces the unequal division of labor in the home. In reconstructing what marriage was like, divorcing women and men pinpoint this fundamental tension in contemporary marriage—between inegalitarian roles, on the one hand, and the ideology of equality, on the other. For women, especially, the costs of this tension are very high.

INEQUALITY: WOMEN'S MEMORIES OF DEVALUATION AND DOMINATION

Modern marriage is predicated on an ideology of equality between the spouses. In wedding vows, the partners agree to "honor" one another and it is understood that husbands' and wives' contributions to the marriage, however different, will both be valued. Marriage is seen as a "joint enterprise," and legally women's contribution to the partnership, even if it is not in the form of income or property, entitles her to a share in "his" estate. Aside from the economic aspect, the ideal vision of a companionate marriage depends on a notion of equality. In order for there to be emotional intimacy, companionship, and mutually satisfying sex between marital partners, spouses must see themselves as individuals, with rights. In order for the gender-linked roles of breadwinner and homemaker to function in a complementary way, each role must be seen as important.[20] The women's liberation movement, advocating, among other things, that wives' work is at least as important as husbands', provides an additional impetus for equality in domestic relations.

Divorcing women remember marriage as anything but equal. Although they may have promised to honor, they may also have promised to obey. Some vividly convey their sense of subordination:

I was in a shell. . . . I was . . . a puppet. (N011)

His narrow philosophy of life chained me in. (N025)

He treated me very much like a child. (L008)

There was no me at all then. . . . I was kind of huddled into a corner, beaten down and bloody. (C017)

Images of the experience of subordination fill some women's accounts—being a child, overwhelmed, buried, chained-in, and controlled. Other women remember instances in which they were devalued and discredited—more subtle forms of domination. Sometimes the issue is physical beauty, as this clerical worker recalls:

> I remember once he screamed at me because, it was in the evening you know, and I'd had a bath and I had no makeup on, only my glasses. I looked more like a granny and he really screamed at me. (C006)

This woman is eight years older than her former husband and thus explains, to herself and the interviewer, "Maybe my age was bothering him." For another woman, it is her physical attractiveness in bed:

> He never told me that he didn't like flannel pajamas. We were wearing bathrobes to bed because it was so cold. And I didn't know and so I went to bed in flannel pajamas and he never touched me. . . . I could never understand. It wasn't until about a year and a half ago, the winter before, when he told me he wished I wouldn't wear flannel pajamas to bed. So I stopped . . . and tried dressing up and then when I did, he thought I was doing it for somebody else. (N026)

In both cases, these women do not question cultural notions of femininity—youth, make-up, and frilly nightgowns—but rather locate blame in their husbands' "lack of respect" for them when they, as wives, did not live up to the cultural standard.

Some women remember being devalued for their modes of thought. The man who screamed at his wife for looking like a "granny" also called her "woolly-minded." She explains it this way:

> Well, I think because Alex had a much higher education than I. He's a scientist, he's very explicit, he knows exactly what he's saying and why he's saying it at all times. . . . I don't. I should start things at the beginning and think them right through. Apparently I don't. (C006)

This woman appears to accept her husband's depiction of her mode of thought as inadequate, but other women do not. A physician sarcastically mocks her husband's descriptions of her:

I was irrational, I couldn't think straight, and I couldn't have an argument that could be followed and I, you know, the way he described me, I could not, you would never believe that I would be able to have a practice and keep one patient for one second. (C010)

A teacher's aide is also critical of her husband's portrayal of her cognitive abilities, using language to mimic him:

He had done a job on me. I was very well trained, I mean, I was the ugly one, I was the stupid one, I was the one that, you know, couldn't go out into the world and make 2 cents for myself, [or] needless to say, you know, keep a job. I couldn't do anything right, I was just a stupid person, a retard, lock her up in the attic and let her out once in a while, don't let the neighbors know she's around. I was in a shell, I was afraid to meet people, I was afraid to talk to people because I thought, Oh my god, you know he's right, I am stupid and I think I'm a little wacko in the head, too. (N011)

Some women speak of even more blatant manifestations of inequality and "lack of respect" in recalling psychological domination by husbands. A few men corroborate women's statements and are self-critical, saying: "I ordered her around like a little Hitler" (N039), "I was too much of a demagogue . . . a dictator" (N019). Wives say their husbands attempted to exert power over a variety of domestic decisions: from the kind of food that would be served and which purchases would be made, to how wives used their time, to what religion they would practice. As wives construct it, husbands both demean their domesticity and try to dominate it, often at the same time. Tessa, a mother on welfare, describes this form of domestic control in a specific incident:

You know, I put some bacon in a meatloaf one time and he threw the whole damn thing out because he didn't want to eat it. So we went hungry that night, just that type of thing. He just made life miserable. It was like living in tyranny, you know, and I never knew what he wanted, 'cause he just wouldn't tell me, he'd just say, "Well, fix supper," and, you know, if I asked him what he wanted, 'cause he just wouldn't tell me, he'd say, "Well, I'll leave it up to you," and when I'd go to do something, he'd say that isn't good enough, you know. (C017)

"Living in tyranny" is not limited to poor women, though its manifestations are subtler sometimes in the middle class. Cynthia, an academic administrator quoted earlier, cared for her husband's three children from a previous marriage. She describes the directives she received from her husband:

> I had to make sure when Manny came home from school that he immediately changed into his play clothes and he only watched a certain amount of television and that he immediately got involved in his piano lessons and his homework and he didn't leave the TV on when he did his homework and, you know, there were just a lot of rules that I had to keep in mind that were rules which had not been generated by me . . . someone else's rules that I had to memorize. (C026)

Cynthia, like others, went along with husband's directives in order to keep peace at home. ("I did what I felt I had to do in order to maintain a somewhat harmonious marriage.") Only later—after the separation and with her family's coaching—does she redefine his behavior, saying she was "personally mistreated and used a great deal."

When women want to return to school or enter the job market, husbands often disapprove, according to wives. Over and over, women from working-class marriages report that their husbands "said no." Again, in order to keep the peace, these women often acquiesce, though not without resentment.

Wives' experience of psychological domination by their husbands attests to what Carol Brown calls "private patriarchy"—the control of the individual husband over the individual wife within the family system. But the husbands' control over their wives' daily labor is upheld by "public patriarchy" as well, for men on average enjoy a monopoly of high-status jobs, knowledge, and property. One woman, who completed a graduate degree after her separation, speaks of her growing consciousness of the structural basis outside the family for her husband's power within the family:

> My husband is a physician, and a lot of the people we knew were graduate students, people becoming various things, attaining different goals. And I think the wives, although it didn't seem to me at the time, as I look back I think the wives were pretty much regarded as supporting these men [to] become lawyers, or physicians, ministers, whatever they were. (C034)

As this woman has come to understand, a professional man's occupational and financial advantage often depends on the "invisible work" that his wife does in the home. Yet women's economic dependence on husbands provides the rationale for men to dominate them in psychological ways.[21]

The economic power of white men creates a serious dilemma for white women: on the one hand, economic support through marriage enables most of these women to live better than they otherwise could; on the other hand, economic subordination creates dependency on men and on marriage, just as it limits women's bargaining power in the home. An academic says:

> He supported me though my first year of graduate school and this financial dependency to me has always been a source of pain. I had no other alternative at the time, but I felt that in making myself financially beholden to Terry, I was thereby set in a very subordinate status to him. (C008)

She goes on to describe the consequences of being "financially beholden":

> I felt that sort of underneath things, all the way along, as long as I could not make my own living, or was not making my own living, I felt indebted to Terry, that I could not call him on his impotence, for example, I could not call him on his emotional insensitivity, I couldn't assert myself or ask that my—a phrase that I loathe—that my needs be fulfilled. Because he was feeding me, he was housing me, he was clothing me, he was schooling me. (C008)

Being fed, housed, clothed, and schooled by their husbands, while beneficial in certain respects, is costly as well, and this woman felt silenced because of her financial dependency. As the woman who finished her graduate degree after her separation put it, "I had to go to my husband for any request" and "there was no sense that any part of that income could be controlled by me" (C034). Money was also used more overtly to control this wife's behavior during a particularly strained period:

> He did things such as refuse to pay my tuition anymore and refuse to pay for gas for me to get to school. (C034)

In a few cases, husbands controlled financial decisions even in the absence of superior earning power. In the experience of many divorcing women, the ideology of equality is far removed from the reality—marriage is not a joint enterprise, in which both spouses are equally entitled to share the fruits of their united efforts.

Women are also subject to the most severe form of domination—physical violence, the ultimate act of inequality in the family. Nearly a quarter of the individuals in the sample describe physical abuse and, like other forms of domination, it is husbands who perpetrate it and wives who are its primary victims, especially poor women.[22]

Although it deeply violates women's beliefs about marriage, physical abuse is not always considered a sufficient cause to leave. Some women leave the first time they are hit, others do not. For a salesclerk who had been abused for years, it is only when her daughter is physically hurt that she begins to move toward separation. Examining the conversation between this interviewee and interviewer, we see how she constructs her divorce account in the context of the research interview itself and, further, where physical abuse fits into her causal reasoning:

Int.: What were the main causes of separation?
Sally: I think, probably, um, I think we were married young and we grew two different ways. I think we don't have anything in common. . . . Our views on almost everything are different. Most especially child rearing. There was a lot of verbal and physical abuse that went on. . . .
Int.: Do you think that hitting them [the children] was one of the major things that led you—
Sally: To see that he would never stop hitting, yeah. . . . The final blow came when he punched our oldest daughter across the living room and then I just told him to get out. . . . He'd punched me out for years but he'd never done that to her and if he was going to start doing that to the kids that was it. . . .
Int.: So, really, the major thing was the abuse?
Sally: Yeah, well, I don't know as I could say that. I guess it was, probably. Even without the abuse, though, it often led to abuse, but even without it like we didn't have much in common and it kind of seems senseless to live with somebody when you have nothing together. You know, we didn't have much between us. It probably would have come

to that eventually anyways, but with the abuse like it just made it come all that much sooner probably. (N015)

Despite the interviewer's suggestion that physical abuse is the "major thing" that led to separation, Sally is clear that it is not the primary cause; the cause is "having nothing in common," or lack of companionship.

More typically, however, abused women do see physical violence as causal in their divorces. As they remember it, physical abuse is the critical incident or turning point in the decision to leave the marriage. A salesclerk says:

That was the last straw. You just don't hit me. . . . I wasn't going to stay around to be hit again. (C024)

Divorcing women resist the devaluation and domination they experienced in their marriages, and one way they do this is by reinterpreting interactions with their husbands in these terms after they have separated. They usually stop short of defining the problem as inequality. For a few women professionals, feminism provides a set of understandings, heightening their awareness of devaluing experiences and providing a language for interpreting them as sexual politics. As one said, "Until I had the words from the women's literature, there was no way I could understand" (C010). For most, however, the language of the women's movement is not overtly present, though in more subtle ways, understandings gleaned from feminism may have changed perceptions about things husbands did and said. Women more often interpret their experiences in private ways, contrasting their realities with what they had thought marriage would provide. Through personal experience they uncover the "oppression, conflict and violence hidden behind a portrait of love and nurturance."[23]

GENDERED REALITIES

Contrary to Tolstoy's assertion that "every unhappy family is unhappy in its own way," the themes in the talk of divorcing individuals suggests certain similarities in the experience of unhappy families, particularly when we take gender into consideration.[24] Women's and men's explanations of what went wrong can be arrayed along a set of common dimensions, with shades of variation around these common understandings both within and between gender groups. Although individuals usually think their experiences are unique, in fact they have much in common.

Building an Account to Explain the Loss of the "Dream"

Individuals make sense of divorce by reviewing their marriage. They develop elaborate accounts of their marital experiences. Reconstructing and reinterpreting the past, as we have seen, is an essential activity in the process of reestablishing control and reconstituting meaning after loss.

Some explicitly acknowledge that they are building accounts, and they do this quite self-consciously as part of a healing process. Al, a craftsman, says:

> I started on my own search to find out what was wrong with our relationship for me. I did two different things, one was to try to construct my way out of the relationship, try to construct a reason why I shouldn't be in it. . . . And the other thing I did was to just think and think and talk and talk. (C032)

An academic comments on his explanation of why his marriage ended, saying, "This is all like a construct that I've really evolved in my own thinking and feeling about it" (C041).

In using the word "construct," both men identify several important features of accounts. First, they are constructed, rather than inherent in the situation; accounts are not "objective" descriptions of the marriage—if such is ever possible. Second, they are built or put together out of a series of elements; they are highly structured rather than randomly organized. Third, accounts "evolve"; they do not spring into existence but are constructed within particular contexts. Finally, accounts are the products of interpretive actors; they are produced interactionally through talk, and the conversation of the interview is one context in which accounts are developed. Put differently, the search for a "good enough" account is a dynamic process. People struggle to integrate disjunctive experiences into their personal biographies, not always as quickly as they might wish, as Al reveals in his question to the interviewer:

> *Al:* People you talk to who have been separated or divorced for a much longer period of time, do they feel more clear as to why?
> *Int.:* People develop accounts of why it happened.
> *Al:* Uh, uh, are they *real?* Who knows . . . Yeah, Sally [wife] has an account and it is a good one. It makes sense to her. Uh, yeah, I guess I'm still trying to get my account together. I haven't got it together. I'm sorry. (C032)

Al articulates his struggle to develop an account in order to "make sense" of what went wrong and "get it together." He feels "sorry" that he is not able to. He thinks that his listener expects an organized explanation for divorce, and he feels deficient in some way because he is not able to provide one.

History and Culture in Private Accounts

Although individuals' accounts have many aspects that were unique, they also draw on many common understandings. Precisely because individuals "take account" of American cultural values about marriage in their explanations of their divorces, the accounts make sense—both to themselves and to their listeners—because they draw on background knowledge and taken-for-granted assumptions about the modern family that many Americans share. They seem natural, transparent, a part of the structure of the world precisely because they incorporate our "native knowledge."[25]

The major cultural theme that these women and men draw on is the ideal of personal fulfillment through a companionate marriage.[26] They have a specific vision of what a love relationship ought to provide, and they explain their divorces on the grounds that the dream was not realized.

This assumption needs to be set in the context of most of human history, where duty to one another, not love, has been the basis of marriage. Stone describes marriage prior to the late eighteenth century:

> Marriages in the past were more than the individual unions of two spouses for affective or procreative purposes. They were that, and

companionship, love and lust certainly helped to bind these unions, but these were all secondary considerations. Marriages created economic partnerships, each spouse being responsible for his or her specialized functions. In any case, marriage offered the only respectable career open to most women, who faced destitution if it was terminated. Marriages were also alliances between families and kin groups, creating social and political ties of crucial importance to large numbers of persons. Finally, marriages acted as the most important vehicles for the transfer of property, far more important than purchase and sale. Small wonder that it was extremely difficult to disentangle this complex web of ties, and few even wanted to do so, however bad the marriage might be.[27]

Americans today believe something quite different, thinking it is their right to find complete happiness, including romantic love, here on earth.[28]

The idea that marriage should be companionate is a relatively recent belief, emerging in the United States around the beginning of the nineteenth century. It served the needs of a capitalist society based on competition and individualism. In the words of historian Elaine Tyler May, people "turned with increasing fervor to the private side of life, perhaps to compensate for a loss of satisfaction elsewhere."[29] What changes are involved in this new vision?

Romantic love, personal attraction, and compatibility became respectable motives for marriage for the first time. As a consequence of this new basis of mate selection, emotional bonds between spouses became the core of family life, and the couple, not the larger world of kin and community, became the principal object of attachment. Put differently, the conjugal family turned more in upon itself. Sexual expression within marriage was elevated in importance, because it exemplified the affectional ties and emotional exclusivity of the couple. As a result, the institution of marriage became sensualized. The companionate marriage was also characterized by a marked division of labor, with sharply differentiated roles for husband and wife. As production moved outside the home, men became solely responsible for providing economically for the family. Domesticity, and the associated roles of mother and homemaker, ascended in importance, with a consequent improvement in the overall situation of women. At the same time, however, the confinement of married women to the home and its moral governance limited their social participation. As the family was increasingly stripped of many of its material functions (production, education, care of the sick), it became redefined primarily in emotional terms—as a source of fulfillment, a place for psychic recharging, and the primary context for personal happiness in an age of "affective individualism." Finally, divorce became an integral part of the new conjugal family, for it was essential to a system of marriage that emphasized the often ephemeral bonds of affection and companionship. Divorce was necessary when free choice, as opposed to family and community interests, became the basis for family formation. In fact, at the turn of the century the pursuit of happiness through marriage took many couples into wedlock and out again; the divorce rate soared.[30]

These changes in marriage (which did not, of course, emerge in such an orderly fashion) went hand in hand with changes both in the ideologies about the "true" natures of women and men and in the rules governing relations between husbands and wives. The recognition that women gained for their domestic roles broke the ancient hierarchy that had assigned superiority to men in all realms of activity. Although hierarchy still prevails among father, mother, and children, the companionate marriage is characterized by greater equality in comparison with other forms of marriage. After all, major hallmarks of the companionate ideal—deepening affection and companionship between spouses—depend upon and in turn foster an ideology of equality between women and men. Too, the importance of romantic love as a basis for marriage depends upon a belief in the self-sufficiency of the marital pair; the couple has to have an existence somewhat separate and apart from kin and community control.[31]

The history of marriage influences individuals' accounts of their divorces today. The companionate ideal is stronger than it ever was. Recent evidence shows that spouses' reliance on one another—both for emotional reassurance and for companionship in leisure—is much greater now than even a generation ago. Some argue the family has become a refuge, a private retreat (particularly for men), as well as the center for a new kind of emotional life where personal fulfillment is the ultimate goal. In addition to history, modern cultural themes also influence divorce accounts by legitimating particular decisions. Ann Swidler discusses the philosophy of "expressive individualism" that is so deeply engrained in the American character that it informs much of what we believe about love. Because the need to realize and explore the self in romantic relations is a quintessential preoccupation, when we can no longer find self-development in the sphere of private life, we define it as the demise of love. U.S. society has provided a home for a primary focus on intimate relations, and, not coincidentally, it places a high value on the individualism and secularism necessary for such a cultural theme to take root. We are a society obsessed with personal life, just as work on the self now constitutes a legitimate form of work.[32]

As the divorce accounts show, the ideal of a "marriage of companions" persists in the imaginations of people, despite a reality that often contradicts it. In holding this view of marriage as the standard, divorcing individuals affirm its romantic vision. Individuals justify their divorces on the grounds that the ideal's central components—emotional intimacy, primacy and companionship, and sexual fulfillment—were lacking. They lament their spouses' performance of the institutionalized roles of husband or wife that are associated with the companionate ideal. And they graphically describe how the preconditions for the companionate marriage as traditionally defined—role differentiation and yet equality—were violated.

Some have argued that the companionate model of marriage is a middle-class phenomenon, and that the ideals of marriage that working-class couples hold for marriage are quite different. Others have argued that over time the model has become more pervasive, infusing the visions of both class groups about what a "good" marriage should provide.[33] The findings here tend to support the latter position: working-class and middle-class interviewees were more often alike than different, though certain complaints tended to cluster in one group and not the other.

On a more general level, then, divorce accounts are more than a set of individualized complaints. The accounts are historically situated and contextually grounded. Though seemingly "private" constructions, they are cultural products, as individuals create personal understandings out of the materials that are available to them, including publicly available meanings. These meanings are by no means universal. In China, for example, individuals "underplay all matters of the heart" and couples depend on a broad array of other individuals, which mitigates the intensity of the emotional bonds of love.[34] The Chinese would thus not interpret divorce (which happens rarely) on the basis of expectations about emotional intimacy and shared leisure interests as Americans now do.

Gender and the Construction of Modern Marriage

Although both women and men draw on the general ideology of a companionate notion of marriage in their accounts, their valuation of its features are not the same. The contemporary vision of marriage is heavily gendered. Women and men have distinctive understandings about how emotional intimacy, primacy and companionship, and sexual fulfillment ought to be realized. For women, marriage flounders because husbands fail to be emotionally intimate in the ways wives expect them to be. This element of the companionate marriage is the centerpiece in women's accounts, working class and middle class alike. For men, the explanatory schema is very different: particularly for more economically advantaged men, the marriage failed because other relationships—with children, kin, and friends—were not subordinated to it; the marital relationship was not self-contained or was not primary enough to the wife. For both husbands and wives there was a failure in companionship; yet the particular activities women and men wanted to "do together" are strikingly different, especially in working-class marriages. And both women and men lament acts of sexual infidelity and incompatibility, though the interpretations they place on these events are not the same. For women, infidelity is an act of betrayal, living proof the marriage is over. Men have complex and differentiated views of infidelity, even as sex is central to their definition of what a good marriage should provide.

Some might argue that these different constructions arise out of the very different personality structures of women and men. Feminist psychological theory suggests that masculinity becomes defined through separation, whereas femininity becomes defined through relationships.[35] Women and men, in bringing these different orientations into marriage, put severe strains on it. Women define the institution of marriage interpersonally. The relationship with the spouse is one of a series of interpersonal ties that coexist for them—not without conflict, of course. Yet at the same time women want marriage to be emotionally intimate through talking about feelings, problems, and daily experiences, and through understandings that go beyond words. Further, they expect talk to be reciprocal: their husbands will disclose to them at the same time as they share with their husbands. Divorced women's accounts describe men who could not or did not express love in these ways, or whose needs for separation, some might argue, precluded this kind of emotional intimacy.

Men want something very different from marriage. Especially prominent is their desire for the undivided attention of their wives. Instead, they discovered they were one among many. Their wives had investments in diverse relationships (with friends, kin, and children), because their socially assigned roles as kinkeepers and mothers required them to tend others in addition to their husbands. Men, in their accounts, lament this. They want the marital relationship to be exclusive and primary; women in contrast, add it to their other relational investments. Men value the autonomy of the marital pair rather than its interconnectedness. They expect to achieve emotional closeness with their wives through sex and a particular kind of companionship. It is these "doing" aspects of marriage that they emphasize.

Although these findings are not inconsistent with feminist scholarship about gender differences in personality, they suggest something further. It is a different *type* of connection that women and men want. It is not separation that men are seeking but connection of a kind entirely different from women's—a particular relationship that is important and primary, where words "are less important than proximity itself," as Rubin describes. Francesca Cancian argues that the masculine style of love emphasizes practical help, shared physical activities, spending time together, and sex—manifestations of love that achieve connection through action rather than talk, just as providing for a family does. This style of love fits well with cultural expectations for men more generally, for achievement, responsibility, instrumentality. [36]

Men's expectations of marriage also make sense in light of their structural position in a capitalist economy. Men are sent into relations of production in order to support families. In this contrast, the home *is* a haven for them, and they seek replenishment from wives. Rayna Rapp notes that "one must work for the sake of the family, and having a family is the 'payoff' for leading a good life." From men's perspective, the primacy of the marital relationship and sexual fulfillment constitute badly needed payoffs. [37]

Women's and men's constructions of marriage raise a further set of questions for feminist scholarship. Despite many common features, the accounts reveal class variation within gender groups. Feminist scholars, particularly those drawn to psychoanalytic theory, have not always attended to class issues and have often drawn on middle-class samples. [38]

Why, for example, was companionship more of an issue in the accounts of the working class? In many jobs that are stripped of autonomy and craft, there is a greater split between living and working. For those who do these jobs, work is typically endured rather than enjoyed, and it serves a delimited instrumental purpose—earning a paycheck. Leisure time becomes highly salient under these conditions. For working-class women whose work is tending a home and raising children on that limited paycheck, moreover, shared adult companionship and activities outside the confines of home represent relief that is sorely needed. For middle-class women and men, in contrast, the split between work and leisure is more blurred and, in some cases, does not exist at all. Put simply, leisure becomes more important when work is alienated, when there is less continuity between what is done during the day and what is done during the evening or on weekends. Lack of companionship, therefore, is more likely to be cited as an explanation for marital failure by those with limited resources. [39]

The complaint that the marital relationship was not primary enough for their wives tends to be voiced more by men with middle-class occupations than by those with a more limited resource base. Working-class men, their wives report, tend to be jealous primarily of women's friendship ties, whereas in middle-class men's minds, relationships with either kin or friends are evidence of a kind of emotional infidelity. Some psychoanalytic investigators have argued that marriage for men replicates the early relationship to the mother and, as such, is emotionally charged in ways that it is not for women. [40] Men thus want an exclusive relationship with their wives—free of kin, friends, and other emotional bonds. But why should middle-class men differ from their working-class counterparts in this desire?

Here again the social experience of different class groups is relevant. Most obviously, middle-class boys are likely to experience an exclusive relationship with a female care giver and hence, perhaps, to want to re-create this model of a relationship in marriage. Working-class men are likely to have experienced care within a kinship system rather than from a single person, because they tend to grow up in families with dense, kin-based networks. Consequently, they do not expect the marital relationship to exist apart from ties to kin and do not define wives' ties to family as problematic, though they do see wives' close friendships as a threat. The very survival of these families often depends on the circulation and pooling of limited resources.[41] Given this reality, there can be no privatizing of the marital relationship apart from kin. In contrast, the middle-class family is more isolated from kin and community and privatized to a much greater degree. Middle-class men turn to the marital relationship to fill a vast array of needs.

Private Meanings for Social Troubles

Neither the women nor the men interviewed, whether working class or middle class, questioned the ideology of the companionate marriage. It was the failure of their particular partners to live up to the ideal that was defined as the problem, not the dream itself. One might argue that there are serious flaws in contemporary beliefs about marriage. Most obviously, it is an idealized image of what a relationship can provide. Few marriages can sustain its core elements, in proper ratio, over time. Given that the essential ingredients of the companionate ideal have different meanings for husbands and wives, a shared consensus is even less likely. Yet personal fulfillment through marriage has become a central preoccupation of American culture—the perpetual quest for the perfect relationship. Paradoxically, these "great expectations" create the very conditions for disappointment and divorce.[42]

How individuals make sense of divorce tells us something, as well, about what people expect when they marry again, for individuals re-create the social order of marriage in the explanatory schemas they invoke to explain its demise. Women and men create very different marital "realities" in their tellings and, by this process, participate in constructing a gendered social world. By holding up the expectation that men should be the primary providers and women should be the caregivers, for example, both women and men reflect and, in turn, reproduce the division of labor that is so consequential for inequality between women and men. In their accounts, they both experience and produce their culture.[43]

There are also inherent strains within the ideal of modern marriage. The realization of the core ingredients of the companionate marriage—emotional intimacy, primacy and companionship, and mutual sexual fulfillment—depends on equality between husbands and wives. Yet institutionalized roles call for differentiation: neither husbands nor wives have been socialized to be equals. The provider role translates into diffuse power within the family and creates inequality between husbands and wives. Wives, in turn, may encourage segregation of roles along traditional lines early in marriage, defining housework and children as their exclusive domain.[44] It is in this context that women become victims and experience subordination. They vividly describe in their accounts how they are financially, psychologically, and physically dominated by their husbands. Women's inequality is incompatible with the formation and maintenance of an equalitarian and companionate partnership.

Yet women are not victims in marriage. As we saw in the accounts of both women and men, women exercised power, often effectively. In thinking about their marriages retrospectively, many are able to make fresh sense of their husbands' domination—redefining the extent to which they are economically dependent, psychologically abused, and physically abused. Beyond these manifestations of control, moreover, women's definitions hold sway over many men (often after the fact), who measure themselves with a feminine ruler and are self-critical of their "doing" style of love. Despite women's structural subordination, their vision about what a relationship ought to be ironically continues to provide a blueprint, feminizing love even while it also intensifies differences between women and men.[45]

In their accounts, women and men seek explanations in their personal situations and psychologies and for the most part eschew structural and political explanations. As Mills reminds us, social problems are often mistaken for individual issues in an individualistic society. The love myth is so powerful precisely because it promises to resolve contradictions; it offers to heal both sides of a duality.[46] Paradoxically, marital difficulties pivot on a duality—gender difference—essential to the definition of marriage itself.

CHAPTER 3

The Teller's Problem

Four Narrative Accounts of Divorce

We tell ourselves stories in order to live. . . . We interpret what we see, select the most workable of the multiple choices. We live entirely . . . by the imposition of a narrative line upon disparate images, by the "ideas" with which we have learned to freeze the shifting phantasmagoria which is our actual experience.

JOAN DIDION, The White Album

What happens when we talk about a divorce? How does a teller convince a listener who was not there that a marriage was seriously troubled, and that he or she was justified in leaving it? How do individuals formulate their accounts, and how and why do they talk about their marriages in such different ways?

These are important questions, because what we do in narrative accounts makes a difference. People are forever composing impressions of themselves, projecting a definition of who they are, and making claims about themselves and the world that they test and negotiate in social interaction. As Goffman remarks, "Participants contribute to a single over-all definition of the situation which involves not so much a real agreement as to what exists but rather a real agreement as to whose claims concerning what issues will be temporarily honored." Humans create their realities through these presentations and responses, and divorcing individuals are no exception. They create who they are, and definitions of their divorce situations, in interaction and through language. We can see the process only by examining, in some detail, longer stretches of talk about when and why they left. There is a reciprocity between form and function, that is, between the way an account is told (*how* it is narrated), the understandings the narrator wants to convey, and the listening process.[1]

AN INTRODUCTION TO NARRATIVE

It is commonplace for people to tell long stories about events that have happened to them. We can all think of times when someone held forth in a conversation, telling in exquisite detail what he said, what she said, what happened next—a recapitulation in chronological order of every seeming nuance of a moment that had special significance for the teller. Narrators hold our attention because they draw us into the world of their story. They build tension by describing the setting, characters, dialogue, and unfolding plot. As Joan Didion suggests, imposing a narrative line on disparate images is not limited to biographers or novelists. We all make sense of disruptive events and heal biographical discontinuities in our lives by constructing storied accounts of them.

Four excerpts from longer narrative accounts will introduce some of the narrative forms we have at our disposal and, at the same time, introduce the people whose experience will be the focus here. The first is told by Tessa, a woman on welfare who lives in a housing project. She is divorcing from her husband because he raped her. She describes what happened in the narrative form most familiar to us— a "story":

> One particular time he had bought me a dozen roses that day, and they were sitting on top of the television which was at the foot of the couch. And he picked up the vase of roses and threw the roses at me, poured the water on me, and dragged me by the arm from the couch to the bedroom, and then proceeded to make love to me. (C017)

In contrast to this graphic story that re-creates a discrete moment in time, Susan narrates what happened to her quite differently. Susan

lives in a middle-class neighborhood, and separated from her husband because of "lack of communication." She says, in a narrative
form I call "habitual narrative":

> And we stopped talking early on in our marriage really. And he spent
> more and more time at work, he didn't want to come home. He'd come
> home and than I would say, "I'd like you to spend a little time with the
> kids." He'd just want to go up and read a book, kind of thing. We just
> didn't communicate really. (N046)

Although the tellers are both women, their marriages could not be
more different, and the same is true of the narrative forms they select
to tell about their experiences. Each woman's experience is rooted in
her specific background, shaped by the realities of life for women in
working-class versus middle-class marriages. The contrasting modes
of presentation vivify difference, not sameness.[2] Susan does not tell a
story, as Tessa does, about a specific instance, but instead narrates
the general course of her marriage over time. The two narratives have
very different effects on us as listeners. Tessa's pulls us into the hor-
ror of the moment, as she invites us to re-experience events *with* her.
Susan's relegates us to a more distant place; we understand, but do
not re-live, her marriage.

Steve is a highway foreman whose avocation is judging dog shows.
He separated because the marriage was not primary enough to his
wife. In the following excerpt he tells of events that he wanted to
happen but that, in fact, never did occur (we learn later that his wife
refused to accompany him on the weekend away):

> I suggested that we leave Friday night. And I would have my room
> Friday night paid for, so no big expense. I would judge the show and
> she would be with me and help me while I'm judging, I do need some
> assistance, and Saturday night we would go into New York after I fin-
> ished the dog show, we would go out to dinner, spend the night in New
> York and come back Sunday. (C040)

I call the form Steve uses a "hypothetical narrative." By contrast Al,
a craftsman who separated from his wife a number of months after

she began an affair, uses the same narrative form Tessa does—a story:

> I finally got up and went into the other room. She was [talking to her lover on the phone] in the laundry room with the door closed. I knocked on the door and said, "When are you going to be done with this?" 'Cause we were going to talk. And she held up her hand like this and went "No." And I got absolutely bullshit and I put my fist through the door. (C032)

The content of Al's story is different from Tessa's story, of course. He tells of a discrete moment in time, of events that culminate in his physical violence, and provides elaboration that helps us visualize the world he is creating in the narrative (his home, its laundry room, his wife's long phone conversation with her lover). As Tessa does in her story, he tells about a particular event and draws us into the story-realm not only by *what* he says, but by the *way* it is told.[3]

As these fragments suggest, individuals narrate their experiences in very different ways, and some are more emotionally affecting that others. In their fuller accounts, some of these narrators combine different narrative genres in their retellings, moving back and forth between them, as we shall see. In this context "genre" refers to types or varieties of narrative that are distinguished by a definite style and are constituted by specific conventions and codes of speech, including verb tense, temporality, sequencing, discourse markers, and other linguistic elements.[4]

Divorcing individuals narrate accounts in such contrasting ways because they face a specific problem in telling about troubled times. As Dennie Wolf describes:

> The problem is, at least in one sense, to convince a listener who wasn't there that these were seriously troubled times and that the speaker hasn't just cooked up this account in order to entertain, lie, or get attention. It, like many other kinds of therapeutic discourse, faces a speaker with justifying her/himself as the main character—both in the sense that s/he was a central agent (not just furniture) and was deeply affected (not indifferent). A speaker also has to prove that the times really did have the qualities s/he says they did. To do this often means

finding some way to provoke a similar state in the listener, at least enough so as to argue, "This is veridical. It did happen. I am justified in having felt as I did."[5]

The divorced also have to convince listeners of another truth: "I was right to *do* what I did, to leave this marriage." In this culture both teller and listener know that marriage is considered a desired and honored state; one cannot walk away from it lightly. In speaking, tellers must render their divorce decisions justifiable or reasonable to their listeners. In the language of Kenneth Burke, the issue is how to persuade through forms of symbolic expression in ways that are rhetorically effective.[6] Narrative genres aid this process.

But narratives are not simply Machiavellian devices to persuade listeners. There is the more basic problem of making sense. As Wolf suggests, the tellers must find a way to make themselves and the times they are describing understandable. Different forms of telling carry with them different understandings. Creating a narrative is an imaginative enterprise, and in them tellers create a context, a special meaning within which they want to be understood. In turn, different narrative styles allow listeners to distinguish between accounts that, on the surface, might appear to be the same. Tessa, Susan, Steve, and Al, in interaction with the listener, each construct an explanation—four different ways of telling. In doing so, they select from a variety of narrative genres (and narrative structures within genre) to make particular points and to create the contexts that allow us to enter into their experiences.

These cases exemplify more general issues of form and content in divorce accounts. The four genres I identify (story, habitual, hypothetical, and episodic narratives) are not idiosyncratic but recur repeatedly in the responses of others in the sample.[7] In the content—what each narrative is about—there is also much commonality with the sample as a whole, though specific details are of course unique. Each of the four narrators draws on a component of the companionate ideal of modern marriage, as we shall see.

Much has been written about narrative. Narrative is a prototypic form of talk—one of the first that we acquire as children and one that is used by all social classes in our culture and, some have argued, in all other cultures and historical epochs as well. "So natural is the impulse to narrate," writes historian Hayden White, that the narrative form is almost inevitable for any report of how things happened. As a solution to a universal human problem—how to translate knowing into telling—narratives link together our experience of the world and our efforts to describe that experience to a listener. Beyond reporting what happened, narratives allow for the construction and expression of meaning. James Gee asserts: "One of the ways—probably *the* primary way—human beings make sense of their experience is by casting it in narrative form."[8]

As sociolinguists define it, a narrative is a general type of text, a discourse organized around time and consequential events in some "world" created by the narrator. Stories are the classic genre, and they can most simply be thought of "as a specific past-time narrative that makes a point," often a moral one. Stories are a kind of cultural envelope into which we pour our experience and signify its importance to others, and the storyworld requires protagonists, inciting conditions, and culminating events. In other words, stories have a typical structure. William Labov shows that a "fully formed" story begins with a plot summary (abstract), contains an orientation (to place, time, characters, and situation), a statement of the events (complicating action) and the attitude of the narrator toward them (evaluation), a resolution of the action, and a coda, or ending, which returns the speaker to the present. With these structures, the narrator creates a storyworld and tells about a change in that world—a problem is overcome, there is a moment of self-revelation. In addition to structure, there are specific rhetorical devices that narrators use to point out particularly important parts of their stories, including word choices, pauses, and expressive phonology. Narrators also, of course, include social understandings in the stories they tell; sometimes they are an effort to set the world straight, a kind of moral telling. Narratives are not solely private and personal constructions of meaning, for they develop in particular social contexts.[9]

The detailed method of transcription used below may not be familiar to all readers. This representation of speech facilitates an analysis of the relationship between narrative form and meaning. To see how individuals actually construct accounts—the linguistic choices narrators make, the structural functions of specific clauses, the role of the listener, and so on—"cleaned-up" speech is not sufficient. The transcripts must be as complete as possible; thus they include both lexical and nonlexical utterances (the actual words as well as other sounds, like "uh-huh") and pauses in the interview interaction (long pauses are noted as "P" and short ones as "p"). The lines are numbered for ease of reference.[10]

TESSA: THE ABSENCE OF EQUALITY

Tessa is a twenty-three-year-old white woman who has been living apart from her husband for two and a half years. She looks much older than she is. It was her decision to separate; he "was completely against it," she says. She lives in a dilapidated housing project, but her apartment is clean and colorful. Her son from her marriage, a preschooler, lives with her, and an older child from a previous relationship is in foster care. Tessa has held a variety of unskilled jobs, mostly in the fast-food industry, and she has just begun to attend a community college part-time. She has always loved music, and her ambition is to be a music teacher some day.

Here is the full text of the first of two parts of Tessa's narrative account of why she divorced:

01 *Int.:* Would you state in your own words what were the main causes of your separation, as you see it?
02 *Tessa:* (P) um the biggest the biggest thing in my mind was the fact that I had been raped three times by him (*I:* mm-hmm)
03   but at that time it didn't, it wasn't *legal* in a probate court (*I:* mm-hmm)
04   you you couldn't get a divorce on those grounds
05   but that was my biggest (p) (*I:* uh-huh) complaint (*I:* uh-huh)
06   total disrespect for me (*I:* uh-huh) (P) (*I:* mm-hmm)
07 *Int.:* Can you tell me a little bit more about that? I know it's hard to talk about.
08 *Tessa:* (laugh/shudder) Well um (p) when it was time to go to bed it was really rough 'cause (p)
09   it was like we had to go together (p) (*I:* uh-huh)
10   and (p) if I wanted to go to bed while he was watching TV
11   he'd say "No, stay up with me" (*I:* uh-huh), you know
12   and um sometimes I just wanted to stay up
13   but he would insist that I go in with him (*I:* mm-hmm)

14   so it was like we had to do it together (p) (*I:* uh-huh)
15   um when I, you know, when I finally *was* in bed, I'd just roll over
        and I just wanted to go to sleep
16   I mean scrubbing the floor every day is kinda rough, you know,
        you're pretty tired (laugh) (*I:* uh-huh)
17   I guess I'm a little sarcastic about it (*I:* uh-huh)
18   *Int.:* Uh-huh, I know what you mean
19   *Tessa:* He'd just grab my shoulder and roll me over
20   and I knew what he was I knew what it was what it was doing
21   I said "I just don't want it tonight," you know
22   "don't you understand, I just don't want anything tonight"
23   "No, you're my wife and in the Bible it says you've got to do
        this" (*I:* uh-huh)
24   and ah I'd say "I just I just don't want it," you know. (*I:* uh-huh)
25   And after debating for 15 or 20 minutes
26   I'm not getting any less tired
27   I'd grab a pillow
28   I'd I'd say, "I'm going to sleep on the couch, you're not going to
        leave me alone"
29   I'd get the pillow and a blanket (*I:* uh-huh)
30   and I went and laid on the couch.
31   Two minutes later he was up out of bed
32   (p) and one particular time he had bought me a dozen roses that
        day (*I:* mm-hmm)
33   and they were sitting on top of the television which was at the
        foot of the couch (p)
34   and he, he picked up the vase of roses
35   threw the roses at me
36   poured the water on me (*I:* mm-hmm)
37   and dragged me by the arm from the couch (*I:* mm-hmm)
38   to the bedroom
39   and then proceeded to (p)
40   to make love to me. (*I:* uh-huh) (p)
41   And uh (P) I didn't know what to do (*I:* mm-hmm)
42   I tried to push him off me
43   and I tried to roll away (*I:* uh-huh)
44   ah I tried to cross (laugh) my legs (laugh)
45   and it didn't (p) work. (*I:* uh-huh)
46   He's six foot seven (p) and I'm five eight. (p)
47   And uh (P) I just had I just closed off my head (*I:* mm-hmm)
48   all I could do was shut off my brain (p)

49   and uh (p) I got very hostile, I— (p)
50   there was no outlet for those feelings. (p)
51   You know that even my neighbors as far as they were concerned
52   you know, they *they* figured that, you know, when people are
         married
53   that they love each other
54   I think, was the assumption.
55   That wasn't so.   (C017)

   The reason Tessa gives for divorcing is rape; as she puts it, her husband by his actions showed "total disrespect" for her. Yet the point she wishes to make is that she escaped her husband's domination and brutality.

   Tessa's account makes explicit the difficulties of leaving a marriage because of sexual abuse ("you couldn't get a divorce on those grounds"). Her recourse to protection from the courts was limited by the law's casual treatment of rape. Until quite recently, in the state in which she resides, a husband could not be prosecuted for forcing sexual intercourse upon his wife as long as they lived together. (In fact, in the late 1980s fewer than half of the states defined marital rape as a crime.) Far from a rare event, sexual abuse of women in marriage remains a closet crime in large part because women are considered the sexual property of husbands. Yet Tessa is able to name the form of her oppression as rape; sexual abuse is a legally defined reason for divorce in the late 1980s in the state in which she filed. Thus an evolving legal discourse shapes her personal discourse and legitimates her experience of sexual abuse.[11]

   How does Tessa construct her compelling account and draw the listener into her point of view? As I will discuss, she structures the narrative episodically to make her points (there are three episodes within which she juxtaposes several kinds of narratives, including stories). Contrasts also bind the complex narrative together (she juxtaposes her views with those of the state, the church, and her neighbors). The strategy of juxtaposition provides coherence to the narrative, at the same time as it marginalizes information that is also suggested in the text.

   If we look at the structure of the narrative, we see that in the first six lines Tessa gives a plot summary, or abstract, for the three episodes she will subsequently relate. Here she also sets forth the key contrast that organizes the narrative—the tension between two realities. At this point, the specific contrast is between her current reality (she was raped) and the reality of prevailing legal doctrine (marital rape wasn't a crime). Using verbal emphasis ("it wasn't *legal* in a probate court"), she draws attention to these contrasting points of view. From Tessa's perspective, which the listener is invited to share, she was a victim both of her husband's sexual violence and of the legal system. Her opening also introduces the main characters of the drama that is about to unfold: Tessa, her husband and, importantly, the social others (in this instance, the legal system) whose definitions of reality Tessa will ultimately overturn. The way she introduces the narrative conveys its overall message—she triumphed over others' definitions of her situation. The narrative she wants to tell is how she made the transition from victim to survivor.

Although Tessa controls the flow of talk in her opening statement, the woman listener is by no means passive. The narrative is frequently punctuated by her nonlexical utterances ("mm-hmm," "uh-huh"), which signal interest and invite the narrator to say more. Also notice how the listener responds to Tessa's long pause at the end of the abstract. Rather than using this as an opportunity to back off from the highly charged subject of marital rape, she waits and, after a pause, conveys through a question that she expects to hear more: "Can you tell me a little bit more about that? I know it's hard to talk about." Without this affiliative comment, Tessa might have stopped after her summary statement. Instead, she goes on to tell a long narrative in which she constructs meaningful totalities out of scattered events. [12]

Tessa's actions are consistent with the process of victimization that Trudy Mills describes. [13] Mills analyzes victimization as a gradual process. She identifies five stages: (1) women usually enter into the relationship at a time when they are feeling particularly vulnerable and are searching for intimacy; (2) women attempt to manage the violence by attaching meanings to it and developing strategies to cope with it (such as placating violent husbands and/or constructing justifications for maintaining the relationship); (3) women experience a loss of self as they withdraw from social interaction in shame their various social identities are diminished and they lose the observing self; (4) at some point women who leave reevaluate the violent relationship (often a specific event triggers this, jarring their previous definition of the situation); and (5) in time, women restructure the self. An important manifestation of the final step is taking on the identity of a survivor rather than seeing oneself as a victim.

Tessa invites the listener into the narrative world on lines 8–14 by orienting her to time, place, and situation. Substantively, she tells about the general case of the bedtime ritual: her husband's rule was that they go together; he would not allow her to go earlier or to stay up alone. Tessa attempts to manage the sexual violence by placating her husband, acquiescing to his demands. Structurally, Tessa communicates the routine and repeated interaction through the habitual narrative genre, indicated here by the conditional past tense ("if I wanted," and "he would insist"). In habitual narratives, events are not unique to a particular moment in time but instead stand for classes of events that happen over and over again. They tell of the general course of events over time, rather than what happened at a specific moment in the past. Tessa continues in the habitual mode by describing in lines 15–31 the usual sequence of events once they were in bed.

Tessa moves in and out of the voices of the characters in the narrative she is building:

20 and I knew what he was I knew what it was what it was doing
21 I said "I just don't want it tonight," you know
22 "don't you understand, I just don't want anything tonight"
23 "No, you're my wife and in the Bible it says you've got to do this" (*I*: uh-huh)
24 and ah I'd say "I just I just don't want it," you know. (*I*: uh-huh)

Strategically, by embedding a dramatization within a narrative, Tessa draws the listener in and, by reenacting the typical argument over sex, mobilizes support for her point of view. She communicates in a vivid way the verbal struggle that preceded the physical struggle—her attempts to resist her husband's unwanted sexual advances with repeated strong statements about her wishes. In line 20 "he" becomes "it"—she merges the man with the act.

In lines 15–31 Tessa also reintroduces the organizing theme of the contrast between two realities. Her juxtaposition of his and her voices achieves this in a powerful way. But the conflict between two realities goes beyond their private conversation, which she suggests here by invoking the Bible. The patriarchal church, as well as the state, colludes with her husband to deny her rights.

There are several important interactions between the two women as interviewer and interviewee in this section. Tessa makes repeated use of the phrase "you know"—affiliative appeals suggesting that the interviewer should understand the implications (and thus the "truth") of Tessa's reality. Perhaps Tessa is also appealing to the interviewer's experience with men and marriage, thereby creating an intersubjective world of meaning between them. There is some evidence that she is successful, judging by the interviewer's nonlexical expressions. Even more, the narrator steps out of the role of storyteller in the midst of a highly dramatic episode (which one might think of as uninterruptable) and, as a woman, makes an active alliance with the woman interviewer. The interviewer responds in kind:

15 um when I, you know, when I finally *was* in bed, I'd just roll over
      and I just wanted to go to sleep
16 I mean scrubbing the floor every day is kinda rough, you know,
      you're pretty tired (laugh) (*I:* uh-huh)
17 I guess I'm a little sarcastic about it (*I:* uh-huh)
18 *Int.:* Uh-huh, I know what you mean

Tessa's statements about housework strike a responsive cord in the interviewer; "I know what you mean" suggests a solidarity between the women is developing. They share the understanding that women are vulnerable, that women do housework, that it's often grueling, repetitive, and boring.

Out of this growing affiliation, perhaps, Tessa goes deeper into her memory:

32 (p) and one particular time he had bought me a dozen roses that
      day (*I:* mm-hmm)
33 and they were sitting on top of the television which was at the
      foot of the couch (p)

Tessa moves from recapitulating the general situation of coercive sex in her marriage to a particular and dramatic instance of it—the rape. As the content shifts, so must the form of the narrative. Tessa changes genres, from a habitual narrative to a story, the first of several she will ultimately tell. She uses the story form in this episode to create a unique past-time world and tells, by reenacting sequential events, of a significant change in that world.

She makes the transition to the story in line 32; it emerges in an almost seamless way from the habitual narrative that preceded it. A short pause signals the shift. (Tessa's speech is fluent, and pauses carry meaning. They had been largely absent from the previous twenty lines of text.) She begins the story by providing the listener with the necessary information needed to follow it. Because the roses will figure prominently in the rape, Tessa introduces these props and their exact placement in the living room, just as a skilled novelist might make the reader aware of a particular physical object that will be used in a later scene.

But the roses are more than a prop. They have symbolic meaning, just as do the television and the couch—Tessa's refuge from her husband's sexual demands. The mention of flowers also introduces an ambiguity into the text. Tessa does not explain why her husband "bought her a dozen roses that day," but such gifts are often a way in U.S. society for men to demonstrate romantic love or ask for forgiveness. Because Tessa's husband has a working-class job, the purchase of a dozen roses may have caused financial strain. In other words, there is a gap in Tessa's story, though the value of the gift is suggested by the fact that she displays the roses on the living room television— the centerpiece of the modern American home. Whatever may have "really" happened, Tessa's juxtaposition of the roses and the rape in the narrative makes *her* interpretation evident. The linguistic choice emphasizes the clash between two realities—romantic love in marriage and Tessa's actual experience, as she has come to define it.

The narrator brings the roses and the rape together in the climax of this first story, told in a series of short, terse, staccato clauses in the simple past tense:

34   and he, he picked up the vase of roses
35   threw the roses at me
36   poured the water on me (*I:* mm-hmm)
37   and dragged me by the arm from the couch (*I:* mm-hmm)

38 to the bedroom
39 and then proceeded to
40 (p) to make love to me. (*I:* uh-huh) (p)

This episode attempts to convince the listener how awful Tessa's marriage was by presenting a sample of it. The story is poignant and effective not only because of its content but because of its expression, and by its contrast to the earlier (habitual) form of the narrative. There is every evidence that the interviewer gets caught up in the story, judging by the frequency and placement of her nonlexical utterances.

But this episode is more than the factual reporting of events. Tessa distinguishes key events in the story in several ways. When describing the rape (lines 39–40), she uses a loaded phrase ("make love"), rich in tenderness, positive connotation, and cultural meaning to describe what she earlier referred to as "rape." As with the roses, there is an ambiguity and a paradox here. Tessa uses pauses to punctuate and thus mark the significance of these lines. She pauses even longer at two other critical points in the story:

41 and uh (P) I didn't know what to do (*I:* mm-hmm)
47 And uh (P) I just had I just closed off my head (*I:* mm-hmm)

Because long pauses are not characteristic of her speech, they draw attention. Structurally, they re-create in the listener the state of feeling of the storyworld and, in this case perhaps, the futility the narrator experienced in trying to protect herself from her husband's sexual advances. Consistent with the victimization process Mills describes, there is a loss of self. Tessa "closed off" her head and "shut off" her brain, the observing ego in the language of psychoanalysis.

Battered women rarely experience their anger directly, in Elaine Carmen's clinical observation: there is "a constant struggle with the self to contain it and control aggressive impulses."[14] Yet Tessa says, in line 49, that she "got very hostile," a statement that, like earlier ones, is ambiguous and invites multiple readings. It may refer to her resistance to the sexual abuse—that she fought back; the previous lines, however, suggest otherwise. The line can also be read as a more generalized statement about her anger—both at the time and as she has reinterpreted it since. This duality of reference moves both Tessa and her listener further away from the specific events and toward the interpretive meaning they have for Tessa.

Structurally, the clause also signals a shift in genres; Tessa is gradually moving out of a story and into a more general kind of moral telling. She justifies her lack of effectiveness in resisting the rape in line 46 through references to men's physical size and associated strength and women's consequent vulnerability to abuse. Some have argued that a woman is likely to be sexually victimized not only because she is physically weaker than her opponent but also because she is socially less powerful. [15] Tessa, developing her account in the context of the 1980s, implicitly draws on these contemporary feminist understandings. She also draws on another aspect of contemporary American culture when she explains both her passivity and her aggression by resorting to an explanatory scheme widely used in our psychologically oriented society—strong feelings require expression. ("There was no outlet for those feelings.") By communicating her moral attitude, Tessa solves the teller's problem. She convinces the listener (as well as herself, perhaps) that she is a good person, that she behaved correctly, and that she did the best that could be expected under the circumstances.

Tessa concludes the first episode by returning to the theme of two realities. This time it is her neighbors' views that she invokes:

51 You know that even my neighbors as far as they were concerned
52 you know, they *they* figured that, you know, when people are
      married
53 that they love each other
54 I think, was the assumption.
55 That wasn't so.

The neighbors, like the legal and religious systems earlier, stand for definitions of the situation that differ from Tessa's own. Through these contrasts between public ideology and private experience, she further defends her reality over that of her husband and others. She also says explicitly that she did not love her husband, a theme to which she later returns.

Structurally, lines 51–55 function to bridge the first episode—

about her husband's physical domination—and a second and closely related episode about her economic inequality, followed by a third one about Tessa's anger at her domination. The episodes are linked by the common theme of powerlessness, as Tessa continues:

56 *Tessa:* I, you know, I married my husband because I wanted to escape
57 but I didn't know that then, I couldn't—
58 *Int.:* Escape from what?
59 *Tessa:* Poverty
60 I had, you know, my first apartment when he proposed to me
61 was two rooms, flea-ridden (p) (*I:* uh-huh)
62 and (p) it had a leaky roof (p) (*I:* mm-hmm)
63 it was just *awful*
64 and I I sort of expected higher, you know, better things. (*I:* mm-hmm)
65 It improved a little bit but (p) there was still very little money and uh (p)
66 he was gone for a couple of weeks at one point
67 with nothing, and there was no food in the house
68 and he couldn't get any money to me cause he was out on a camping thing with the Army (p)
69 and uh (p) his friends (p) went and got some food for us
70 from the kitchens of the (p) the mess halls, I guess
71 and they brought my son and I a whole great big box of food.
72 You know, it wasn't the best, there wasn't any fresh (*I:* mm-hmm) vegetables or fruit
73 but it was meat and cake and stuff like that
74 so we ate. (p)
75 But I was totally uh dependent (*I:* uh-huh) and powerless at the same time (*I:* uh-huh)
76 I was just like I was when I was raped. (*I:* uh-huh) (p)
77 And those things, you know, those things happen.
78 As far as I'm concerned, I was raped I was raped from the first day (p) (*I:* mm-hmm)
79 but I didn't feel so hostile about it at that point. (p) (*I:* mm-hmm)
80 I just felt like it was something that you had to go through because you were married.
81 *Int.:* (p) And then what made the difference so that you wanted to get out of that relationship?

82   *Tessa:* (p) Oh, when I found myself, when I realized that I was
        throwing myself at him be–
83   out of hostility (p) rather than out of self-defense (*I:* uh-huh)
84   it was a little bit of both.
85   But I was so angry at one point when he was moving his things
        out (p)
86   he had promised, he had told me
87   as an example, he *told* me he'd give me the TV, okay.
88   At the last minute he decided he wanted it. (p) (*I:* mm-hmm)
89   And I was so *mad* (p)
90   I threw myself at him
91   I went to punch him (*I:* mm-hmm)
92   and I passed out (*I:* mm-hmm)
93   I was so mad. (*I:* mm-hmm)
94   (laugh/shudder) It's, my God, there's nothing like it
95   I don't *ever* want to feel that again, never (p) (*I:* mm-hmm)
96   I'd sooner scream at somebody and (p) and pound
97   I've punched my fists into walls
98   I punched in the front door in that apartment on Main Street (*I:*
        uh-huh)
99   and unlocked it.
100 He put my son out on the front porch at one point and I was
101 it made me so violently angry
102 that I I literally punched in the front door
103 and it was just about as thick as the front door here. (*I:* uh-huh)
104 (p) And uh (p) I, you know, after that incident
105 I lived in Rocky Falls with my mother (*I:* uh-huh) and my fa-
        ther, my stepfather, for three weeks (p)
106 and I tried to get a restraining order
107 and the and the person at the courthouse said it's not worth it.
        (p)
108 But he did tell me that what I *could* do is go back to him, to my
        husband
109 and say "if you're not out of here I'll have the police after you."
        (*I:* mm-hmm) (p)
110 So I did that
111 and he left reluctantly (*I:* uh-huh) (p)
112 but he did leave. (*I:* uh-huh)   (C017)

The second episode begins, as did the first, with a plot summary:
Tessa says she married to escape (lines 56–57). Because of the inter-

viewer's interruption ("Escape from what?"), Tessa elaborates. Also as in the first episode, she orients the listener to time, place, and social circumstances—the "flea-ridden" apartment with a leaky roof that was all she could afford before she married. Going back in time and shifting scenes, Tessa seeks to explain her divorce to her listener by explaining why she married in the first place. In this flashback she again sets up a contrast: her reason for marriage as she understands it now, compared with what she thought then. She says she married her husband to escape her poverty, not because she loved him. (Listeners may begin to feel some empathy for Tessa's husband at this point, and reinterpret her earlier story about the roses. Was he trying to woo her, to persuade her to love him?)

The content of the second episode is consistent with Mills's analysis of victimization. Tessa entered into the relationship at a time when she was feeling particularly vulnerable. Like other women before and since, Tessa's susceptibility to poverty was, in large part, a consequence of her gender. She had the sole responsibility for care of a child, an inadequate welfare allowance, and limited job possibilities. As a member of U.S. culture, however, she "expected better, you know, higher things." Her solution, consistent with the American dream for white women, was to find a man; the traditional conjugal family would improve her circumstances, she thought. Although marriage hardly proved to be a protective haven for her or her child, it did help their economic situation. Yet, she says, "there was still very little money."

In this episode, too, Tessa moves into the story form, providing an illustration to persuade the listener how difficult things were (line 66). She tells of a sequence of events: her husband could not provide for her financially and his friends did, getting food from Army mess halls. Although the story lacks the linguistic elaboration of the first story about the rape, and hence the associated tension and drama, it nevertheless makes its point. If we have any doubt about the causal link that ties the two episodes together, Tessa states it explicitly:

75 But I was totally uh dependent (*I:* uh-huh) and powerless at the same time (*I:* uh-huh)
76 I was just like I was when I was raped. (*I:* uh-huh) (p)
77 And those things, you know, those things happen.

78 As far as I'm concerned, I was raped I was raped from the first
    day (p) (*I:* mm-hmm)
79 but I didn't feel so hostile about it at that point. (p) (*I:* mm-hmm)
80 I just felt like it was something that you had to go through be-
    cause you were married.

In these lines Tessa tells the listener directly how to interpret the two
stories and, more generally, her episodic narrative. She creates her
own private image to give meaning to her past: the metaphor of rape
epitomizes her total domination—financial, psychological, and
physical. She moves away from the specific events with interpretive
meanings and contrasts how she felt about them at the time and how
she feels about them now. Through metaphor, Tessa makes a moral
point: marriage based on women's subordination is not the way marriage ought to be. In creating a narrative to explain her particular separation, she has produced a discourse about inequality in marriage in
general.

But there may be another meaning here. In addition to linking
powerlessness and rape metaphorically (to refer to women's structural subordination in the institution of marriage), Tessa may be referring more specifically to her experience of sex: "It was something
you had to go through because you were married." Again, the ambiguity in meaning may call Tessa's interpretation of events into question for some readers. Because we have only her narrative, the
ambiguities cannot be resolved.

Tessa has not yet mentioned what prompted her to reevaluate the
violent relationship from a position outside it. The listener, sensing a
missing piece, pauses and asks about it ("And then what made the
difference so that you wanted to get out of that relationship?"). Tessa
responds by developing a third narrative episode, in lines 85–103, on a
topic she has hinted at several times earlier—*her* violent response to
her husband. She says that she went beyond "self-defense" and began
"throwing" herself at him "out of hostility." Unlike Tessa's controlled
way of telling in the previous episodes, here her control slips: the emotions of the last days of her marriage break through.[16]

In the third episode, Tessa moves into the story form to recount a
specific instance of her rage (lines 85–95), intimating that for her the
triggering event—the fourth stage in Mill's model—was her own ag-

gression. Although the precipitant is seemingly minor (certainly when compared to the sexual abuse in the earlier story), her husband's change of mind about the television provokes a violent response, which she describes in a series of tightly ordered clauses:

89 And I was so *mad* (p)
90 I threw myself at him
91 I went to punch him (*I:* mm-hmm)
92 and I passed out (*I:* mm-hmm)
93 I was so mad. (*I:* mm-hmm)

Her anger (which perhaps includes her pent-up rage about the rapes) is unacceptable to her. She makes this clear in a series of affect-laden evaluative clauses using a variety of rhetorical devices, including verbal emphasis, an explicative, and expressive speech (a shudder).

94 (laugh/shudder) It's, my God, there's nothing like it
95 I don't *ever* want to feel that way again, never (p) (*I:* mm-hmm)

The clustering of these devices marks this episode as the peak of the action in the narrative. We learn later in a series of story fragments that this dynamic—his actions provoking rage and physical violence in her—had occurred throughout the marriage (lines 97–103). The point is that Tessa can no longer contain her *own* aggression; this is the turning point. She has taken on the identity of a survivor, rather than that of a victim, the change that is the final stage is Mill's model. [17]

Tessa's detailed account is one woman's understanding of how male dominance leads to rage and, consequently, to divorce. All the forms of inequality Tessa experienced—physical, psychological, and financial—can provoke fury in the subordinate. Yet her point is that she surmounted powerlessness and victimization. Ironically, she took control by losing control and broke out of a violent relationship when she could no longer contain her own violence. She filed for divorce, even though her husband "was completely against it."

Tessa realizes these themes through language. She organizes the narrative she tells around her definition of the situation, set against the contrary definitions of others—her husband, the state, the church, her neighbors. She gives shape to her experience and makes it meaningful by talking about power and subordination, just as she persuades the listener that these were seriously troubled times in her construction of the narrative. She tells a series of linked stories, episodes about how intolerable it was at highly memorable moments, set against a backdrop of how intolerable it was in general (the habitual narrative). The rape story is quintessential, a dramatic incident that illustrates her overall theme. Through narration Tessa not only reconstructs the temporal sequence of events that led to the separation but invests these events with meaning and morality. She constructs a reality and a surviving self that are sealed inside the narrative—a reality that is accomplished as much by the way she structures the account as by what she says.[18]

Although Tessa's text is a deeply personal statement, it is also a cultural product, situated historically, with assumptions and formulations that could not have been made in another historical period or by women in many parts of the world today. At numerous points a specifically American cultural discourse shapes the personal discourse, most obviously by enabling Tessa to articulate the issue as marital rape. Going beyond a formalist analysis of the text, I suggest that a narrative cannot be fully interpreted without investigating the condition in society of the person who produces the text. The narrative is contextual in this additional sense because it speaks to the aspects of a survivor's identity with which gender is intimately intertwined, namely race and class. Tessa's narrative does not reflect some essentialist view of women in general but speaks of the unique experiences of a white, working-class woman who came to define her marital experience as rape. It was also told to a white, middle-class feminist interviewer who "heard" the account in a particular way, to some extent shaping the narrative by her questions and nonlexical responses, just as it was told in a cultural context where feminism and personal psychology provided legitimating vocabularies of motive. The narrative implies how extensively some psychological concepts and assumptions about women's rights have fed back into popular thought in the United States. Tessa's "private" story is embedded in a social discourse in which it is taken for granted that strong feelings require expression and that marital rape is a crime.[19]

Tessa solves the teller's problem by narrating about events in her marriage. She persuades by letting us into her experience, communicating how she wants to be understood by the way she conveys it, linking key points in her life into a complex, episodically structured narrative.

SUSAN: THE ABSENCE OF EMOTIONAL INTIMACY AND RECIPROCITY

Susan is a white divorced woman who lives with her three children (ages ten, eight, and five). She is thirty-six years old and college educated, and she has been living apart from her husband for almost three years. Currently unemployed and looking for a job, she receives regular support payments from her former husband and still lives in the house, in a middle-class neighborhood, that her mother helped them buy. Nevertheless, she experiences considerable financial strain. Her income is barely half what it was when she was married and the costs of raising her children have increased. As is true for many women in her situation, her divorce was a financial catastrophe; yet by the usual sociological indicators of level of education and type of neighborhood, Susan would be considered middle class. Here is a section from Susan's long account of why she divorced:[20]

01 *Int.:* Would you state in your own words what were the main causes of your separation?
02 *Susan:* Ahhh (p) lack of communication (p) um (P)
03 um (p) we started to resent each other (P) um (p)
04 *Int.:* Say more about about the communication and the resentment
05 *Susan:* Well (p) um (P) I don't know where to begin
06 do you want me just sort of go up just explain about about our marriage and go into all that
07 *Int.:* Yeah, and what led to the separation
08 *Susan:* Uh-mm, let's see (p) I was twenty-five when I was married
09 and I was pregnant
10 and I wasn't um (p)
11 didn't really have my head on very well I guess I (p)
12 I kind of decided I should get married
13 I was pregnant

14 I didn't really give it that much thought
15 I don't think I would have married Bill if I had not been pregnant
16 I think we would eventually would have gone off our own ways.
      (p)
17 He was a Irishman from Boston whose mother had (p)
18 um (p) done a lot, done *everything* for him, you know
19 and he went into a marriage without realizing there's a lot of give
      and take.
20 And basically I had the children (p) um (p)
21 from day one [tape unclear]
22 uhm (p) he did *not* help out
23 it was not a give and take
24 I really carried 99 percent of the brunt of everything that had to
      be done
25 and I resented it. (p) (*I:* mm-hmm)
26 You know the years went by
27 and I built up this resentment. (p) (*I:* mm-hmm)
28 And (p) uh we didn't know each other very well and
29 a lot of the things about his personality
30 uh (p) things that I had found sort of complex and interesting
31 which I really was, I didn't really know what these things were
      but
32 I grew to (p) kind of
33 there was a lot of selfishness in him (*I:* uh-huh) and
34 he wasn't he didn't give a lot. (p)
35 You know besides not helping he some–
36 a real loner
37 hard to communicate with.
38 His idea of having an argument (p)
39 was not to discuss it at all
40 it was just to go into another room
41 and not communicate, kind of thing.
42 And so (p) uh (p) I just built up a lot of hostilities.
43 And we stopped talking
44 early on in our marriage really (p)
45 um and he spent more and more time at work (p)
46 he didn't want to come home
47 he'd come home and (p)
48 and then *I* would say
49 "I'd like you to spend a little time with the kids" and he (p)
50 he'd just wanted to go up and read a book, kind of thing.

51 We just didn't communicate really.
52 um (P) What else? um (P)
53 You know we continued to have children
54 I think, you would think that (p)
55 you you bury yourself in the things that have to be done on a
     daily basis
56 and that's one way of not having to discuss
57 what's lacking in your *own* marriage.
58 And I think we had more children
59 that took up a lot of time
60 there were always family things (p)
61 and we just didn't deal with our problems. (p)
62 And (p) he just started coming home less and less
63 and making up excuses for
64 for being at work and
65 and I had all these young children running around
66 I had *no* time for myself
67 and I buried all of what *I* needed for myself
68 for years and years and years.
69 (p) We had a bad marriage
70 we really had a bad marriage.   (N046)

Susan blames her divorce on "lack of communication," which she elaborates by talking about not talking: her husband's "idea of having an argument was not to discuss it at all"; they "stopped talking"; they absorbed themselves "in things that had to be done on a daily basis," not "discussing" their problems. This definition of a bad marriage—not talking—recurs in the accounts of many women, as we have seen; as many women understand it, intimacy with a husband ought to be realized through verbal interaction and sharing. Susan also expects give and take, a theme common to women's accounts. Communication for Susan means not only talking but spending time together and sharing domestic labor. She says she built up resentment because she "carried 99 percent of the brunt of everything that had to be done," meaning housework and child care. In keeping with the institutionalized roles of husband and wife in modern marriage, he occupied himself with his work and she managed the home and children.

The content of Susan's experience is less extreme and harsh than

Tessa's, and the form of her narrative is also different. Susan uses the habitual narrative genre throughout. She never tells a story, in the formal sense of the term, about a specific incident or a group of incidents in the form of episodes. Instead, she tells of the general course of the marriage over time, a tale about gradually growing apart. She uses the conditional past tense—a hallmark of the habitual narrative—in lieu of the simple past in this dramatization:

47 he'd come home and (p)
48 and then *I* would say
49 "I'd like you to spend a little time with the kids" and he (p)
50 he'd just wanted to go up and read a book, kind of thing.
51 We just didn't communicate really.

For Susan there is no single incident, no moment in time that changed the course of the marriage, at least from her current vantage point. Unlike many others we interviewed, Susan never says, "I decided to leave" or, "then he decided to leave." Rather, she seeks to convey a slow downward spiral—a sequence that is well suited to a habitual rather than a specific past-time narrative (or story). Because of her understanding of why she divorced, Susan solves the teller's problem by re-creating the quality of the marriage for the listener, not incidentally (as in a story about roses and rape) but habitually— the sense of chronic, enduring difficulties that refused to go away and could not be resolved by specific actions.

Although this account does not take the form of a story, it is nevertheless temporally organized. Linear time, in fact, is the organizing principle of the narrative, just as contrasts and episodes organized Tessa's. Susan explains her divorce by starting at the beginning— when she was twenty-five and decided to marry because she was pregnant. Like Tessa's account (and others', as well), Susan's has a three-part structure—the reasons for marriage, what it was like, and why it was unworkable—but unlike Tessa's (and some others'), the parts are presented sequentially, in chronological order, with no flashbacks. Because the narrative is organized by sequential time, it begins with the decision to marry, progresses through the years of the marriage, and ends with a summary statement, or coda, explain-

ing the separation ("we really had a bad marriage"). Temporal ordering of events into a narrative is a classic form in which individuals
remember and recapitulate past experience—a form that, though
not universal, is a generally available form of retelling in U.S. culture, one that is keyed to middle-class listeners' expectations.[21] Certain utterances demonstrate the centrality of chronological time in
the account:

08	. . . I was twenty-five when I was married
20–21	. . . I had the children . . . from day one
26	. . . the years went by
43–44	. . . we stopped talking early on in our marriage
53	. . . we continued to have children
58–59	. . . we had more children / that took up a lot of time

Nothing is out of place. By using linear time as an organizing frame
and by staying within the habitual narrative mode, Susan brings a
particular kind of order to her memories of her marriage to help the
listener understand it. The invariant order of Susan's account also
conveys the inherent dullness of her marriage. As she understands it,
nothing unusual ever happened; things just plodded along in their
unsatisfactory way until they arrived at the end. Tessa has a more
dramatic sense of her marriage and thus uses a more dramatic narrative form to convey its character and quality.

Although both Susan and Tessa have been living apart from their
husbands for nearly the same amount of time and, as stress theorists
might argue, are equally distant from the "objective" stressor, their
styles of speech suggest that they may be at very different points in a
recovery process. (They also have very different experiences of marriage from which to recover.) Perhaps Susan uses linear time to structure her account because she has continued to move forward, putting
her marriage behind her. She recalls it to make her divorce decision
comprehensible to the interviewer, but she does not re-live it or
re-present the particular instances that may have turned the tide—
events that may have occurred but have fallen away from her present understanding. There is consequently a striking lack of emotion in the narrative, in sharp contrast to Tessa's. An alternative

interpretation, of course, is that each speaker has a preferred style of speech—Tessa tells by storifying, Susan by chronicling—which, in turn, shapes the presentation of emotion in the two narratives.[22]

At the same time that Susan uses linear time to order her memories, she also employs time in a contradictory way. Although time is tight and sequential, it is also blurred and unending. This kind of temporality is expressed by the habitual genre she chooses, which conveys the repetitious nature of events that wore her down rather than emphasizing critical moments. Her husband's unavailability was not a one-time occurrence; it happened over and over. The theme of blurred time gets expressed most fully later on in the interview:

```
123    . . . as I look back it's amazing that (p)
124    that you accept things and you just (p)
125    know that they're wrong
126    but you just kind of go along and (p)
127    take each day and
128    and the days become weeks
129    and the weeks become months
130    and suddenly you have three children and (p)
131    you're communicating less and less
132    but you're just kind of existing.
133    (p) We were just existing.
```

The feeling of heavy hanging time is re-created in the listener: days become weeks, weeks become months, and months become years. Susan repeats and emphasizes to signal the special salience of these lines; they are present insights about the past, when she saw herself as "just existing" through time.

In this passage Susan also changes pronouns, from the personal "we," "I," and "he" she used earlier in the narrative to the general "you," and then back to "we" at the end. These shifts, and especially the use of the impersonal "you" to describe a distinctly personal perception, communicate her alienation at the time of the marriage from the self she now perceives herself to be. She has grown, and she is groping to integrate her earlier feelings with her present ones. When she "look(s) back it's amazing"—even to herself—to see how far she has come. She feels distant from her past self, yet to some degree she must re-create this self to make the narrative believable to a listener.

Susan searches for a metaphor to stand for her experience and to persuade the listener. Although not as overtly stated as Tessa's association of rape and powerlessness, a metaphor is strongly suggested in several lines:

55   . . . you bury yourself in the things that have to be done
67   and I buried all of what *I* needed for myself
136   the anger was all buried

Coupled with Susan's statements about "just existing," we infer a deadening quality to her marriage, compared with the life she feels now. The self, as she has come to know it, was submerged. Her choice of genre is significant in this regard too: she re-creates the feeling in the listener of deadness, of heavy, hanging time, precisely by *not* telling a story.

Susan too constructs her narrative in a way that makes a broader moral point about inequality in marriage, albeit in more muted tones than Tessa's graphic discourse on marriage as rape. Susan defines herself as someone who values talk and reciprocity—"give and take"—and defines her husband as the other—by his "selfishness" and his unwillingness to "give a lot." Although these can be read as psychological interpretations of "his" and "her" character, on another level they are value statements about how people ought to be. Although she does not explicitly draw upon a feminist explanatory system, her understanding of her marriage is quite consistent with such a schema. She assumes that domestic labor should be shared, and she faults his mother in passing (who did "*everything*" for him) and her husband repeatedly ("he did *not* help out") for failing to live up to this moral standard. Susan's account can be read as a discourse about traditional middle-class marriage. She describes a gender-based division of labor and the burden she felt caring for three small children with little help from her husband, who occupied himself with his profession. Susan's "private" narrative contains a cultural discourse—a commentary on the sexual politics of modern marriage and one woman's growing awareness of what Betty Friedan calls "the problem with no name."[23]

Susan solves the teller's problem in a way that can be distinguished from Tessa's. Susan strategically persuades us that these were troubled times and that she was right to leave, but she builds her case around a different set of understandings and, consequently, a different narrative form. There are some similarities in the content of the two women's narratives (both carried the burden of household labor, both encountered inequality in marriage), but there are also striking differences, not the least of which is the extent of oppression and the harshness of its manifestations. These differences are rooted to a great extent in their contrasting class positions.

In narrative form, the accounts of Susan and Tessa could not be more different. Rather than constructing a complex narrative as Tessa does—linked episodes with flashbacks and embedded stories, framed by a habitual narrative about what things were generally like—Susan tells in a linear way of the gradual growing apart, the general downward course as she now views it. She chooses the habitual narrative genre and the metaphor of death. This form of narrative, Charlotte Linde says, "tells how we used to do something; even if the actions reported were completely common at the time . . . , they have become rare or obsolete at the time of narration, and hence are reportable."[24] A story would not capture Susan's distinctive understandings of this divorcing process, not would a mere listing of marital complaints. She helps the listener enter into her understandings by her strategic use of form.

STEVE: THE ABSENCE OF PRIMACY AND COMPANIONSHIP

Steve is a thirty-nine-year-old white man who has had some college. He has been separated from his wife for two and a half years and now lives alone. Married for sixteen years, he has two children (ages five and thirteen) who live with his former wife and whom he sees once a week. As is true for many men in his situation, his contact with his children has been severely limited by his divorce. From his perspective, not being able to spend time with his kids is the major difficulty he has had in the separation process. Employed by the highway department, Steve pays $5,000 a year in child support, but he says he does not experience much financial strain because his support payments constitute less than a quarter of his current income. In fact,

Steve says that his economic situation is much better now than it was when he was married; recently he received a raise and was promoted to supervisor. Although his job is working-class, he is financially comfortable.

Steve answers the woman interviewer's question about the reasons for divorce as follows:

01 *Int.:* Would you state, in your own words, what were the main
     causes of your separation?
02 *Steve:* (P) Ah, let's see, main causes?
03 (P) My (P, clears throat) my desire of wanting (p) a wife
04 (p) a wife, a lover (p)
05 uh let's put it this way, a lover, a wife, and a mother (p)
06 in that order (*I:* uh-huh)
07 someone who would be (p) interested in (p) *me*
08 and (p) find it important to be involved with *me*
09 my interests
10 me with her interests
11 and (p) the the children involved, yes (*I:* mm-hmm)
12 but willing to spend time one-on-one with each other.
13 And I didn't get this kind of (*I:* uh-huh) relationship.
14 It was always (p) the children first, the children second
15 and (p) maybe (p) there'd be room down the end. (*I:* uh-huh)
16 And I'll clarify this with, with an example.
17 *Int.:* O.K.
18 *Steve:* Uh one month before we separated
19 uh (p) I mentioned before I'm involved with show dogs
20 and I do a lot of judging in dog shows (*I:* uh-huh)
21 and (p) when I go to judge, my expenses are paid
22 (p) and I mean *expenses*
23 mileage on my car, room, board, everything (*I:* uh-huh)
24 and (p) this one month before we separated
25 I had a (p) a dog show to judge
26 north of New York the town's not important but
27 uh (p) it was on a Saturday. (*I:* uh-huh)
28 I suggested that we leave Friday night
29 (p) and I (p) would have my room Friday night paid for for my-
     self so
30 you know, no big expense.
31 Uh (p) we would I would judge the show

32   she would (p) be with me and help me while I'm judging (*I:* uh-huh)
33   I do need some assistance
34   and (p) Saturday night we would go into New York after I finished the dog show
35   we would go out to dinner
36   spend the night in New York and come back Sunday. (*I:* uh-huh)
37   And I was told "Who would take care of the kids?"
38   I suggested "How about your mother?"
39   (p) "She doesn't want to."
40   "How about *my* mother?"
41   "I don't want her to." (*I:* uh-huh)
42   "Well, we'll hire a nurse."
43   (p) "We can't afford it. (p)
44   What about the dogs?"
45   "We'll put 'em in a kennel."
46   (p) "We can't afford that."
47   And (p) as a point to to relate to the "can't afford"
48   we had close to ten thousand dollars in the stock market. (*I:* mm-hmm)
49   (p) I took this to mean
50   (p) she didn't want to *go.*
51   So I went anyway. (*I:* uh-huh)
52   I had to go.
53   I went the night before
54   and (p) judged and came back. (*I:* uh-huh)
55   But (p) that is a classic (*I:* mm-hmm) example of the whole (*I:* mm-hmm) relationship.
56   She chose (p) *not* to be with *me* (*I:* uh-huh)
57   and in the long run I chose not to be with *her* (*I:* uh-huh)
58   and she made no effort one way or the other (*I:* mm-hmm)

(C040)

Steve's narrative portrays expectations and disappointments. Steve says he wanted primacy—"one-on-one" time with his wife—a desire consistent with the vision of marriage that a number of men described. For his wife, however, he says that the children "came first." As an expression of the primacy of the marital bond, Steve expected to share his leisure avocation—judging dog shows—with his wife. Instead of companionship with her and freedom from the demands of the children on a weekend vacation at a dog show, he is forced to go alone. Thematically, the narrative is organized around a moral opposition—what a marriage ought to be like and what it was actually like. Structurally, this moral point is achieved in a tightly organized narrative that juxtaposes several genres.

Steve begins the narrative by testing the waters with an enumeration or listing—what he wants from a wife and what he expects from marriage (lines 2–12)—setting the stage for the events he will describe in the subsequent narrative. The story that Steve eventually tells about the dog show is worth telling precisely because he sets up an explanatory system at the onset—the male vision of marriage— from which his wife's behavior deviates. He struggles with frequent pauses and false starts while he ranks the three roles of a married woman as he defines them—wife, lover, mother—and his final ordering stresses the importance of marital sex; his spouse, first and foremost, should be a lover for him. He goes on to emphasize shared leisure; he expected that a spouse would be involved in his interests and, almost as an afterthought, that he would be involved in hers. He places the role of mother to his children last. He says he wants someone whose primary interest would be in *him*. Steve juxtaposes the ideal he has constructed with reality: he "didn't get this kind of relationship." His wife put "the children first, the children second" and, he adds sadly, "maybe there'd be room down the end" for him.

Steve expands these understandings and provides evidence to encourage the listener to believe him by narrating a specific instance. He signals the transition with "entrance talk," announcing that a story is about to be told (he says he'll give an example), to which the listener responds affirmatively (lines 16–17).[25] But the formal narrative (lines 18–53) is more complex than a story, in the linguistic sense of the term. Its structure includes a lengthy orientation, followed by a hypothetical narrative (about events that did not happen), capped off by a story (about events that did happen). He juxtaposes fantasy and reality, expectations and disappointment. He draws the listener in by providing a hypothetical contrast—a vision of what marriage might have been.

In the orientation (lines 18–27), Steve provides what the listener needs to interpret the next two parts of the narrative. He identifies the time: the events he will tell about took place "one month before we separated." He describes his avocation of showing dogs, including his generous expense account. He introduces the particular dog show that the story will be about. By providing the context for the events he will subsequently talk about, he makes sure they will be believable to someone who was not there.

With this background established, Steve develops the plot of the story, beginning with a narrative clause in the simple past tense ("I suggested that we leave Friday night"). He then leaves the story genre and moves into the hypothetical narrative, signaled by a shift in verb tense. Using the subjunctive, he describes a conjectural sequence of events—his fantasy of how he had wanted the weekend to go (lines 29–36). Substantively, his plan for the weekend includes a tightly sequenced series of events from Friday to Sunday, with his wife accompanying him throughout. Steve's choice of genre—a temporally ordered hypothetical narrative—is a good rhetorical device. Not only does it describe the fantasy from start to finish but it is convincing because it builds drama, momentarily suspending the action of the story he began a few lines earlier. The listener is primed, wanting to know what happened next.

In order to tell about the weekend, Steve returns to the story form and to dramatization—an especially effective method for drawing listeners in and making events vivid. Just as Tessa did, Steve replays a marital conversation, but for him it forms the climax of the story:

37 And I was told "Who would take care of the kids?"
38 I suggested "How about your mother?"
39 (p) "She doesn't want to."
40 "How about *my* mother?"
41 "I don't want her to." (*I:* uh-huh)
42 "Well, we'll hire a nurse."
43 (p) "We can't afford it. (p)
44 What about the dogs?"
45 "We'll put 'em in a kennel."
46 (p) "We can't afford that."

The short pauses before his wife's replies to his proposals make the turns in the conversation even more dramatic. She withholds herself from him at every turn. The phrase "I was told," which he chooses to introduce his wife's utterances, depersonalizes her and makes her sound like an authority figure. To further convince the listener, he mentions the fact that he and his wife had nearly $10,000 in the stock market (lines 46–48), thereby suggesting that they could clearly afford to hire a nurse. In his construction of this moment, he seeks to persuade the listener how bad the marriage was.

Before resolving the action, Steve steps back from it and tells the listener how he interprets the events ("I took this to mean / she didn't want to *go*"). Here, he hints at the "point" of the story and its moral message: I am a good person, one who wants to share important events in my life with my wife; she is the one who does not want to be close.

Steve finishes his story by returning to the place and time of the storyworld and resolving the action:

51 So I went anyway. (*I:* uh-huh)
52 I had to go.
53 I went the night before
54 and (p) judged and came back. (*I:* uh-huh)

Through succinct clauses, he tells what finally happened. Their starkness contrasts vividly with the elaborate clauses he uses in his hypothetical narrative. Linguistically, this contrast serves once again to juxtapose the fantasy of his marital expectations with the reality of his actual relationship.

Like other storytellers, Steve needs to bring the listener out of the past and back into the present. He does this and at the same time sums up the meaning he sees in the chain of events he has reported:

55 But (p) that is a classic (*I:* mm-hmm) example of the whole (*I:* mm-hmm) relationship.
56 She chose (p) *not* to be with *me* (*I:* uh-huh)
57 and in the long run I chose not to be with *her* (*I:* uh-huh)
58 and she made no effort one way or the other (*I:* mm-hmm)

Just as entrance talk and the word "example" take the narrator into the storyworld (on line 16), exit talk and the same word choice get him out of that world and back to the present. He backs off from the specific events, saying they were "classic," which also establishes their "reportability."[26] They are worthy of a story, he implies, because they are emblematic—a conversation between Steve and his wife about going to a dog show for the weekend, a rather ordinary event, is significant because it is similar to other instances. Steve is justified in leaving his wife because she repeatedly refused his requests for primacy, companionship, and sexual fulfillment—to go away with him to a hotel room, without the kids.

Lest listener have any doubt about the moral of the story, Steve says it explicitly and with verbal emphasis to underscore his evaluation of his wife's actions. By deciding not to come with him to the dog show, "she chose *not* to be with *me*." Steve's moral evaluation draws on background knowledge about modern marriage: marriage requires effort and work from *both* spouses.[27] This, of course, is part of the ideology of the companionate marriage. Steve draws on this cultural discourse and constructs a story that shows how he put effort into marriage and his wife did not. Steve's account helps the listener understand his definition of his marriage by pairing a hypothetical narrative and a brief story. He persuades by juxtaposing what might have been and what was.

AL: INFIDELITY AND ITS MEANINGS

Al is a thirty-five-year-old white man who completed several years of graduate training in an academic discipline before he decided to change careers. Currently self-employed as a potter, he has been separated from his wife for one and a half years. Al has two children (ages thirteen and six) from his fifteen-year marriage; they live with him for half the week and with his former wife for the other half. He fought for this arrangement and won it because he had actively participated in the care of his children from infancy. Although not well off financially, he has enough money to make ends meet and has a decidedly middle-class style of life.

Al's narrative about why he divorced emerges in conversation about another topic entirely, not in response to the woman interviewer's question about reasons for separation.[28] In response to that question, he says tersely, "her relationship with Tony," but we only know what this means by the conversation that precedes it:

01   *Int.:* You'd split then in (p) April and this was—
02   *Al:* Well, we actually uh
03   I don't date things from April.
04   I don't date things from when we separated.
05   What I, you know, I date 'em from when all
06   from when I found out, out about her affair
07   because that really seems like the crucial (*I:* uh-huh) time.
08   *Int.:* And when was that?
09   *Al:* That was in December, you know, of (p) '82. (*I:* uh-huh)
10   (p) God!
11   *Int.:* So you lived together a long time—
12   *Al:* Yeah, for the better part of half a year.
13   *Int.:* I see.
14   *Al:* And that was just *nuts*
15   it was ab*surd* because (p) uh
16   (p) she would have these *long* telephone conversations with Tony
17   you know, I'd be in here or somewhere
18   (p) and (p) just (p) in absolute agony
19   and still not even able to (*I:* mm-hmm) able to, able to admit that.
20   I remember lying down here once
21   and I had certain records that I would play that would calm me down
22   'cause I *hate* being angry
23   I just, you know, I have a hard time with anger. (*I:* uh-huh)
24   And I remember lying here
25   and she was talking with Tony on the phone
26   and we were supposed to be talking about something.
27   And I could just feel this (p) anger ri– rising up in me
28   and then I would listen to this music and it would go away again.
29   It was a Palestrina Mass (*I:* uh-huh) that I *really* like and really
30   and (p) finally, ah it's, this is actually a crucial incident
31   because I *finally* got up and (p)
32   and (p) went into the other room
33   (p) she was in the laundry room with the door closed and
34   (p) knocked on the door and said
35   "When are you going to be done with this?"
36   'cause we, we were going to talk.
37   And she kind of held up her hand like this and went "no."
38   And I got absolutely bullshit
39   I put my *fist* through the door (*I:* uh-huh)

40   which is not the kind of stuff that I, that I do, you know
41   I'm *not* a real physically violent person at *all*.
42   um (p) and uh (p) she yelled and
43   hung up the phone
44   and then kind of came at me
45   started hitting me.
46   And we'd never done that before or ever since
47   there was never any physical (p) violence.
48   I'm very *controlled*, I think, about that.
49   Um (p) it just didn't even *occur* to me, you know
50   it's not the thing, it was one of the things that, that's
51   that was impossible to figure out
52   when she said she was scared of me
53   there was, there was a physical fear involved in that.
54   And it's a thing I can't relate to
55   because I've *never* (p) except for then (p)
56   felt like hitting her or hurting her at all.
57   (p) Consciously.
58   Um (p) and I hit her (p) then (p) and
59   (p) she picked up a stick of wood
60   and I said she "better not do that."
61   And she stopped.
62   But it was at that point that I realized that this is,
63   this was no good (*I:* uh-huh)
64   that it was just going to be, that
65   it couldn't get any better and that, or
66   or just that, that living together—
67   That must have been close to the time that we started separating
68   I mean, that we did the, the half-time deal. (*I:* uh-huh)
69   'Cause I remember feeling that, that this was just
70   no good for me at all
71   that, that uh I felt like I was subjecting myself to
72   uh I felt like I was being masochistic.
73   There wasn't any, any *reason* to *be* there other than
74   other than to hurt
75   that that was all, that was all that was going on.
76   Um (p) so (p) I'm afraid I got a little lost
77   we were talking about the stages—   (C032)

Through narration Al links his wife's open infidelity, his emotional pain, his violent response, and the decision to divorce. As is true for other men, his spouse's affair is not necessarily a sufficient cause for ending the marriage. The affair becomes significant only in the context of other events—in Al's case, his physical violence.

It is clear from the first thirteen lines that the narrative emerges out of an interchange about the date of his separation. Al's explanation for his divorce is provoked by the interviewer's query about timing and, following this, a question about the stages of adjustment he has gone through. Instead of answering the question directly, Al re-defines it; he is an active agent in the interview, not simply a passive "respondent." He tells when *he* dates the separation—the month when he found out about his wife's affair—though he and his wife lived together for five months after this discovery.

Al's account is constructed interactionally in a very explicit way. The interviewer's comment, "you lived together for a long time (after you found out)," is the critical stimulus for the narrative: her words make manifest a puzzlement, a problem that the teller must resolve to make sense to this particular listener. It also seems that Al's expla-nation has not solidified nearly to the same degree that those of Tessa, Susan, and Steve have, perhaps because Al has not lived apart from his spouse as long as they have. Maybe the narrative has not been told this way before; certainly, it has not been rehearsed. In a very explicit way, it is being constituted in the very course of the tell-ing. Al's answers stumble and slide into memories, associations, rev-eries, with the listener's questions, as Marianne Paget says, "poking gently at perplexities."[29]

To resolve for the listener the issue of why he continued to live with his wife for so many months after finding out about her affair, Al begins a narrative that re-creates the quality of those months. He evokes the feelings that belong to this period, ones that the listener has no way of knowing about, by stressing key words (nuts, absurd, long) and intensifying words to signal salience ("*long* telephone con-versations"; "absolute agony"). He pauses a number of times, as well, suggesting his strong feelings and, perhaps, that he is having diffi-culty putting a narrative together. With halting speech, Al reestab-lishes the mood of the past and communicates "how it was"—that the emotions were almost unbearable.

Having set out how it was emotionally, Al draws the listener in more deeply as he moves into an illustration, a re-presentation of what he sees as a quintessential moment. Like Tessa, Al tells a habitual narrative, which he then backs up with a story. He orients the listener to the *general* state of affairs during the five months by describing events in the indefinite past ("she would have these *long* telephone conversations with Tony"). Through the habitual narrative genre, Al relates that during this period his wife made a display of her outside involvement and, further, that this routinely put him "in absolute agony." Her actions produced a strong emotional response in him, but no action.

To tell about the time when he *did* act, Al leaves the habitual genre and begins a story. This is signaled lexically by a narrative clause told in the simple past tense ("I remember lying down here once"). The picture he is painting for the listener requires a concrete example. He locates the events for her: they took place "here" and "once." Folktales begin with certain rhetorical conventions—such as "once upon a time"—and Al moves similarly into his storyworld. The listener is about to be told about events that took place under particular circumstances, involving particular characters, and that resulted in a change in the habitual state of the marriage. Because the story will be about a change—a time when Al expresses his anger—he establishes his usual emotional state as a baseline. He breaks into the story and backs up to say that he "hate(s) being angry" and has "a hard time with anger" (lines 22–23).[30] Having communicated this essential fact about himself, Al returns to the plot and repeats himself in line 24 so the listener will know he is returning to the story begun in line 20. He continues by dramatizing his emotional state at that instant ("And I could just feel this (p) anger ri– rising up in me"). To build the plot further, and to contextualize even more the violence he will shortly describe, Al suspends the immediate action and returns to a description of his usual routine when he felt angry:

28   . . . I would listen to this music and it would go away again.
29   It was a Palestrina Mass (*I:* uh-huh) that I *really* like . . .

This interlude conveys the waves of feeling that were taking possession of the protagonist. The juxtaposition of images—anger and religious music—is very effective.[31]

Having set the stage and primed the listener, Al tells what happened—the "crucial incident," perhaps not unlike the "trigger event" Mills refers to—in a dramatization, an almost unbroken sequence of temporally ordered narrative clauses in the simple past tense:

31   . . . I *finally* got up and (p)
32   and (p) went into the other room
33   (p) she was in the laundry room with the door closed and
34   (p) knocked on the door and said
35   "When are you going to be done with this?"
36   'cause we, we were going to talk.
37   And she kind of held up her hand like this and went "no."
38   And I got absolutely bullshit
39   I put my *fist* through the door (*I*: uh-huh)

This "blow-by-blow" form of telling, unlike a summation, pulls the listener into the specific moment. The untoward nature of the events stand out precisely because Al has provided so much background material to make the listener aware of his customary quiet nature and his usual ways of calming his anger.

At this moment in the narrative, Al leaves the storyworld. At a moment of high drama, he enters the interview context, commenting once again to the woman listener about his nonviolent nature ("I'm *not* a real physically violent person at *all*"). He says explicitly the point he wants to make with his story—that it depicts behavior that is totally out of character. He makes certain that the listener will not misunderstand and assume he is normally given to violent behavior. This content may be designed, at least in part, for this particular listener. Al may need to justify himself and his actions repeatedly because he is reporting violence toward a woman, to a woman.[32]

Al brings his story to its climax and concludes it:

58   Um (p) and I hit her (p) then (p) and
59   (p) she picked up a stick of wood
60   and I said she "better not do that."
61   And she stopped.

Line 58 is the most important in the narrative. It forms the turning point in the story because it changes Al's consciousness. (As previously, the pauses in his otherwise fluent discourse signal the special importance of the utterance.) Because of his many statements about his usual nature, the listener can understand how this eruption of violence would change the marriage, as Al comments immediately in lines 62–68. These lines, too, are replete with false starts, ideas that the narrator breaks off midstream, suggesting his confusion and turmoil.

How Al depicts the violence is significant. It was a one-time event, not part of a habitual pattern. It is also mutual, though Al does not emphasize this. After he puts his fist through the door, his wife comes at him and starts hitting him (lines 44–45). The half of the story that Al does not choose to develop is that his wife hit him before he hit her. Instead, he feels at fault for the violence.

Al has a rhetorical task to accomplish: he must move out of the story genre and back into the here-and-now of the conversation. In lines 62–68, with phrases such as "at that point" and "close to that time," he gradually distances himself from the events and time line of the storyworld and moves into the present and an interpretive mode. He begins to return to the issue that prompted his narrative—the date when he separated from his wife—by making reference to "the half-time deal" (the shared custody arrangement).

Before returning to the present, however, Al makes one last comment about the meaning of the events he has reported:

69   'Cause I remember feeling that, that this was just
70   no good for me at all
71   that, that uh I felt like I was subjecting myself to
72   uh I felt like I was being masochistic.
73   There wasn't any, any *reason* to *be* there other than
74   other than to hurt
75   that that was all, that was all that was going on.

Al began his narrative by describing strong feelings, and he ends it this way. He interprets what has happened to him in psychological terms, referring to the concept of masochism. Instead of placing blame on his wife and her open display of affection for another man, Al blames himself. He stayed in the marriage when he was being mistreated because of his need for punishment. This understanding is echoed at earlier points in the narrative, where he invokes the psychoanalytic concept of the unconscious (for example, he says he did not "consciously" want to hurt his wife in line 57). Both the beginning and the end of the narrative are tied together by feelings and psychodynamic formulations of his theme (he begins by saying it was "nuts" and he was in "agony" and ends with his "hurt" and "masochism"). Just as Tessa's narrative was permeated with a cultural discourse, so is Al's, but in his case it is the theory of psychoanalysis—a distinctly middle-class idiom of explanation in American culture for complex behavior.

Through his narrative, Al resolves the listener's uncertainty about why he continued to live with his wife after the emotional separation that began with the affair. He creates a context for understanding, making explicit how he wants the listener to interpret the events surrounding his divorce decision. Further, he establishes his positive social identity and nonviolent values, despite the fact that the key event in his account is his physical violence toward his wife. His choice of genre helps him with the teller's problem, for stories allow a split between speaker and protagonist; the speaker can be shown to be a "good person who recognizes that the protagonist did wrong."[33]

Having resolved the teller's problem, Al must get out of the narrative and back into conversation. His sensitivity to interactional norms is vividly displayed with "exit talk":

76   Um (p) so (p) I'm afraid I got a little lost
77   we were talking about the stages—

The structured portion of the interview can proceed. The listener can ask the next question.

Al's account shows how one man constructs a narrative to make sense, to heal the hurt and compose an impression of himself; structurally he does this by combining the habitual form with a story. At first glance it would appear that Al left his wife because she was having an affair (he says this elsewhere in the interview), but the narrative he constructs shows that the reality is more complicated. In this instance, too, he develops his definition of the situation interactionally with a woman listener. The fact that the narrative is about physical violence towards his wife makes the interactional context especially significant and overtly shapes the way he tells it.

NARRATIVE: A WAY OF MAKING SENSE

At the most basic level, the four case studies reveal how individuals impose an intelligible and followable order on their memories of marriage by constructing narratives about them. Each narrator posits a central dilemma, two characters with opposing goals (husband and wife), and resolves the dilemma. The process provides coherence to a disjunctive life course and helps the divorced reconstruct who they are. Out of the trauma of marital difficulty, divorcing individuals begin an intense process of searching from which new understandings of marital events have to evolve, and these new meanings, as well as the process of meaning construction more generally, are revealed in their lengthy narrative accounts. The narrator's present sense of herself or himself determines how the past is viewed. Jerome Bruner refers to this process as subjectification, "the depiction of reality not through an omniscient eye that views a timeless reality, but through the filter of the consciousness of the protagonist of the story." In their accounts divorcing individuals are active speaking agents, who mull over and evaluate their experience in the very process of retelling it. [34]

By attending to longer stretches of talk, rather than to specific complaints, we can uncover how individuals give meaning to the events that have happened to them. Tessa tells about physical abuse and Al tells about marital infidelity, for example—two "complaints" that are common in divorce accounts and, previous research suggests, also occur in many marriages that do not end in divorce. But as Tessa and Al make clear, it is the meaning placed on these events by individual husbands and wives that gives the incidents their dynamic power in the separation process. Nor are initially stated "complaints" always what they seem. Narrative analysis lays bare the interpretive work and the complexity of the divorce process.

The close analysis of particular accounts reveals how a theme—like physical violence or marital infidelity—is an active force, not a static category. In examining accounts we find a sequence of events, a process that links together what individuals remember from their marriages, their emotional responses, and their decision making about divorce. Individuals do not merely report events but also actively interpret them, putting them into a narrative sequence to gain understanding. Nor are the events themselves—however terrible—

always the "cause" of the divorce, as Tessa and Al make clear. Unearthing distinctive themes or meanings is possible only when we examine larger units of talk, such as narratives, that preserve subjects' ways of organizing and making sense of their experience.

Each of the four accounts has a distinctive architecture, with each narrator actively constructing his or her divorce explanation by using and combining (often in very complex ways) a variety of narrative genres, or forms of narrative. Although previous investigations have focused on the story as the prototypic form, analysis of these accounts suggest that this is only one of several genres that individuals use to organize and convey the meaning of personal experience. Habitual and hypothetical narratives, either alone or in combination with stories, and episodically structured narratives are other forms frequently employed.

Although there are a variety of narrative types, narrators do not arbitrarily choose them, nor are they interchangeable. An account's structure is influenced by two interrelated aspects— the meaning of events and the teller's problem. The speakers convey distinctive understandings of marital events through the particular linguistic choices they make, including the choice of narrative genre. Susan uses the habitual form to convey the sense of being gradually worn down by her marriage. Tessa, Steve, and Al each tell stories of instances that result in change. Each expresses through a way of telling what the experience of marriage was like. This does not mean that the use of stories necessarily signals one type of understanding and the use of a different narrative another, for stories may function in different ways and accomplish different communicative aims. But in general I find a relationship between the "point" a narrator makes and the form of expression he or she chooses. In a reciprocal fashion, structure flows from meaning, with subsequent understandings allowing narrators to interpret particular events as turning points in consciousness. In focusing more closely on language, we see the extent to which interpretation depends on the form of telling, rather than existing solely in the content of what is told.

But the construction of meaning is not a private psychological process: it is socially accomplished. Narratives require an audience, and making sense of narratives is an interactional process in which tellers try to persuade listeners. Interviewers also enter into the narrative—

as questioners, listeners, and commentators. Reciprocally, tellers enter into the perspective of listeners, and this can be seen in the way tellers construct their texts. (Where the reader enters in is a topic for another book.)

Tessa, Susan, Steve, and Al actively confront the teller's problem. They all employ the strategy of narrating their experience (albeit in very different ways) rather than merely listing a set of complaints. Narratives allow tellers to draw listeners into their worlds, to recreate the feeling of a past time, to tell of events that caused a change in that world. This way of telling, unlike a listing or a report, allows individuals to persuade a listener who was not there that their marriages were deeply troubled and that they were right to leave them. Their accounts make sense, in large part, because of the strategic choices they make in constructing their accounts in interaction with a listener.[35]

To emphasize this performance aspect of narration is not to undermine the "truth" of what each narrator said, or the point made earlier that narrating can bind a life disrupted by loss. Although the four texts were interactionally produced, coauthored by listener and teller, the marital experiences the texts relate certainly were not. Whatever "really" may have happened in each marriage, we must assume that the narrator's selection represents a reality, albeit not the only one. Narratives are probably some combination of fact and fiction; they are presentations of the world, not copies of it. Yet an interpretive approach to the narratives need not entail what Paul Ricoeur calls a "hermeneutics of suspicion."[36] Attention to the strategic uses of narrative is not intended to undermine the narrators' claims about their lives.

Some have argued that narrative structures are universal, that they always emerge—a self solving a problem in its own world.[37] Although it is true that narrative genres and other structural features of narration are widely available in U.S. culture, I suggest that how and when they are invoked by tellers is a social process, emerging out of interaction and shaped by context.

The four case studies display some of the genres that tellers call upon to solve the teller's problem. Habitual narratives tell of the general course of events over time; hypothetical narratives present a vision of how it might have been; stories recount specific events so that the listener will believe they "actually" happened; and episodic narratives are stitched together by themes rather than by time, making a general point through a series of snapshots.[38] Each of these genres provides a way for the teller to go deeper, to illustrate what it was "truly" like. Within each genre, narrators can capture a listener's imagination even more deeply by dramatizing events. Structures help tellers draw in and persuade listeners, and examining structures helps us understand how narration works. It is in the telling that events "happen" for the listener, and thus the *how* of telling becomes important.

Related to the teller's problem and to the interactional context of the construction of meaning more generally, are the affiliations with particular listeners that narrators develop. This link is displayed in the talk between them, especially in nonlexical utterances. Genre itself may be a function of how "deep" the teller is willing to go, how much trust there is between teller and listener. Tessa's narrative, especially, suggests that as she came to trust the listener and as the listener demonstrated that she was not going to back off from difficult topics, the narrative deepened and the "unspeakable" could be spoken.

Narrative accounts are socially constructed in other ways, as well. They are infused with cultural discourses and taken-for-granted knowledge; Tessa took a feminist understanding of rape for granted, for example, and she and Al each built upon psychoanalytic notions. Accounts are also moral tales that argue "this is not the way the world ought to be"; they argue that something went wrong between husbands and wives, a position that necessitates commentary and evaluation within the narrative itself.[39] In Tessa's discourse on inequality in marriage and Al's on the inappropriateness of physical violence between husbands and wives, each developed a narrative to make a moral evaluation or implied critical judgment about the world they shared with other people. On another level, narrative accounts are moral tales allowing narrators to preserve a positive social identity in the face of getting divorced—behavior that, even in the 1980s, carries a stigma. Individuals narrate to achieve social ends, making a claim for a valid social identity—"I am a good person despite my divorce." By storifying their accounts as they do, the four narrators provide evidence for their moral adequacy.

CHAPTER 4

Personal Trauma in Women and Men

The Private Experience of Social Trouble

But first I must tell you
That I should really like to think there's something wrong with me—
Because, if there isn't, then there's something wrong,
Or at least, very different from what it seemed to be,
With the world itself—and that's much more frightening!
That would be terrible.

—T. S. ELIOT, The Cocktail Party

Cynthia sat across the kitchen table and described the emotional roller coaster she had been on since she had decided to leave her husband a week before. The most recently separated person who agreed to be interviewed, she was especially articulate in describing her alternating feelings of despair and elation, fear and freedom. She conveyed her sense of having lost control of her life, saying she felt "like a deck of cards that has been thrown up into the air." She described the inner turmoil that came from the "whole structure falling apart." Structure for her meant the purpose and organization that marriage, and gender roles within marriage, had given to her life, as well as the social approval that came with being someone's wife. In her words:

[When you're married] you know what you are supposed to do from the time you get up 'til the time you go to bed. . . . There isn't much doubt that when you get up, you have to make sure that everyone has breakfast and gets off to school and the house is somewhat organized, before you have any time for yourself. Everybody approves of these functions and it gives you a sense of validation as a person. Then, when you don't have that, you have to make all these decisions about what you're gonna do from one minute to the next, as well as developing your own grand design for your life. (C026)

Cynthia says she feels sad and anxious a good deal of the time, and guilty, too, because she is not there to care for her husband.

Bob, a thirty-four-year-old man separated much longer than Cynthia, is less sad but also expresses the same sense of dislocation, albeit with a different metaphor:

My family was the centerpiece, and everything revolved around that, and that was knocked out, with nothing to hold the pieces together. (N006)

"Nothing to hold the pieces together" and "a deck of cards thrown up in the air"—these phrases express the sense of dislocation that marital separation brings, giving rise to turbulent emotions. As Marris describes, loss creates a crisis of discontinuity, causing intense grieving for structures of the past.[1] In addition to losing an attachment to a specific person (however ambivalently regarded), divorcing individuals lose marriage, itself a kind of linchpin that holds together various spheres of life. When a marriage dissolves, daily routines are disrupted and a variety of decisions, previously taken for granted—everyday concerns such as where to live, how to survive economically, how to spend time, whom to spend time with, to name but a few—are opened up, creating both disruption and opportunity. As Cynthia put it, the divorced must develop their "own grand design for . . . life."

Both women and men experience disruption and upheaval during this important life transition—a time of both threat and promise. They may have feelings of distress, depression, and anxiety, and they may display the actions that can accompany emotionally upsetting states, such as drinking and bodily responses in the form of

121

physical symptoms. (These reflections of emotional upset are experienced by all of us at some point in our lives, and are not necessarily clinically significant states.) How do women and men express the personal trauma of loss and change? How do they interpret their feelings and actions?

The search here for answers to these questions integrates three sources of data—markedly different representations of personal trauma. I begin with the symptom scores of women and men on an established depression scale, and then move from this quantitative analysis to two kinds of qualitative representations—individuals' own constructions of their psychological states, first, in spontaneous comments and, second, in two longer narratives. The two longer accounts, selected because they exemplify in a vivid way gender differences in vocabularies of distress, allow us to examine how a woman interprets why she feels depressed and, correspondingly, how a man does.

Each source tells us something different about gender and the trauma of divorce—the patterned occurrence of certain symptoms, on the one hand, and the experience of distress "from the native's point of view," on the other. To borrow from Clifford Geertz, the quantitative approach to understanding emotions is "experience-distant," and the qualitative approach is more "experience-near," focusing on the immediacies and vernacular of the individuals themselves. As he argues, neither is to be preferred over the other; both are needed "to produce an interpretation of the way a people lives which is neither imprisoned within their mental horizons, an ethnography of witchcraft as written by a witch, nor systematically deaf to the distinctive tonalities of their existence, an ethnography of witchcraft as written by a geometer."[2]

WHO IS MORE DEPRESSED? THE QUANTITATIVE EVIDENCE

The separated and divorced express their trauma in high levels of depressive symptoms. As a group, they have more intense symptoms than individuals who have not gone through the divorcing process.[3] In a national study comparing the married and the divorced on the Center for Epidemiological Studies Depression (CES-D) scale, the married have an average score of 8 (on a scale from 0 to 60).[4] The average for my sample of divorcing and divorced individuals is 16—somewhat higher, in fact, than the average for the divorced in other studies, probably because this study includes such a large percentage of the recently separated, who are in the most acute stages of the grieving process. The most recently separated (those living apart for less than a year) are significantly more depressed than those who have lived apart for longer, and women as a group are significantly more depressed than men as a group. The average score for women is 19, compared to 13 for men ($p < .01$).[5]

Why do women experience significantly more depression then men after divorce? To explore the reasons for these gender differences, I began with a series of statistical analyses of the answers given by the divorcing people I and my colleagues had interviewed. My analysis was guided by what mental health investigators term the "differential exposure" hypothesis.[6] It is well known that when marriages end women face particular hardships from which men tend to be shielded. Women, for example, are more likely than men both to reside with children and to be responsible for their daily care. They are also likely to experience a decline in income at the same time that their parental responsibilities increase. Women are more likely to depend on support payments from their former spouses, and these may be irregular and insufficient. Women are also likely to have lost the help that husbands provided in household management. Not simply discrete stressors or events, these are the persistent circumstances of daily life that can often induce strain and on-going difficulty. To what extent does exposure to these life strains explain variation in depression?

Children, after a separation, have a strong impact on psychological distress for the women interviewed but not for the men. Women who have children are twice as likely to be depressed as those who do not ($p < .01$). Further, when the role demands of parenting are greater, there is a corresponding increase in symptoms: separated women with a child less than six years old in the household are significantly more depressed than women whose youngest child is over the age of six ($p < .05$). And, irrespective of their ages, as the number of children in the household increases so, too, does women's depression. In contrast, men's depression is not related to their parental status or to the age or number of their children, even in those few cases where fathers either have custody or actively co-parent. Fathers without custody who have more contact with their children (that is, fathers who often see and talk on the phone with them) tend to be somewhat less depressed than fathers with less contact, but only marginally ($p < .07$).[7]

Separated women are also likely to be depressed when they are under economic strain. Women with children display the most symptoms of depression when they also report having difficulty affording food, clothing, medical care, leisure activities, and essential household items that needed to be replaced ($p < .05$). Interestingly, there is also a trend for single-parent fathers to be more depressed when they are financially strained in these ways, but this association is not statistically significant, perhaps because of the small number of single-parent fathers in the sample.[8]

In addition to the general issue of not having enough money to afford basic necessities, there is a specific kind of financial strain that is particularly relevant to separated and divorced women—worry about support payments. When asked how often in the last month they had worried about alimony or child support, 25 percent of the women said they worried either fairly often, very often, or all the time about this issue. In a reaction similar to the effects of financial strain in general, women are significantly more likely to be depressed if they have to worry about receiving support payments, especially if they have children ($p < .01$).[9]

An additional strain in separation—the loss of help that a spouse provides—is not so tied to gender. For a woman, however, the availability of aid from others after marital separation can be especially crucial, because it can partially mitigate the stresses of poverty and parenting alone to which she is more likely, as a consequence of her gender, to be exposed.

The more people a woman has to rely on—to help around the house, to do small favors, to loan money, to socialize and discuss personal matters with, to help make decisions, to talk to on a daily basis—the less likely she is to be depressed. These forms of support also reduce depression significantly for women with children ($p < .01$). The degree to which men experience depression is not affected by the receipt of help.[10]

I have identified some of the key life strains that contribute to depression among separated and divorced women. (I have been much less successful in identifying the sources of men's psychological distress—a point I will return to below.) Although it is true that other research shows some of these persistent problems—primary responsibility for the care of young children, financial strain, absence of help, for example—to be linked to depression for married women as well, being unmarried greatly increases women's chances of being exposed to these strains and thus of being psychologically hurt by them.

Which of these strains is most important? In other words, what are the relative and additive effects of children, money, worry, and lack of help on women's psychological distress? Testing a model that combines these four life strains (and education, a predictor of psychological distress because it is an indicator of social class), I find that a significant proportion of women's depression is predicted by the cumulative effects of the variables in the model—42 percent of the variance, or 34 percent if one is more conservative and adjusts for the number of variables.[11] A more detailed look shows the order of importance of each factor, with the others held constant. Worry about support payments is the most important factor increasing women's depression (beta = .37), and the help women receive with a variety of practical and personal tasks is the second most important (beta = −.32). The presence of children and the perception of financial strain, though they have sizable effects, are no longer significant once the other factors are taken into account. In other words, the responsibility of caring for children increases separated and divorced women's depression, but only when they are forced to do so without adequate and regular support payments from their former spouses and when they have few people to turn to for support and aid. It is this social and economic context that is deleterious to women's mental health, not single parenting per se.

When we look at the aggregated mental health scores across all cases, we see that women appear to be at considerably higher risk for psychological distress when marriage ends than are men. The findings also provide evidence that depression in separated and divorced women is socially produced, grounded in the structured and institutionalized arrangements that expose women, more than men, to toxic conditions in life, such as money worries and unaided child care. In the language of epidemiology, women's greater exposure to enduring life strains following divorce plays a large part in accounting for their distress. A different kind of data—a more personal language—can help us understand more deeply what these statistical relationships mean for women. It will also allow us, in later sections, to examine the trauma associated with divorce for men that statistical analysis did not reveal.

WOMEN AND THE COSTS OF CARING

Women have extensive vocabularies for conveying the experience of emotional distress. Unlike men, as we shall see, they have no difficulty talking about it at length. They often use relational metaphors. A recently separated factory worker said, "It's like losing your best friend," and she added, "It's just like when someone dies" (N026). Another said, "It's like a part of me was gone" (N024). An interpersonal orientation is manifested in the language women choose, yet this orientation carries high costs for them personally.

When women spontaneously spoke about personal trauma in the interviews, they often did so when discussing problems in the lives of others—people for whom they felt responsible, particularly children and former spouses. It may be that having children in the home contributes to women's depression because women tend to identify with their children's difficulties—their material losses as well as the emotional ones—taking in and then expressing children's feelings for them. As one woman said:

> I want her [daughter] to know that she has a daddy that loves her. . . .
> I'm not entirely sure he does and that hurts me. It is almost like I'm
> taking it personally, but it hurts me for her. (C033)

In addition to identifying with their children's hurt, mothers try to be both parents to their children, a desire Sally expresses:

> I'm not with them all day and I feel that I should be spending time with
> them. Perhaps even more time because he doesn't spend it. (N015)

Given that most single mothers are employed and running households, too, there is role overload, general fatigue, and a scarcity of time. Women respond to economic and emotional demands they cannot meet by feeling guilty. In the words of a factory worker:

> If I had the time to be with them, I would. I would rather be with them than be working because it's hurting them more than me. Tommie's withdrawn symptoms and Jeannie's little problems . . . it makes me want to cry all the time, all over again, inside and out. To see that happening. I can't do everything. I can't be here and there at the same time. I have to be a provider first and be a part-time mother. Just wish I could give them more. (N026)

On one level, these women feel guilty for not being "good enough" mothers, for not being able to do it all. But they are saying something more. They are aware of the ways that divorce has hurt their children, and they carry both the burden for this and the desire to remedy it. As individuals, they cannot make up, either economically or emotionally, for the absence of fathers. Yet, in the language of C. Wright Mills, they transform the public issue—the lack of social provisions for single women and their children—into their own private "trouble." Individually, they carry the sadness for a society that has failed to respond to women and failed to attend to children.[12]

Ruby—the exotic dancer—is a case in point. She reports many symptoms of distress, and her depression score is close to the top of the range (CES-D = 50). She says the greatest difficulty she faces is "the kids." What she means by this is not that it is difficult to care for them alone (though it is), but rather that she senses that they are having emotional difficulties without their father. Although "it was brutal" when he was in the house because he physically abused her, she has empathy for their suffering now, even as she acknowledges the "peace of mind" that divorce has brought to her. When she describes what divorce means for her son, she measures his distress as greater than her own:

> When he [her former husband] first stopped coming over, my older son thought it was because he was such a rotten kid, his father didn't love him anymore and didn't want to see him. . . . The kids suffer very, very greatly. Very greatly. The parents suffer, in comparison, on a scale from one to ten, I feel the adults involved suffer maybe one, and the children suffer nine. (N018)

An even more poignant statement of this issue is voiced by a woman with a young daughter, who had a middle-class style of life before her husband left but who is now on welfare. She has been separated a little more than a year and has the highest depression score of anyone in the study (CES-D = 53). She cried often during the interview, speaking of "this terrible thing that's eating away at me inside." Often her tears came when the conversation turned to the meaning of her daughter in her life. When asked about dating, she said:

> I don't feel I should, I think I do want to, but I don't really know how to approach this life again, you know. Especially when you have a little girl, you're a package deal now, it's not like when you were single. I don't know why I'm getting like this (starts crying). (N016)

When asked about the "greatest difficulties" in the process of separating, she said:

> I didn't have a, you know, a very happy childhood myself and I guess I always wanted to give Joanie a lot and, you know, be with her. Not that I was opposed to working part-time or anything. . . . I think preschool is good for her, but I wanted to be with her until she went to school . . . be there in the afternoon when she got out. And now I feel I'm just trapped. I don't have a house anymore, she doesn't have a yard to play in . . . he [ex-husband] doesn't go out of his way to do anything for her. He did before he got this new woman in his life. (N016)

Crying as she speaks, she goes on to talk, in a habitual narrative, about the problems her daughter had right after the separation:

> When he first left . . . she went through vomiting spells where every night at supper when he wouldn't come home she would cry, she would vomit, she was sick a couple of times in the hospital with dehydration, when she would get sick from vomiting. . . . I would sit here for a month, night after night, and she would just vomit her dinner. Now, I think she's pretty much adjusted, but she will say things like, "It was really nice with my Daddy, when we were all together." (N016)

This woman acknowledges that she has many issues impinging on her mental health—past and present—but her experience also dem-

128

onstrates that the social circumstances of a divorced woman's life can create distress.

Some women also take responsibility for the adjustment problems of their former spouses. A teacher expressed concern about her husband's mental health:

> After the conversation I had with him last week, I was worried about him. . . . I don't think he's okay. . . . And he said, "I'm fine now. I've gone through all this stuff and I've had some problems and I'm okay," but you talk to him and he still doesn't make sense the way most people do and I worry about him. (L014)

A similar concern is expressed by Cynthia, separated only a few days, whose statement about the dislocation of separation opened this chapter. The welfare of her husband and his children from a previous marriage haunt her:

> My husband has been very angry and upset about it . . . he's threatened that he can't manage by himself and that's been very hard for me to tolerate. . . . I feel very guilty because I feel as though I've been important to that household and that it will be hard for him to function on his own. And he also has a potential operation coming up. (C026)

Reporting a number of symptoms of depression (CES-D = 37), Cynthia feels guilt that centers on her belief that her strivings for independence (epitomized in her decision to end the marriage) are causing pain to others. Another woman, also with a significant depression score (CES-D = 32), describes a similar sense of responsibility for causing her husband pain:

> Sometimes I feel guilty. Not because I didn't save the marriage but because the way he is now, he looks like defeated, like he lost everything. And I know that if I were to say to him, "Let's go back again," he would. I see him as being so lonely. (N024)

Breaking the bonds of dependency on spouses is difficult for a number of women. They blame themselves and experience high distress levels when they put their own interests first. Even as women leave their husbands, they display empathy for them. Jean Baker

Miller argues on the basis of clinical evidence that women often link the exercise of their own power with others' destruction.[13]

Women's emotional responsiveness to others' difficulties upon divorce continues a pattern that is characteristic of marriage. Women are the socioemotional experts in modern marriage. Their "invisible work" includes the emotional tending of husbands.[14] As one woman put it, as she mused about her marriage, "I picked up his emotions as well as my own" (C042). Upon divorce, this woman, like others, continued to "pick up" emotions, for example, as they divided up the marital property:

> I just took the minimum of what I needed. . . . I remember taking one poster down off the wall and him sort of dying over that, and me realizing that I can't leave any spaces for him to deal with. He can't deal with it. (C042)

Although there is value in women's orientation toward others, there are also some costs for women personally. When women are responsible for children and those children display their distress about divorce, women are more likely than men to worry and to blame themselves. When women are responsible for caregiving in a marriage and the marriage ends, women are more likely than men to anticipate the spouse's distress and experience sadness and guilt. This contagion of stress from husbands to wives and from children to mothers makes women more vulnerable to the emotional effects of events in others' lives. The fuller interview responses of women in this study bear witness to these costs of caring.[15]

THE EXPERIENCE OF DEPRESSION: CINDY'S NARRATIVE

To understand more about the particular features of personal trauma for divorcing women, it is useful to examine one case in detail, and to attend closely to the language that gives form and meaning to this woman's emotional experience. This analysis draws on the methods of narrative analysis used in Chapter 3, but adds an additional focus: it examines the poetic structure of the narrative. As we shall see, "stanzas" bind this account together, and the narrator conveys subtle information about her life and her emotions through the way she structures her speech. From this case, we get a richer and more complex picture of what the variables in the quantitative analysis mean, that is, how children, money problems, worry about support, and lack of help combine to create distress in one woman's life. We see the costs of caring up close.

Cindy is a twenty-six-year-old white woman who has been separated one and a half years. Her narrative about the trauma of her divorce came about three-quarters of the way into our lengthy interview with her. Its emergence was a bit of a surprise, for up until that point, Cindy had been using every opportunity to describe her feelings of freedom, even ecstasy, since she had left her husband—the positive side of the divorcing process that I will turn to in Chapter 5. Her husband had been a member of a religious community and, though she had known about the importance of his beliefs before she married him, it was not until she moved into the community with him and had a child that she experienced the full import of its severe constraints. Every aspect of her life was regulated by rules, and after much difficulty she decided to leave her husband, taking their three-year-old son with her. The period since had been filled with self-discovery and innovation, which she described to the listener with pleasure and excitement.

At this point the interviewer administered the CES-D scale, and Cindy reported many symptoms. She said, for example, that she "felt sad" and "felt depressed" a moderate amount of time (three to four days during the previous week), and that most of the time (five to seven of the previous week) she "felt lonely" and everything she "did was an effort." Her depression score on the CES-D scale was 30, markedly higher than the average of 19 for women in the sample. It was in this context that the interviewer departed from the structured set of questions and asked about "things that had been hard" lately. Cindy's response, which has been displayed in clauses to facilitate analysis of its stanzas, is as follows:

01 About (p) things that are hard?
02 Well um I don't know what's hard (laughs)
03 I've been walking around
04 in this for the last month or so
05 feeling that things are very very hard

06 like I have a cloud over me
07 and I'm very *confused*
08 and I can't (P)
09 I feel like
10 I am too burdened
11 and I can't imagine how
12 to be less burdened
13 I feel like
14 I I *need* to be doing everything I'm doing
15 (P) and so I don't know how to
16 take some of the burden
17 off of myself (P)
18 *Int.:* Why do you think you need to be doing everything?
19 *Cindy:* (P) Well ah I I need to work
20 in order to earn a living.
21 (p) I need to ah
22 go to school
23 so that I won't always have to work for nothing.
24 I need to
25 be a good mother
26 'cause that's very important to me.
27 (P) And (P) I'd like to
28 find a little free time
29 if I can (laughs).
30 *Int.:* (P) So it it's been particularly in the last month that you've
felt
31 (p) everything's piled up, or?
32 *Cindy:* Yeah, well
33 a lot of it has to do with the welfare system changing
34 *Int.:* What happened?
35 *Cindy:* Well I used to be on welfare
36 but um with them talking about
37 number one they cut me a whole lot
38 because I work also
39 *Int.:* Was this recent?
40 *Cindy:* No it was like Novem– the end of November
41 and ah so I got cut way down
42 and um (p) they cut me so low in fact that
43 my ex-husband was paying them more
44 than they were paying me
45 so (laughs) which I think is even illegal

46 I think it's
47 they would have sooner or later caught it themselves
48 but uh (P) so my choice at that point was
49 either to go off completely
50 and get money from him
51 or (p) quit working
52 and I
53 at that point it sounded like a good idea
54 to quit working
55 so that I could
56 go to school and not feel
57 like I had so many things to do
58 but um financially I just couldn't do it
59 there was no way I could do it.
60 And also with workfare looming ahead
61 I was worried that I'd get
62 forced out of school
63 and I only have like a year to go
64 so um (P) because I didn't want to take a chance
65 of being forced out of school
66 I just quit welfare.
67 And so all this financial stuff came up
68 and trying to decide what to do
69 and uh (P) and not being on welfare
70 I don't have anything to fall back on so
71 and my job is also
72 (p) because of a lot of restructuring and
73 the way money is changing
74 the assessment stuff
75 I don't know how long my job is going to hold out
76 so I really need to be looking
77 for a new job.
78 So my financial situation is just
79 completely unstable at this point.
80 And (p) I ended up taking two incompletes
81 out of the three classes I was taking in school.
82 (p) So it's making me think that
83 trying to go to school
84 *and* work and be a mother is too much
85 but I don't know how I can not do it.
86 And uh (p) at the same time for some reason

87 my son's going through a really clingy spell again.
88 And uh (P) he probably does it right when I can least (laughs)
89 afford to deal with it you know.
90 (p) So it's just a lot of stuff all at once
91 in the last month or so.
92 (P) And so I've been
93 with all this other stuff I've been
94 actually needy myself
95 you know wanting
96 wanting someone to come home to
97 who would say "Hey sit down
98 I'll fix you a drink
99 let's chit chat about the day,"
100 you know someone to nurture *me*.
101 And so I've been more aware of not having that person.
102 (PP) (both laughing and crying?) I I feel like
103 I have to make a decision
104 but I don't I don't
105 I don't know what to decide so
106 (p) I'm walking around waiting to decide.   (N029)

To facilitate and summarize my analysis of Cindy's narrative, I have redisplayed portions of its text, organized in terms of its structure and revealing some of its poetic features, in Transcript 1.[16] Cindy begins with a metaphor—a primary method of expressing emotion—likening her state of mind to walking, with a cloud over her, unable to see clearly. She refers to her unsettled emotions with this same image again at the end of the narrative ("I'm walking around waiting to decide"). In addition to unifying her account, the repeated references to walking, first in the past and then in the present tense, suggest motion and lack of resolution.

Cindy's vocabulary of emotion is not clinical and detached but immediate and experiential. She refers to her distress as "feeling that things are very very hard," rather than labeling it depression. She continues to develop her own vernacular about the sense of being "burdened."

Cindy's speech (probably like all speech, linguists argue) has a stanza form and, in this case, it joins the narrative. Stanzas are a series of lines that have a parallel structure and that sound as if they go together by tending to be said at the same rate and with little hesitation between the lines. James Gee argues that stanzas are a universal unit in planning speech and that poetry, in fact, builds on what we each do all the time. Poetry "fossilizes" and ritualizes what is in everyday speech. In Cindy's case, she gives in stanzas 3–6 a four-part explanation for why she feels so burdened, an explanation that she later expands into a narrative. As she lists the four areas that in her mind are causing her such difficulty—money, school, child care, and no time for herself—she moves from the outside in, from the most macro to the most micro. The tight stanza structure articulates a sense of constraint; the roles of provider, student, and mother create conflict because the expectations of each are so discordant, creating insoluble emotional dilemmas. In moving from the social to the personal, the stanzas also suggest that Cindy has turned the responsibility for change from the outside in. She feels that the dilemma is *hers* to resolve, personally and privately, despite the fact that the sources of this distress are social.[17]

Having outlined her four problems in four stanzas, Cindy develops each theme, amplifying in sequential order each of the causes of her distress in four episodes. In the first she explores the problem of money. She describes her struggle to support herself and explicitly locates the cause of the problem in the social environment ("a lot of it has to do with the welfare system changing"). She tells a narrative to explain "what happened," reconstructing and interpreting how budget cuts, changing welfare policies, workfare, and the uncertainties of her job have made her financial situation "completely unstable."[18]

Cindy is experiencing the effects of the first of the Reagan budget cuts in welfare expenditures and the beginnings of a new workfare program, which requires that she register for job training as soon as her child turns six (he is five and a half). Because she is in a four-year baccalaureate program (not considered "training" by the welfare department in her state), she stands a good chance of being "forced out of school," with only one year to go before she gets her degree and, presumably, becomes more employable. Caught in the irrationality of these policies, Cindy decides to quit welfare. As a consequence, she must rely on child support payments from her former spouse that, she tells us elsewhere in the interview, are irregular and thus a source for worry. (In answering interview questions designed to

TRANSCRIPT 1.   CINDY'S EPISODIC NARRATIVE

Frame

03	I've been walking around	
04	in this for the last month or so	
05	feeling that things are very very bad	
06–07	like I have a cloud over me and I'm very *confused*	

Affect and Conflict

09	I feel like	Stanza 1
10	I am too burdened	
11	and I can't imagine how	
12	to be less burdened	
13	I feel like	Stanza 2
14	I *need* to be doing everything I'm doing	
15	and so I don't know how to	
16	take some of the burden	
17	off of myself	

Source: Enduring Role Strains

19	Well I need to work	Stanza 3
20	in order to earn a living	(money)
21	I need to	Stanza 4
22	go to school	(school)
23	so that I won't always have to work for nothing	
24	I need to	Stanza 5
25	be a good mother	(care of children)
26	'cause that's very important to me	
27	And I'd like to	Stanza 6
28	find a little free time	(time for
29	if I can	self)

Transcript 1.   Cindy's Episodic Narrative (continued)

Episode 1: Money (core narrative)

33	a lot of it has to do with the welfare system changing
35	Well I used to be on welfare
37	. . . they cut me a whole lot
38	because I work also
48	but so my choice at that point was
49	either to go off completely
50	and get money from him
51	or quit working
52	and I
53	at that point it sounded like a good idea
54	to quit work
55	so that I could
56	go to school and not feel
57	like I had so many things to do
58	but um financially I just couldn't do it
59	there was no way I could do it.
60	And also with workfare looming ahead
61	I was worried that I'd get
62	forced out of school
63	and I only have like a year to do
64	so because I didn't want to take a chance
65	of being forced out of school
66	I just quit welfare.
75	I don't know how long my job is going to hold out
78	So my financial situation is just
79	completely unstable at this point.

Episode 2: School

80	And I ended up taking two incompletes
81	out of three classes I was taking in school.

SUMMARY

82	So it's making me think that
83	trying to go to school
84	*and* work and be a mother is too much
85	but I don't know how I can not do it.

(continued)

Transcript 1.   Cindy's Episodic Narrative (continued)

Episode 3: Care of Children

86	And at the same time for some reason
87	my son's going through a really clingy spell again
88	And he probably does it right when I can least
89	afford to deal with it you know.

SUMMARY

90	So it's just a lot of stuff all at once
91	in the last month or so.

Episode 4: Self (hypothetical narrative)

92	And so I've been
93	with all this other stuff I've been
94	actually needy myself
95	you know wanting
96	wanting someone to come home to
97	who would say "Hey sit down
98	I'll fix you a drink
99	let's chit chat about the day"
100	you know someone to nurture *me*.
101	And so I've been more aware of not having that person

Frame (Return to affect and conflict)

102	I feel like	Stanza 7
103	I have to make a decision	
105	I don't know what to decide so	
106	I'm walking around waiting to decide.	

---

measure financial strain, she indicated she is worried "all the time" about her financial situation and "often" doesn't have enough money to afford basic necessities; at the end of the month she usually ends up with "not enough money to make ends meet.")

Cindy leaves the narrative mode after summarizing the first episode in lines 78–79. She does not tell another narrative again until later, and instead uses non-narrative forms in the two middle episodes (episodes 2 and 3 of the transcript) to explain the sources of her distress and the conflicts they create in her emotionally. The second episode—about the strain associated with school—merely reports in a couplet, succinctly and tersely, how she resolved the dilemma of role overload. Like her earlier statement about financial strain ("I just quit welfare"), the active voice here says how she resolved her dilemmas ("I ended up taking two incompletes"). As if to summarize, she then explicitly restates the theme of being burdened in a four-line stanza in lines 82–85. This passage captures the essence of the bind that welfare policies have created for Cindy: holding a job is necessary because of welfare cuts and workfare, but going to school is necessary to get a decent job.

In the third episode, Cindy elaborates on her problems being a good parent—her five-year-old son is "going through a really clingy spell again." He's doing this at a time when she can "least afford to deal with it." The irony in her choice of the word "afford" is apparent: her emotional resources for parenting are as limited as are her financial ones. Like other single mothers, she empathizes with her son's distress, experiencing his pain as her own.

In the summarizing couplet of lines 90–91, Cindy makes a statement that ties the three episodes together. The recent past has been especially difficult, she says, because of the combination of money, school, and child-care demands—"a lot of stuff all at once." It is the piling up of role strains that makes her feel "burdened," not any single problem.

The fourth episode, lines 92–101, picks up on a theme Cindy put forward earlier—no time for herself—but gives it a twist. In the context of "all this other stuff," she's been feeling "actually needy" herself. It is not time alone that she wants as much somebody to support and nurture her.

The focus of the fourth episode is not events that have happened, but events she *wishes* would happen, and consequently she tells a hypothetical narrative. Through dialogue, she creates a text within a text, a multivoiced narrative episode with texture and dimensionality that is emotionally affecting both because of what she says and how she says it.[19] To convey the fantasy, she constructs a hypothetical conversation in lines 96–101, ending with a coda that returns the action to the present moment.[20] Like her son, she wants someone to cling to.

Cindy concludes the narrative but does not resolve the dilemmas it sets forth. Unlike the divorce narratives in Chapter 3, this one, concerning role strain and distress, lacks firm resolution and closure, for the narrator is still in the middle of the conflict. She returns to the metaphor of walking, her feelings, the present tense ("I feel like"), and the stanza structure with which she began in lines 102–106.[21] She is preoccupied with making a decision (mentioning this three times in the four lines), but exactly what decision is ambiguous. What is clear is that Cindy feels overwhelmed in the face of multiple pressures, with no one to help. Although at one level the origins of her problems are distinctly public, her experience of them is personal and private. As she assesses her situation, it will be "resolved" by some decision *she* has yet to make.[22] In the words of T. S. Eliot, Cindy verges on saying, "There's something wrong with me," when in fact there's something wrong "with the world itself."

Cindy's narrative is quite consistent with the quantitative analysis of the sample. When we examine women's emotional distress from her point of view, we see that she forges the links between enduring role strains and personal trauma, between her position in the social structure and her feelings. Her experience amplifies how particular sources of stress are built into the lives of divorced women, causing psychological distress.

This close analysis of Cindy's case provides a "thick description," giving a depth and texture to our understanding of the general problems women face upon divorce.[23] Emotional distress occurs in context. Lack of money is more than a variable that is correlated with depression: emotional distress is produced in Cindy's case by social policies that force women to make choices, between job, school, and welfare eligibility, that compromise their efforts to become self-supporting and bring depression in their stead. Similarly, Cindy's experience with a "clingy" son and her longing for care herself show what other variables in the quantitative model—child care and lack of help—actually mean in context.

The close analysis of one woman's talk also shows how emotional life is constituted in language. Individuals go through an interpretive process to make sense of their distress, and when left to their own devices rather than analyzed with depression scales, they give meaning to particular stressful events by constructing narratives about them, using poetic structures such as stanzas, couplets, and metaphors. The form of the explanation is not something separate and apart from its message, but reinforcing and mirroring of it.

PUBLIC SOLUTIONS FOR PRIVATE DISTRESS

The findings here on women's psychological distress are consistent across three types of evidence: quantitative comparisons, qualitative excerpts, and a narrative account. The quantitative findings show that women are exposed to particular hardships when marriage ends from which men tend to be shielded, and that these enduring strains—daily care of children, lack of money, worry about support payments, and lack of help—have direct consequences for women's mental health. Compounding this is the meaning that these hardships have for women. The qualitative evidence suggests that women's empathy for children and their spouses leads to guilt, self-blame, and sadness. Although some have argued that women are more vulnerable in the face of stress than men, results here suggest an alternative interpretation: women are emotionally responsive to the difficulties of others.[24] Finally, the detailed study of one woman's narrative shows how depression is experienced and interpreted in context. All three kinds of data point to the social origins of women's psychological distress, and the case study shows how one woman transforms the social trouble into an individual problem.

The fact is that the sources of many of Cindy's problems, and those of divorced women more generally, are amenable to public solutions. The particular strains that are built into the lives of divorced women and cause distress could be remedied, for example, by the set of social welfare proposals developed by a group at the Institute for Policy Studies.[25] The recommendations include (1) universal, federally supported child care; (2) guaranteed child support payments from noncustodial parents (typically fathers), subsidized by the state when income is insufficient; and (3) economic and employment policies, such as job creation and an increase in the minimum wage, equal opportunity and pay equity in the workplace, vocational education, and job training. A full discussion of these proposals is

141

beyond the scope of this book, but they suggest a direction for needed changes. If these policies and service structures to ensure their implementation were in place, the sources of stress for divorced women with young children would be considerably lessened.

MEN'S PSYCHOLOGICAL DISTRESS

The trauma that men experience when marriage ends is not as easy to identify. It might even be said that this trauma is less susceptible to remedy than that of women, at least at the level of social policy. In addition, men's idioms of distress are more varied than women's and, consequently, more difficult to quantify.

As noted earlier, men had significantly lower depression scores than women did, and the quantitative analysis was not successful in predicting their emotional distress.[26] Yet in the interviews many spoke of their distress and, like Cindy, some developed narratives about it. The distinctive ways men experience and express the personal trauma of divorce can be better understood in two ways: through a detailed analysis of the words of one narrator and through an examination of the patterns of qualitative response of all the men in the sample.

"Running Right on the Edge"

Rick is a thirty-three-year-old academic, without children, who has been separated for two years.[27] His wife left him precipitously, in the middle of "a stupid argument," and he found out later that she had been involved with someone else for some time. His initial reaction was, in his words, "bleak depression." He responded by pouring himself into his work and by "going out with just sort of random women—two, three, four, half a dozen perhaps"—on the "spur of the moment with no commitment whatsoever," until he met a woman with whom he ultimately formed a relationship. Yet he says he is "not very happy" with his life and is quite lonely, especially because he has recently taken a new job that, though lucrative, is far away from his lover and the college community of which he felt such a part. Still, he has few symptoms of depression on the CES-D scale. He says he feels sad only "some or a little of the time," depressed or lonely "none of the time," and hopeful about the future "a moderate amount of the time." His depression score, 4, places him below the mean for men in general and considerably below the average for women.

Rick elaborates on his feelings after his wife left by telling a narrative. This began when, about halfway into the interview (before Rick completed the CES-D scale), the interviewer departed from the structured set of questions to inquire what "bleak depression" was like—the words he used to describe the phase immediately after his separation. Rather than describing feelings of sadness and personal vulnerability usually thought typical of depression, Rick's response suggests an entirely different idiom of distress—frantic activity and heavy drinking:

01 *Rick:* (PP) I got a feeling that
02 I'd never experienced before
03 which was almost
04 a cer– certain fran*t*icity
05 um *fran*tic feeling
06 I don't know what I'm doing
07 I don't know what—you know it's almost like (*I:* mm-hmm)
08 like I was running *right* on the edge (*I:* mm-hmm)
09 (p) and I don't know on the edge of *what*
10 I was never able to (p) (*I:* uh-huh) you know
11 put that (p) into *words* very well
12 but I had the feeling that
13 (p) almost something's got to give.
14 Now nothing ever gave
15 that I can see
16 things just sort of backed off and eased out.
17 But I was running
18 sort of like wide open
19 ninety miles an hour
20 down a dead-end street (*I:* uh-huh)
21 as the song goes (*I:* uh-huh)
22 um (p) and uh (P)
23 yeah I started drinking much more
24 just because (*I:* uh-huh)
25 (p) it was something to do
26 I'd stop at the bar (*I:* mm-hmm)
27 be– between Greenboro and home

28 there was this little comfortable bar (*I:* mm-hmm)
29 where everybody used to gather about five o'clock (*I:* mm-hmm)
30 and uh (p) we were drinking pretty heavily
31 and uh (p) which is something I you know
32 I used to (p) *party* pretty well
33 but you know drinking that heavily
34 uh (p) it was just something different
35 it was a it was a whole a total reaction
36 and living
37 just much more wildly
38 as I said (*I:* uh-huh) just more (p) you know
39 it was like I said
40 just driving faster
41 and just *push*ing it
42 just (p) (*I:* uh-huh) just, that was, I can tell ya
43 funny kind of a feeling just uh
44 (p) kind of hard to put into words (*I:* uh-huh)
45 I never really could
46 when it was going on (*I:* uh-huh)
47 I'd say to people
48 "well you know I feel like I'm on the *edge* of something" (*I:* uh-huh)
49 but I didn't know what (*I:* uh-huh)
50 I still can't describe it very well
51 that's not an accurate description
52 *Int.:* No it's it makes it clearer
53 *Rick:* but it's 'bout the best I can do right now. (*I:* yeah, mm-hmm)
54 And uh I I was monumentally unhappy (*I:* mm-hmm)
55 I did *not* want her to leave
56 which I discovered after she left, you know. (*I:* mm-hmm)
57 (p) But there's lots of songs about that too you know
58 so (laughs) what can you do.
59 *Int.:* That helps to understand what that was like for you.
   (Rick goes on to talk about his music avocation and writing
      songs after separation—"maudlin sorts of things in a country
      vein.")   (C035)

Transcript 2 redisplays key sections of this narrative. Like all narratives, Rick's is saturated with pattern. Its point is very different, as is its form, from Cindy's. But like Cindy, Rick relies on metaphor to express emotion rather than on abstract clinical language, and he repeats one of them—"running on the edge" (lines 8 and 48). Pressure metaphors also recur throughout the text ("something's got to give," "running wide open," "driving faster," "just pushing it"), and they are in sharp contrast to the overt images of emptiness, loss, and vulnerability and behaviors like crying that are more consistent with depression in women's talk. Rick's machine-gun style of delivery (evident in listening to the tape) is different, too, from women's styles. He rushes through his account of his emotions, not dwelling on the topic as the women tend to do in their accounts. The language also suggests a fear of loss of control—he is on the edge of disorganization, and whatever restraints that usually contain his strong feelings are breaking down. Whether the issue is overwhelming anger or the sorrow of loss, the prevailing image is of running from it.

Rick's narrative is not easy to classify into one of the four genres described in the last chapter. It may represent a fifth form, a kind of reminiscence, a hunt to reconstruct and name a past feeling or state.[28] Whatever we call it, it is a form of narrative that allows for talking about the search itself, which is, for Rick, "kind of hard to put into words." Evaluative and metaphoric naming of emotional states take over, overshadowing events that would usually organize a narrative. As Dennie Wolf has commented about this account, "If there is a 'story,' it is the tale of being able to convey what it was like 'back then.' "[29]

Rick's narrative form is meaningful, because his choice allows him to tell about strong feelings and then to retreat from them. The narrative is organized by an alternation between explication and avoidance. Rick states a feeling, backs off from it, restates it, and backs off again, in repeated cycles. This might also be described as repeatedly interrupting the flow of discourse about his emotions to say he does not have a vocabulary for them, and attempting to capture them using descriptions that are not his own, borrowed from songs. This refrain is, in fact, a manifestation of his distress. Not having the words, particularly for an academic, is a way of saying, "I'm not located, I'm out of place in this field." Although he has an advanced degree, he defines himself as inarticulate in the realm of feelings and emotions, and gets away from them by constantly apologizing for his lack of the right word.

TRANSCRIPT 2.   RICK'S EXPLANATORY NARRATIVE

Affect

01	I got a feeling that	Stanza 1
02	I'd never experienced before	
04	a certain fran*tic*ity	
05	*fran*tic feeling	
08	like I was running *right* on the edge	Stanza 2
09	and I don't know on the edge of *what*	

Backing Off

10	I was never able to
11	put that into *words* very well

Affect

12	but I had the feeling that	Stanza 2
13	almost something's got to give	(cont.)

Backing Off

14	Now nothing ever gave	Stanza 3
15	that I can see	
16	things just sort of backed off and eased out	

Affect

17	But I was running	Stanza 4
18	sort of like wide open	
19	ninety miles an hour	
20	down a dead-end street	
21	as the song goes	

Backing Off (habitual narrative)

23	I started drinking much more
24	just because
25	it was something to do
26	I'd stop at the bar
27	between Greenboro and home
28	there was this little comfortable bar

Transcript 2.   Rick's Explanatory Narrative (continued)

---

29   where everybody used to gather about five
         o'clock
30   we were drinking pretty heavily
32   I used to *party* pretty well
33   but drinking that heavily
34   it was just something different

SUMMARY
35   it was a total reaction

Affect

36   and living   Stanza 5
37   just much more wildly
40   just driving much faster
41   and just *push*ing it

Backing Off

43   funny kind of feeling
44   kind of hard to put into words
45   I never really could
46   when it was going on

47   I'd say to people
48   ". . . I feel like I'm on the *edge* of something"
49   but I didn't know what

50   I still can't describe it very well
51   that's not an accurate description
53   it's 'bout the best I can do right now.

Coda: Affect and Backing Off

54   I was monumentally unhappy
55   I did *not* want her to leave
56   which I discovered after she left

57   But there's lots of songs about that too
58   so what can you do

Note how Rick breaks up stanza 2 with a parenthetic remark ("I was never able to / put that into *words* very well"), truncating what is otherwise a key stanza in a sequence of four that build toward the figurative language Rick finally seizes upon that "gets it." He finds a metaphor in popular culture:

17 But I was running
18 sort of like wide open
19 ninety miles an hour
20 down a dead-end street
21 as the song goes

Rick uses the lyrics of a country western song to describe his distress. He also returns to the theme of using song lyrics as a language for emotions at the end of the narrative ("But there's lots of songs about that too"). A contradiction is apparent throughout: Rick is an academic and yet the vocabulary he finds most meaningful is street language. Perhaps only there can he find a masculine idiom for his feelings.

Drinking, also a stereotypically masculine idiom, is another way that Rick deals with his feelings. To tell about it, however, he still backs off from the emotions. He moves away from the figure of the speeding car in stanza 4 and begins a habitual narrative fragment about "this little comfortable bar" (lines 23–34). The plot does not concern a specific time or incident but describes his general routine at the end of the day, which fits the habitual narrative genre. Using conventional narrative devices, Rick orients the listener to the particular bar, the group of people, and the time each day that he drank and conveys the meaning that these events now have for him in lines 25 and 33–35.

As he sums it up, it was "a total reaction." His response to his wife's departure was to avoid his emotions by drinking and running, just as he responds to the listener's request to tell about his "bleak depression" with an approach/avoidance narrative strategy.

Nowhere in the narrative does Rick make reference to feeling hurt. Until the very end, there are no statements about loss, missing the attachment to a spouse, or the routines of marriage. In sharp contrast to the content of Cindy's narrative, which is interpersonal and full of statements about connection (both to people and to institutions), Rick's narrative pivots on separateness—a solo driver barreling down a "dead-end street." Indirectly this too is a powerful image of emptiness, of having nothing and going nowhere.

Ending the narrative, Rick makes its point explicit. In lines 55–56 he momentarily breaks into the structure that he has set up to organize it, and openly tells of his emotional response to his wife's actions ("I was monumentally unhappy / I did *not* want her to leave"). He quickly pulls back, however, and distances himself in lines 57–58. He follows with a laugh and a change of topic—further signals that he has fled from sadness.

Other men in the sample also ran and drank to deal with distress and repeatedly said they had no way to name what they felt. Rick's narrative articulates themes that appeared in the talk of the men as a group. It is not that they did not have feelings, or that they failed to express them in the interview. Rather, as Rick illustrates, men do not have an easy language for feelings and emotions and, importantly, quantitative measures (like the CES-D scale) do not provide one as they do for women.[30] From a close analysis of the one, we have, in fact, learned a great deal about the many.

Men's Idioms of Distress

When men spontaneously describe their emotional responses to separation, these are patterned in distinctive ways that Rick's narrative anticipates fairly well. Many divorcing men deal with their distress by heavy drinking, with 20 percent of the men (versus 10 percent of the women) intimating that they use alcohol as a major method of stress relief after divorce.[31] As one man said, "my loneliness is drowned out by alcohol" (C023). Others talk of getting "totally smashed" (C011), getting "loaded to try to forget about everything" (C031), "imbibing a little bit too much" (C019), and drinking "to pass the time away" (C021).

Although drinking may have also been a coping pattern for some while they were married, for others it seems to develop as a consequence of the divorce process, with heavy drinking beginning in the period immediately after separation (the pattern Rick displayed). As a factory worker put it, "my first year separated I spent in bars." He describes how he currently does a lot of drinking in between romantic relationships and makes explicit his ongoing difficulty in handling feelings in any other way:

> It is difficult. It is lonely, that is what it is. I can't afford to go out every night, so you have to pull yourself together and do your own thing. Because . . . you could drink yourself to death. Either that or let nerves bother you to the point where there is no return. Nerves can do a number on you. (C018)

He, like virtually all the other men in the sample who mention drinking, scores below the average for men on the depression scale. Some have argued that seeking solace in alcohol may mitigate men's depression. To put it differently, men drink "to drive the blues away"—a lyric that recurs in American jazz. In this case, folk wisdom and recent psychiatric research agree: there is strong evidence that depression is a major cause of drinking (rather than the other way around).[32]

Beyond the relief of stress, drinking seems to serve another purpose for men. It appears to be a medium through which they develop and sustain relationships with others, particularly during the early phases of the divorce process. Separated and divorced men encounter problems with time management and the organization of their daily lives.[33] When they lose a wife, they also have less access to a number of important relationships, most notably with kin and children. They attempt to manage loneliness by re-creating a social network in bars. Rick describes drinking as "something to do," especially at five o'clock, when "everybody used to gather" at a particular bar. For him as for other men, the bar provides an alternative routine and an instant network of new friends to ease loneliness—people to whom men can tell their stories and from whom they can gain sympathy and companionship.

For the factory worker, the bar is where he learns about a singles group (Parents without Partners):

> I heard about it [PWP] at a bar. . . . I was talking to this older person and he was telling me different things. . . . He said, "Are you newly divorced?" He said, "Why don't you join PWP?" I never heard of them. So he told me to go up to [hotel] on the first Thursday of the month. (C018)

But the bar as a forum for sociability can become a habit, as a machinist comments:

> Yeah, when things close in I go out. And . . . say you go down there to have a couple and you end up having six, you know. (N021)

Drinking also has a paradoxical effect on the very feelings of loneliness that men are trying to avoid. A businessman says he feels most lonely and lacking attention when he gets drunk:

> I guess you want to have your arm around somebody. That's the only time I feel lonely. (N044)

The factory worker expresses the problem more directly:

> Did a lot of drinking and felt very lonely. Because drinking is a depressant, right, alcohol is a depressant, and I would come home very depressed. (C018)

Men also try to handle their loneliness after separation by pouring energy into the job—a pattern of response seen in Rick. When the workday is over, or on weekends, many men have trouble. Nor is work a refuge only for professionals. A factory foreman describes it this way (I have used narrative conventions here to capture better the cadence of his talk):

```
84  (p) Work was the best thing for me.
85  I hated weekends
86  I'd rather be working than have a weekend
87  there was nothing for me to do on a weekend
88  I was just run—
89  constantly going somewhere
90  getting nowhere
91  just in a hurry to get someplace
```

Reconstructing his experience of restlessness at being alone on a typical weekend, he goes on to tell a fragment of a habitual narrative:

```
92  I didn't want to just sit at home by myself
93  so I'd—off I'd go down to my mother's house
```

94   next thing I'd get there
95   and I wasn't
96   content or anythin'
97   and I'd be up to Tom's house
98   (P) I, I—so work was the best thing.   (N027)

Like Rick, he expresses his inner turmoil by constant activity and running, desperately trying to fill the time he is not at his job. Another man refers to this male pattern of extreme restlessness as his "hyper tendency" (C041). The defensive features of this mode of handling distress is made explicit by an insurance salesman: "As long as I kept moving I was great" (L012). Constant motion seems to counter these men's feelings of sadness and loneliness.

This pattern of coping is understandable from what we know about gender and divorce more generally. For men much more than for women, divorce brings massive change in daily routines. Men typically do not have the care of children to provide continuing structure and meaning, and for many, contact with children can be irregular and sometimes unrewarding.[34]

Often men lose the family home—a cultural symbol of power and success for them as well as a place to put energy into on weekends. More generally, men's power in the family is lessened or lost altogether, as is their primary or sole confidante—an activity wives perform for husbands that benefits men's mental health.[35] The job becomes a refuge from all these losses because it is an alternative source of power, gratification, and routines and because it provides the easy company of others to ease loneliness.

Yet some men have trouble concentrating at work. At the same time that men say the job was a refuge after separation, they also describe how their job performance suffered. The factory foreman quoted earlier says that in the months immediately after his wife left he "had a hard time at work":

Doin' paperwork, I couldn't concentrate. My mind would be off somewhere else all the time. (N027)

Another working-class man—an electrical contractor—describes how he "wasn't able to function" at work for quite some time after his separation and "lost maybe thousands of dollars as a result of it" (C047). A number of other men, but few women, also spontaneously mention difficulties on the job after separation, especially if they are self-employed and these problems of achievement evoke a good deal of self-criticism.[36] Yet employment remains a source of comfort for men, especially in the context of other difficulties in their lives.

Some men manifest their distress in a more extreme way—losing control altogether. This too is present in Rick's narrative, though in a much less extreme way (he, in fact, talks of the fear of *losing* control). A few men describe overt power displays, explosive outbursts that are often directed at their former wives. The struggle with destructiveness is particularly salient for men in general, and being abandoned by a wife seems to bring this struggle out in full force.[37] Charles, separated six months, tells a story about seeing his former wife and her friend on a motorcycle:

> It really hurt because I could see her wearing the same colored motorcycle jacket that he had on, she had a fake diamond ring that I assume he bought her and leather gloves. (C021)

He "took off after them" in his car until the police stopped him. Nor was this an isolated incident. Apparently a law-abiding citizen while married (he had been employed as a security guard), at the time of the interview he had a long list of criminal charges against him:

> So as it stands right now, I've been convicted of annoying phone calls, I've been convicted of larceny over $100—I've appealed both of these. My wife brought a complaint against me for destroying the car, which I did. Monday, I'm going to court in Greenboro for violation of a restraining order, operating to endanger, two counts of assault with a dangerous weapon, two counts of attempted murder. (C021)

Despite his many difficulties, Charles has few symptoms of depression on the rating scale. Feelings of sadness, helplessness, and personal vulnerability are clearly not his idiom.

Men's various manifestations of distress have one thing in common: the distancing of the self from feelings of sadness. The most extreme manifestations of this pattern are the few men who had scores of zero on the depression scale—something no woman achieved. Despite divorce and the many life changes associated with it, these men appear on the scale as if they felt no pain whatsoever. Steve, whose narrative was analyzed in Chapter 3, is one such man. When the interviewer pressed him to talk about any difficulties he'd had since the separation, he said:

> Alright, one thing. The first night I got separated, the fact that she made absolutely no effort to say, "Why don't we talk it over," "Why don't we reconsider," "Why don't we do something," that upset me for one night. And I can honestly say that's the only bad thing that I've had with the whole separation. The next day, I moved out, I moved into my apartment the next day and felt good about myself, about the situation, and it's gotten better all along and I really have no bad feelings about it at all. I feel I did the right thing at the right time. In fact, I feel I know I did. (C040)

A more common mode of distancing the self from any depressed feelings is manifested in some men's choice of language. The machinist, separated two years, names the phases he has been through—"depression, anxiety, whatever you want to call it"—but then adds, "I never let it bother me, I head out when anything bothers me" (N021). An apartment superintendent, separated for nine months, says:

> I'm not hurting, I'm never depressed anymore or anything. It's been a long time since I've been depressed, long time. I can't even remember. I've been happy ever since. (N017)

Depression is talked about as if it were a thing of the past, as the following three men—all middle-class—describe:

> I, in fact, did go through a very serious depression and, as I look back, in retrospect, there was, in fact, a time when I wasn't at all sure that I was going to make it. (C027)

> I was depressed for a long time afterward because I did not know why it had happened. I couldn't figure it out really. (N040)

> The first time we were separated I was very depressed. I didn't know what depression was. Later I realized what it was. (N043)

Significantly, though all these men are vocal about feelings and use clinical language, at the time of the interview not one had a depression score above the mean for men in general. They apparently accept the psychiatric category of depression, but they do not use this label to interpret their current subjective experiences. Women in the sample, even those separated the same length of time as these men, tend not to employ the past tense to describe emotional distress or to talk about depressed feelings in an abstract way, which suggests either that these feelings are ongoing or that they have less need to distance themselves from them.

Another way men seem to separate themselves from the direct manifestations of sadness is to express emotions in a physical form. A factory foreman recalls that the first four months after his separation he "threw up every morning" (N027). Others also speak of physical problems—ulcers, colitis, low-grade infections—and intimate that these were related to the emotional strain they were under during the divorce process. One man describes how his "intestines got into a flip-flop," attributing this to the stress of a holiday:

> I can tell you, it was due to this—the separation—because it was Thanksgiving, the first year when I was separated, and we all went over to the house, my ex-wife and the kids and all that. . . . It was a very stressful thing. Ended up in the hospital that night. (C031)

Somatization—locating distress in the body rather than in emotional life—is a way to distance feelings and concerns elsewhere and, as Arthur and Joan Kleinman have shown, is often employed when overt expression of psychological distress is not culturally approved.[38]

A few men do seem to find the idiom of depression compatible with their style of expressing distress. One of these is a maintenance supervisor who had a CES-D score of 25—higher than the average for women. When asked about the greatest difficulties he'd experienced since his separation, Bill responded, "Well, not having my kids." When asked to say more about that, he answered cryptically:

> Well, I just don't have them now. I always wanted to have kids all my life and now I don't. That's the worst thing about it. That sums it up right there. It's too hard to talk about or say a lot about . . . (C046)

When the interviewer pressed, Bill added:

> Not having them [his children] like with me, that's been the real hardest thing. Just leaving the woman wouldn't be that much, but leaving, you know, the family. I always wanted a family.
> *Int.:* What's that mean to you, "a family"?
> *Bill:* What do you mean, what does it mean to me? It means—what do I interpret? What is my impression of it? Being complete, a man and a woman and kids. Just a man and a woman isn't a total family to me. (C046)

This man, unlike others, does not distance himself from feelings of sadness and loss, even though he has difficulty describing the feelings. He mentions missing his children and his limited access to them as a source of pain, which corroborates a quantitative finding that men were somewhat more likely to be depressed if they had less contact with children than they wanted. Bill's explanation for his distress is also interpersonal; unlike Rick, for example, he builds his account around attachments to others, notably his children. At the same time that Bill's account is interpersonal, however, it is also ideological. He does not only miss specific people; he also misses the family as an institution ("just a man and a woman isn't a total family to me"). For this man the loss of the daily anchors of family life is particularly meaningful. He too, however, echoes the refrain that recurs so often in men's talk: "It's too hard to talk about or say a lot about." For many men, emotions are hard to put into words.

THE FEMINIZATION OF PSYCHOLOGICAL DISTRESS

Different vocabularies of emotion are available to women and men when a marriage ends. The extent of gender relativity in their responses reveals just how socially constructed emotions are.[39] Women and men make different sense of marriage, and they also make very different emotional sense of the loss and dislocation of divorce.

Men are far from immune to the emotional effects of marital dissolution, though their modes of distress do not translate into high scores for men as a group on a depression inventory. Men do not report the usual symptoms of depression, because these are not the culturally approved idioms for men. Many, however, have responses that, unlike sadness, are stereotypically masculine, that they have a ready vocabulary for, that they can disclose without conflict, and for which they do not need to feel ashamed.

More generally, the subtleties of gender differences in emotional response to marital separation are missed in aggregate comparisons of women and men. The quantitative measures usually employed in community studies of psychological distress considerably underestimate men's emotional difficulties after separation, and skew the findings in the direction of more symptoms of depression for women and the appearance that men do considerably better than women separated for the same amount of time.[40] Although the focus here has been on a single life event—marital dissolution—the same issues would arise in any study of life events. It seems that the survey interview context may be constructing emotional distress in ways that are ill-suited to men's styles, giving the illusion that women are more vulnerable to psychological problems. In a word, there is a serious gender bias in measurement: psychological distress has been feminized by mental health investigators.[41]

As we have seen, men are quite capable of emotional expression. When allowed to use their own vocabularies, men evidence their emotional pain and their ways of coping with it, as in Rick's narrative, especially its pressure metaphors and use of lyrics from a country western song. Yet questions that might have tapped his idiom, as well as those of other men, are generally missing from quantitative inventories. Because psychological distress scales are constructed on a feminine model, organized around women's response patterns (crying, sadness, eating disturbances), they not only give an incomplete picture but also, paradoxically, make it look as though there is something wrong with men because they seem not to feel anything after divorce.

Why is psychological distress manifested in such different ways by men and women? Psychoanalytic theory, which argues that varying surface behaviors can have a similar underlying meaning, has something to contribute here. Both women and men may experience depression upon divorce, but the vocabularies for it may be quite distinctive.

The issue of gender differences in symptom patterns is not new in psychiatric epidemiology.[42] But why is it that men do not express their distress after marital separation in the form of symptoms of depression—the affect usually associated with loss—and rely instead on frantic activity, drinking, somatic symptoms, and a tendency (for a few) to lose control altogether? Although a thorough discussion of this important question too is beyond the scope of this chapter, lines of inquiry may be suggested.

Most obviously, individuals are socialized in particular historical contexts to become gendered personalities, and the appropriate experience and display of emotional distress is an important way that gender distinctions are maintained. Acknowledging sadness and crying are not consistent with masculinity in U.S. culture, and consequently the prohibitions against these behaviors are strong for men. Nor have men been socialized to value affective experience or to be introspective.[43] Gerald Gurin and his colleagues argue further that sex-role socialization may produce different coping styles in the face of problems and difficulties that, in turn, may influence the reporting of symptoms:

> The male role is closely linked to an active, coping interaction with the world, and a man's masculine identity is closely linked to his success in coping with his environment, to his strength in the face of difficulties. It would not be surprising then, if a man defended against feelings that attested to his failure in this respect, and not only experienced such feelings less often than women, but also was less likely to report them if they were experienced.[44]

Consistent with this view is the suggestion that some men may be nondisclosers, acquiring patterns of defense that push feelings of sadness and personal vulnerability out of their awareness, and thus they report fewer symptoms of depression than do women. Some have even suggested that men are engaging unconsciously in a massive cover-up operation: "A man may find depression an intolerable condition because it makes him feel like a woman."[45]

Certainly, men's patterns following divorce can be interpreted this way. It can be argued that they fend off ongoing feelings of depression with physical illnesses, restlessness, overwork, explosive outbursts, and drinking or that they deny distress altogether. Their emphasis is on doing and action, rather than on being and feeling. Not comfortable just sitting with sadness, as women seem able to do, they do everything possible to get away from it.

The problem with this line of argument is that it tends to set up women's modes of expressing distress as the standard against which men are evaluated—and found wanting. (The interpretation's strength, of course, is that unlike previous theories about women, it places their high rates of emotional distress in perspective, redefining "depression" as sadness and personal vulnerability in the face of difficult life circumstances, rather than as simply personal psychopathology.)

Different modes of experiencing and displaying emotions are suited to different socially assigned roles. Men's socialization toward doing and action prepares them for work roles in the economic system, especially a capitalist system. An interpersonal orientation and an openness to emphasis on talk about emotions among men might create tensions in (but also potentially change) the work settings where they spend the bulk of their lives. Women's socialization toward the interpersonal prepares them for caregiving roles. Modern marriage is also predicated on this division of labor, as we have seen, with men primarily responsible for the economic support of the family and women primarily responsible for the care and nurturing of family members. When a marriage ends, there is personal havoc for both women and men, yet the ways in which each group experiences and expresses distress is consistent with both early socialization and the division of emotions in marriage. Men are unaccustomed to the realm of talk about emotions, for they are the products of families where women did the work of feeling.[46] They have trained incapacities in the language of feelings, and in particular, they do not know how to talk about sadness. But they do know how to act, and thus they take their distress into the realm of action.

Psychological distress in divorce is socially produced for women, as it is for men, but in a very different way. For women, the central problem is one of material conditions. Environmental stressors, such as parenting in poverty, create distress for divorced women. The culture paradoxically provides for the emotional demoralization of women by supplying them with a language for emotions at the same time that it fails to provide for the material distress that occasions many of those emotions. As outlined earlier, public solutions to women's problems are possible. For men, the issues are complex, but they too are socially produced. The problem lies in the way masculinity is defined in this culture and the associated institutional arrangements that keep such definitions in place. At the same time that the culture provides for men's material advantage, it does not provide for their emotional development in certain key respects. The result for individual men is that they are deprived of a language for their feelings. Talking about emotions is the domain of women.

The lack of vocabulary of emotion may have serious consequences for men's lives. After divorce men are at greater relative risk than women for more severe physical and mental health outcomes, including mortality and hospitalization of all types.[47] It appears that the patterns of response to the loss of a spouse that many men describe—distancing, physical illnesses, restless activity, explosive outbursts, and drinking—may fend off difficult feelings in the short run but carry serious risks for men's physical and mental health in the long run. As Joy Newmann states: "The capacity to experience and express feelings of sadness in the face of loss is generally viewed as a mark of mental health and may be an effective deterrent to the development of more severe symptomatology."[48] The conditions of men's lives do not easily allow for the development of this voice of sadness.

CHAPTER 5

Starting a New Life

The Positive Consequences
of Divorce

You want to ask, am I lonely?
Well, of course, lonely
as a woman driving across country
day after day, leaving behind
mile after mile
little towns she might have stopped
and lived and died in, lonely.

—ADRIENNE RICH, "Song"

Divorce requires individuals to reorder their lives in major ways. In the "restless search to recover meaning" they become innovators, developing accounts of positives in the divorcing process and taking charge of their own recoveries and of others' views of them by acting on their worlds.[1] As most of them understand it, divorce is not only a loss, but a gain. One woman, separated almost two years, muses about this:

> People say you're gonna start a new life, and I have in a sense. It's not what they think. It's not a whirlwind of activity and a thousand dates knocking at my door. It's a whole growth process. (N023)

Making sense of the positives of divorce is an interpretive process, not an "objective" recounting of change and growth. Both women and men make claims about their identity in their talk. They select evidence that portrays a reconstituted self to a listener, a self that has not been totally destroyed by divorce. The areas of personal development one woman lists recur in the talk of others, as well:

> A lot of very good things happened to me after the separation, for sure. I developed a whole sense of myself that I didn't have before. I certainly did things that I had never done before. It's unlikely that I would have left everything and traveled across the country if I had stayed married, and I loved that. . . . It's unlikely that I would have gotten to know as much as I do now about therapy . . . and considered for a while very seriously becoming a therapist . . . that's a whole area that I sort of stumbled into because of the experience. I probably never would have [taken a sales job] if I'd stayed married, and I loved that. I probably would never have gotten as involved with the group of women friends that I have now if I'd stayed married. I certainly wouldn't have known the men that I've known since then if I'd stayed married. Which is not to say that all this has been wonderful . . . there have been many down cycles in all of this, too. I just don't know how to sum it all up. (L003)

She goes on, not only to "sum it all up," but to make an essential point about the significance of the present context in making sense of the past:

> I think a lot of the things that I've chosen to do are things that I wouldn't have done if I'd been in the marriage. And yet, at the same time I would be the first person to say had the marriage worked, I probably wouldn't have missed any of the things that have happened in the last few years. . . . My life has certainly turned out to be very different than I expected. (L003)

Precisely because divorce is regarded as deviant, it requires that individuals reinterpret their lives to others and forge new identities, convincing themselves and others that leaving their marriage was "worth it." The process is not without its dark side, but neither is it entirely negative.

There has been little research on how people construct positive sense out of loss. Interviewees in this study were asked about the difficulties of the separation process, but they were also asked to describe in their own words "the greatest benefits." Their lengthy replies help us to answer several questions: Are those who experience positive emotions a different group than those who report depressive symptoms? How do individuals construct positive meanings out of the massive changes of divorce and what do they draw on from U.S. culture to give form to these experiences? What do women, compared to men, single out as the "missing pieces" in their married lives that divorce allows them to fill in?[2] Who is more likely to interpret life outside of marriage in positive terms, women or men, and why?

LEARNING TO SURVIVE: "A BLESSING AND A BURDEN"

Most of those interviewed had no difficulty identifying divorce's benefits, which many—some explicitly and some implicitly—summarized as "freedom." (The 15 percent who could identify no benefits of divorce were all men, to be discussed later.) The positive changes in their lives cluster around three general areas: competence in the management of daily life, changing meaning of social relationships, and a fuller sense of a whole identity. More often than not, these positives coexist with feelings of distress. Some with above-average depression scores are also those who note considerable personal growth and change for the better, a finding that helps confirm the suspicion that psychological health is not a single continuum between healthy and sick poles, as Antonovsky argues it is.[3] Instead, individuals feel distressed in certain contexts and elated in others; some aspects of their lives may make for depression, others may engender happiness. Even the same experiences can engender ambivalent and contradictory feelings, which suggests that positive and negative responses to events are not opposites, but qualitatively different states.[4]

A woman teacher, separated almost three years, expresses this theme:

Like having to carry everything yourself—a total burden on your back about the house, finances, maintenance, and the career. You feel like

163

everything's there, all of a sudden. It's the responsibility, it's like a blessing and a burden. Two ends of the pole are both there. Like you know you can do it, but who needs it? But there's a lot of satisfaction in doing it all, too. (L002)

"Having to carry everything yourself" and the satisfaction this brings—this refrain occurs over and over. Demonstrating the ability to survive on one's own is a core component of the divorce experience, constituting "proof" to others that divorce is not entirely bad. Self-reliance is highly valued in American culture, and being more self-reliant is a way to construct a positive identity in the face of behavior—like divorce—that violates deeply held social norms. Moreover, the divorced are struggling to make positive sense of their new lives in the light of a contradictory value of modern marriage— that it provides what are seen as essential forms of social support. However problematic a marriage may have been, a spouse was usually there—for economic support, perhaps, or help with parenting and maintaining a home, or just so one did not feel so alone. The structure and expectations of the companionate marriage encourage husbands and wives to be not only psychologically dependent on each other but dependent in a variety of concrete, trivial, and gender-linked ways that are often taken for granted. At the same time the ideology of marriage encourages a myth of self-sufficiency as a couple—husband and wife are not dependent on an outside world, but on one another.[5] One woman sums up this issue:

Marriage assumes that you are, that the couple is self-sufficient. It's harder to reach out. It's funny, I hadn't thought about this but it's true. You're not supposed to be needy when you're married. It's like a betrayal . . . of this myth that marriage provides everything. (C002)

Divorce necessitates breaking these modes of thought and reclaiming aspects of the self that had been given over to the other to manage. Both women and men wonder whether they can survive on their own, whether self-sufficiency is really possible. Both construct accounts to show that they can manage, but because "his" and "her" dependency in marriage is so different, so are "his" and "her" understandings of change in divorce.

For both women and men, the quintessential American task of "finding oneself" provides a context for their psychological journey.[6] Both construct meanings out of a core value in American culture—freedom—a word that appears repeatedly in men's and women's talk. Yet a closer look reveals that they mean very different things by "freedom," and they manifest it in contrasting ways. Consistent with these contrasting meanings, women and men tend to define three areas of growth—in the management of daily life, social relationships, and identity—differently, as well.

FREEDOM FROM SUBORDINATION

To convey the positive side of divorce, women use vivid imagery:

> I feel like I'm living again. I feel like I was dying a slow death in that relationship. There's joy in my life. . . . I feel energized and liberated. I feel a real emotional release. (N008)

This woman—mother of two, recently separated, and an unemployed musician—is not atypical. The idea that divorce brings "liberation," "control," and "independence" recurs in interviews with women, working-class and middle-class alike. More than half the women in the sample, particularly those separated less than a year, actively engaged in reconstructing a self, emphasize this outcome. They say they "got born" (C012), have "the freedom to be myself" (C017), feel "more like a free person" (L010).

With this vocabulary women are making a connection between what their marriages were like and what their lives are like now. As they understand it, marriage brought subordination and divorce brings freedom. They revel in a new sense of ownership of themselves. Despite all the hardships—economic strain, role strain, and loneliness—women with children, as well as those without, experience more control than before over a variety of aspects of their lives and, concomitantly, a seeming zest and delight:

> I can go do the things that I like. (C016)

> I'm being independent . . . making my own decisions and following through with my own decisions. It's a good feeling. (L008)

I can feel inside as though I can do things again. (C013)

I have more freedom to think about what I want. (C026)

I can have it [the house] the way I want it. (C042)

I have more time to myself. I feel more in control of my fate. (N003)

Parenting alone has contradictory effects. Even though unrelieved child care causes distress, children provide a sense of purpose to some women's lives, and in managing children after separation women draw on skills and resilience they did not know they had. Some women say they enjoy their children more, in part because they have occasional relief when fathers take children out of the house. Others enjoy relating to children in their own ways, without the constraint of their husbands, as the unemployed musician, recently separated, says:

> My relationship with the children, with the pain of it all, there's so much pleasure in terms of the fact of being free, of being able to relate to my children the way I want to relate to them, and not feeling the tension or disapproval, the way my husband expected me to relate to them. (N008)

The language of freedom is especially pronounced among women who have been physically abused by husbands, though escape from subtler forms of male authority is prized as well. Listing the good things that accompany separation, this woman includes freedom from physical abuse as only one item among several:

> Letting the house be a mess, not having to make supper, being my own person and not having to answer to anybody for it, not getting beat up. (N028)

Ruby responds with a narrative to the interviewer's request to "give more specifics" about the benefits of separation:

> Okay, take for instance if I want to take the kids and just split for the beach for the day, I don't have to turn around and say, "Oh, honey,

would you like to go to the beach today?" . . . "Nah, I'm too tired."
And you sit there and you argue. If you want to go out for a couple of
drinks, you go out. You want to go out with your friends . . . hey, go
ahead. If you don't want to, if you just want to hang around the house
and do nothing, you do. You want to go out to eat, if you've got the
money, you pack the kids in the car and you go. . . . You have your life
back, you know? This is how I feel . . . I don't have to live in fear that
I'm gonna, if I come in the door a few minutes late, I'm gonna walk into
a fist. Or walk into an argument, if I'm late. I have nobody to answer
to. (N018)

"You have your own life back," a number of women said, to explain
what freedom means. They no longer needed to be responsive to or
worry about the reactions of a disgruntled spouse. In developing this
theme, Ruby constructs a hypothetical narrative, contrasting what
events might have been like, had she stayed married, with what they
are actually like after separation. Her sense of freedom is not con
tingent on being alone, because caring for children figures prominently in her narrative, as it does for most of the women quoted
earlier on the pleasures of their new-found freedom. It is important
to Ruby, too, not merely that she is free from physical abuse but that
she is free to be self-directing in a variety of ways. As Tessa says,
"instead of freedom *from* someone, I'm free to do what it is that is
within my abilities" (C017).

In using the language of freedom so often, what are women saying? As they try to make sense of who they are all over again, apart
from husbands and apart from marriage, women intimate that marriage had been different for them than it had been for their husbands.
For these women, the individuality that U.S. culture so highly
prizes was submerged in marriage. In the words of Robert Bellah and
his colleagues, "The sharing and commitment in a love relationship
can seem, for some, to swallow up the individual, making her (more
often than him) lose sight of her own interests, opinions, and de-
sires."[7] Divorced women draw on these cultural themes and reconstruct their marriages as filled with constraint, subservience, and
vulnerability to the authority of husbands. In this context, they
make positive sense of divorce by seeing it as an opportunity to "take
back" their lives.

COMPETENCE IN THE MANAGEMENT OF DAILY LIFE

Women also describe changes in their daily lives when they argue that things are better than they used to be. They alter aspects of their current environments and feel that positive consequences flow from their efforts. The experience produces what Robert White posits is a necessary condition for psychological development—the feeling of efficacy.[8]

Learning to Fix Things

To survive without husbands, women must manage households, including making necessary repairs. Trivial as many may seem, the fact that women repeatedly mention them as benefits suggests how significant they are in developing a new self:

> I can really take care of myself, up to and including taking care of my old Ford. That's very nice. (C008)

> I'm learning how to do things . . . there's no mystery about it now, I can get out an electric drill. . . . I got satisfaction from putting a bookcase together. (C016)

> I've even mastered [things] since he's not been there, like when I fix a leaky faucet or something. That makes me feel a little better or a little more capable. (N015)

As women understand it, house and car repairs were the province of their husbands in their marriages, and they did not have the opportunities or the desire to develop or exercise mechanical capabilities. But with divorce they find they, too, can fix things:

> I know I'm a better household mechanic than Terry [her former spouse] was . . . but as long as I was living with [him], it never would have occurred to me to push him aside and say . . . "I'll do it." Now I can just go ahead and repair the toilet and say to myself, "You did that all by yourself, by golly." (C008)

Why does fixing a toilet or arranging to have the car repaired warrant such satisfaction? Growing beyond dependency on husbands in these ways is analogous to studies of infants' play. Although women are obviously not infants, conceptually there are some parallels. Piaget argued that shaking a rattle and playing hide-and-seek are "serious business," because it is through these mundane tasks that infants first learn they can affect the world.[9] Similarly, seemingly trivial activities are one arena where divorced women's explorations of their competency occur and where important new learnings take place. At a time when they are feeling vulnerable, these activities offer tangible proof to the world and to themselves that they can survive on their own.

Money: Having Less But Controlling It More

Although most women have a lower standard of living after divorce and considerable financial hardship, one-quarter of the women interviewed spontaneously expressed happiness at their greater control over money. (This is undoubtedly an underestimate, because they were not specifically asked about feelings associated with managing money.) Though middle-class women may no longer drive Volvos, they adapt to their new circumstances and achieve a measure of financial independence. One describes supporting herself as "a kick . . . a shot in the arm" (C008). Nor is pride in making do with less confined only to middle-class women, as two recently separated mothers—one a waitress and the other a salesclerk—make clear:

I do what I want with my paycheck. . . . I feel more independent. . . . I've got all the bills for the house in my name. (C038).

Handling the money, just the pride in being able to handle everything. My bills are paid every month. I've never bounced a check. I feel very good about myself. (L008)

This last woman adds, "I celebrated the day I opened my own checking account." Managing money is an area of novelty for many women, a new aspect of their environments to explore.

Handling finances is another arena to master, and a place where women can directly argue that divorce isn't so bad. We know from other research that money is typically the province of men in marriage. Particularly in middle-class couples, husbands support wives economically and consequently usually control major decisions about how money in the family is to be spent.[10] With separation, money management becomes women's work. Contrary to expectation, even managing with less is a source of pride, especially for recently separated women, who are the most hard-hit economically. However meager the resources, women portray how they survive economically. Employed women discover one tangible thing that is theirs—the paycheck—even if it is a slim one. Though they may not have experience managing money, they discover that they can learn how.

In reconstructing their histories with money, some women describe how husbands had dominated decisions and what a sense of power they now have when they decide on major purchases on their own. An unemployed woman living on very limited means speaks proudly of furnishing her apartment:

> I've managed to get almost everything I've wanted. . . . Everything you see here I bought, this is all mine, I have done it in less than two years. I did this, while with him I never got anything. It was either "We can't afford it" or "We need the money for something else." (N013)

Women sometimes enjoy obtaining their own credit—a symbol of status in the United States—because it means financial independence from financially irresponsible spouses. A physician, whose settlement is not final as she speaks and who anticipates paying alimony to her husband, talks explicitly about control:

> I may not have even as much money as I had before . . . and I feel very, very angry about that, but there's nothing I can do. . . . I don't have control, you know, if I have to pay him thirty or forty or fifty thousand dollars, but I have control, you know, in a larger sense, day-to-day control right now . . . that feels very good. (C010)

Rather than being victims of their poorer circumstances, women present themselves as active agents, taking charge by opening bank accounts, establishing credit, and deciding how to spend whatever they have. Like fixing toilets, managing money is both a symbolic and a tangible way to measure freedom and to project a new and positive self.

Entry into Jobs and School

For women surviving economically often means looking for a job, or taking a job more seriously than before. An elementary school teacher said she reexamined her career "after the initial pain," adding that divorce "forces you to do that" (L004). Jobs take on a new salience, beyond their economic purpose, as women—especially middle-class women whose jobs offer opportunity—construct new selves and find fulfillment through work outside the home.[11]

A few working-class women also experience feelings of efficacy through paid work. Lynn, a woman with two young children and separated for two years, is an emblematic case. She makes positive sense of divorce by making negative sense of marriage:

> Life was always the same when I was married, you know, same thing every day, watch the soap operas and had my friends in for coffee or whatever, and 11 o'clock was always bedtime. Same thing day in and day out, and that was going to be my life for the rest of my life. At the time I had no complaints, I mean, that's pretty much what I expected, I guess. (C022)

After discovering her husband's affairs, Lynn divorced and took a job for the first time, in a hospital where the workers were trying to organize. She became a leader in the union movement, eventually leading a strike—an action that she says her husband "would have forbid." She tells a story about it:

> I had no voice, I lost my voice on the second day [of the strike], but I was the spokesman . . . they said, "You're the one that's got to go [to the meeting], they're ready to endorse this." And I can't even talk. Well, nobody else could do it, so off we rushed . . . and I spoke to all those people and TV and radio. (C022)

The success of the strike and "feeling like a leader" gave her confidence to look for a better job:

> I met so many intelligent people, going to talk to the [students and professors at the local college]. It made me feel like maybe I could do more with my life than fold up laundry at the Ashland Hospital. (C022)

Other women make the same point: paid work, unlike housework, leads to a fuller identity as they develop competence, confidence, and status outside the home.

171

Some women return to school, which, though stressful, also benefits self-confidence. Tessa began to attend a community college and says, "I took an English class and got a B+ in it," adding that she "was really surprised" because "I didn't think I had any ability" (C017). Another woman cites going back to college as a major benefit of her divorce, saying she "always wanted to go back to school and finish," but her husband had not supported her aspirations. Without him, she says, "I got my self-confidence back" (N013). As Sally, a recently separated salesclerk, understands it, divorce frees her from her husband's authority and alters her vision of future possibilities:

> He [husband] didn't want me to do things before and rather than . . . cause a fight, I'd just do what he said to do. And if I want to go back to school, like when I figure out how I can do that financially, then maybe someday I can do that. (N015)

Asked why she had not gone back to school when she was married she reconstructs a typical marital conversation:

> It was a waste of time, it was a waste of money. I should be home taking care of the kids. There was no need for me to have any more education. (N015)

The few women who had financial resources and returned to graduate school began careers that in turn stabilized their confidence:

> I feel much more secure, independently of him. . . . Not only with the experience [of divorce], but just having gone to graduate school. (C034)

CHANGES IN SOCIAL RELATIONSHIPS

Women must juggle the roles of mother, worker, and sometimes student, and they frequently turn to others for help. Because of the exigencies of their lives, they cannot maintain the myth of self-sufficiency. There is an unanticipated benefit to these structural pressures: divorced women solidify ties with kin, construct social networks that provide material and emotional aid, and generally intensify their relationships with others. [12] As one woman says, "Being on my own I need those significant others all the more" (L015).

"Coming Out of a Shell"

Women construct a new self after divorce through social relationships, and as with the other areas, they interpret their growth in this area by contrasting current experiences with marital experiences.[13] No longer "half a couple" and subsumed by husbands, they begin to feel free to be leaders themselves, as this clerical worker who had been married to a scientist describes:

> When I was with Alex [husband], I tended to let him speak and I'd be quite happy, I wouldn't resent it or anything. Now I'm on my own, I feel I have to contribute. . . . I make more of an effort. (C006)

Some women believe that divorce frees them from tendencies to be empathic at the expense of themselves. One woman, whose husband had been unemployed, felt she had to "make excuses for him," be "protective of him" in company, and explain to others why he was not working. The costs of carrying his burdens were high, and the relief at setting them down is great; she says she can now speak as a "full person" (C010). Susan tells how she buried her sociability in deference to her husband:

> I was much more outgoing and, I think when we were together, I was conscious of that, that I was more of a talker. . . . I buried somewhat of my outgoingness 'cause I always felt a little guilt about it, that he was much quieter. (N046)

She adds that now, "I can sort of be myself more."

A common metaphor that women use—especially those with working-class jobs—is "coming out of a shell." A teacher's aide whose husband had defined her as crazy says:

> I was in a shell and when I found out, it was like whammo, you know, I was like a butterfly coming out of a cocoon. I just started meeting more people and talking and goofing around and I said, Hey, you know, I'm crazy but people like me this way, you know. I started to become the person that I was. I was no longer a puppet. (N011)

This woman's figurative language is significant. In a shell, in a cocoon, being a puppet—these phrases evoke an image of constraint and subservience in marriage.

But women are saying something more. They had submerged themselves and were protective of their spouses because their husbands were a reflection of the choices that they, the women, had made. Not only did the particular man need defending—especially if he was unemployed or professionally unsuccessful—a wife's choice of him as a husband needed to be defended as well. Husbands are a reflection of who wives are; the social standing of the family is predicated on the husband's status. In U.S. culture, too, where individual choice is the basis of marriage (as distinct from cultures where marriage is arranged), the choice of a particular partner needs to be defended constantly. Only as the relationship begins to come apart can women let the secrets out and move toward others more freely.[14]

From the perspective of many women, the companionship that marriage ought to provide is found in relationships with kin and friends, as a school administrator describes:

> One of the biggest adjustments I had to make was when I wanted to do something, there wasn't somebody there to do it with. I had to make an effort, I had to become much more extroverted. I had to call up people and ask them . . . if I could do things with them. (L001)

A teacher, afraid of loneliness, makes a discovery: "I found out that I didn't have to be, if I didn't want to be" (L002). Middle-class women speak about opening up emotionally to their women friends, confiding in ways that previously might have been reserved for husbands, which, in turn, intensifies women's friendships:

> I think my relationships with my . . . close friends became much more close because I needed to confide and seek their advice more and that, in turn, made them willing to do that with me. Where before I would have gotten that advice and confidence from my husband. (L001)

Women's relationships with their friends had been constrained in marriage, as we saw earlier, and these relationships are freed up after divorce. Greater equality accompanies the reciprocity of exchange:

> One of my friends said to me, "Gee, it's real nice to know that you bleed like everyone else." (L011)

174

Although women generally view their greater sociability very positively, a few feel guilty about the time that they take up talking about their problems in their interactions with friends and relatives and about being so oriented toward themselves. Sally says she spends more time with friends, talking about her children and her life, but adds:

It's probably more centered around me when I'm with friends . . . like before I think it wasn't so self-centered. (N015)

Managing Aloneness

Divorced women do not spend all their time in the company of others, nor can they rely on others for everything their spouses provided. Learning how to be alone—physically and psychologically—is a central issue, and one for which they are not well prepared by their culture.[15]

Although divorce confronts some women with their worst fear, many women come to relish it. Single parents wish they had more time alone. One says wistfully, "About the only time I'm alone is when I'm in the car driving from one place to another" (L008). Those without children learn how to tolerate being alone and derive satisfaction from mastering their fear. The school administrator, who has no children, says she never even went to a movie by herself until she separated, and now describes going places alone as "learning kinds of things and positive" (L001). She sums up one of the "greatest benefits" of divorce for many women:

I've learned to live alone and enjoy it and to rely on myself without the benefit of anyone else being there. (L001)

Women who have more resources—those with middle-class jobs—develop elaborate rituals for alone times. An academic recalls a particular time right after her separation when she took care of her needs with a flourish:

I can remember the first week I was in that apartment, it was very cold, the apartment had a fireplace that works, and what I would do, I would come home from work, and I would consciously say . . . I am going to pamper myself, I am going to do things for myself now, just for me, for my own satisfaction, my own pleasure. (C008)

She continues with her habitual narrative:

So, I'd come home from work, put a chicken in the oven, open a split of champagne, start a fire, put Bach on the stereo, drink champagne, and have a marvelous dinner all to myself. I can spoil myself if I wish and there's no one else I need to think of. (C008)

Women who develop rituals for themselves or who enjoy time alone often seem to justify their behavior, which suggests that they see their actions as deviant in some way.[16] Because a woman's role in the family is to tend to others, tending herself is often confused with "selfishness."

Although it is undoubtedly true that divorced women sometimes feel lonely and miss the easy companionship that marriage can provide, it is significant that so many portray being alone positively. They seem to seize on this feature of divorce, almost to prove that it is not as bad as they expected. Nearly a third, with and without children, differentiate "alone time" from loneliness. Jennifer, a graphic artist with two small children, says:

I don't usually feel lonely 'cause I feel I like to be by myself and I know that people love me and are nearby and are an important part of my life. (C004)

Sally, who has two school-aged children and is separated less than a year, makes positive sense of being alone this way:

I have more time, even if it's like just to sit and read and do something quiet, that I didn't have time like to do before, or felt guilty doing it before because I should have been out helping him, or down [in] the cellar helping him make something, or helping him do something if he was working around the house. (N015)

New Competency, New Confidence

Divorce forces a number of changes in the structure of women's daily lives. Women describe themselves as gaining "freedom" from husbands who held the power. By and large, they do not portray themselves as casualties of their circumstances; rather they present selves that display considerable innovation, competence, and mastery. They tell how they shape their environments and reorder their lives in meaningful ways, diversifying their emotional investments rather than putting them only into the family.[17] Out of the experience of success in managing difficulty and change, their feelings about themselves flourish. The public manifestations of independence—managing households and money, moving into jobs and school, constructing social networks, and learning to be alone—seem to have effects on women's private psychological lives. Reciprocally, new confidence leads to further changes in their social circumstances. Whatever the causal order, as women reclaim themselves and reanalyze who they are, they say they see themselves in new and different ways.

TRANSFORMATIONS IN IDENTITY:
SELF-RELIANCE AND SELF-ESTEEM

Personality theory has argued that identity and intimacy are inextricably fused in women, with intimate relations playing a central role in women's sense of who they are. Because their married identities were fused with intimacy, being divorced means women are free to have their own, separate, identity. Many divorcing women construct identities around a very different set of principles, with greater reliance on the self than on intimacy with a man.[18] Jennifer reflects on her new identity:

> Realizing that I'm it, in terms of the children, in terms of money, in terms of decisions, in terms of scheduling, in terms of not having a partner to help, to nourish me or to help me have what I need. (C004)

As many women understand it, marriage had promised that they would be taken care of, provided for, and "protected" by a man. Because this myth failed them, they reason that learning to take care of themselves is a positive outcome of divorce. This process is evident in the talk of nearly one-third of women in the sample. Growing beyond the childlike dependency that traditional marriage engenders, they repeatedly use metaphors of maturation to describe themselves (most, but not all, had married at a young age):

> I'm growing up, that's what I'm doing . . . becoming a responsible adult. (C024)

> I feel like an adult, this year, for the first time in my life. (L008)

> I feel like I'm becoming a woman . . . learning to take care of myself. (N031)

> I got born . . . the experience [of divorce] all of a sudden forced me to grow up. (C012)

A key step in this process is seeing themselves as separate people—often for the first times in their lives. Divorced women portray this as a watershed in their development. Sometimes insights come from therapy, as for Cindy:

> I didn't see myself as separate . . . it's like me was always us. . . . Now I'm realizing me is me (N029)

Others, like this woman, recently separated and working as a cook, make sense of this issue on their own:

> For the first time [I'm] getting some self-sufficiency, getting some rapport with who I am, being my own best friend. . . . I hadn't developed that to any degree . . . if Bill [husband] wanted to move in one direction, I would move too. I wasn't a separate entity, with my own, just my own reality. (N031)

Viewed psychologically, these women's development had proceeded along a path typical for white women—toward orientation to others, connectedness, and interdependence.[19] Divorce forces them to expand this orientation, to differentiate themselves more, to strike a balance between relatedness and self-reliance.

Although valuing relationships is sometimes discussed as if it is an essential and innate psychological characteristic of women, thus neglecting the social context, it arises, at least in part, because of the inequality between women and men. Jean Baker Miller argues that in a male-dominated society women adapt to their subordination, and learning to affiliate with men serves this purpose, just as it fits well with women's socially assigned roles. Further, an affiliative style is encouraged in women, but not in men, at key points in development. Some observers have gone so far as to argue that white female socialization is largely training *for* dependency, for "learned helplessness."[20]

Little girls are trained to ask for help, to feel they need help, and, at least until recently, their primary, crowning achievement was a form of affiliation—getting married and having children. In order not to limit marriage options, young white women put other parts of their personal identities on hold, which often results in a "moratorium in the development of a self concept"—a self based on more autonomous aspects, that is. Elizabeth Douvan puts it succinctly: "Girls wait till marriage to 'become.'" The structure of modern marriage further encourages white women to put aspects of themselves away in exchange for being taken care of and in order to take care of others.[21]

Divorce demands that women move beyond these customary ways of being in the world and to act in ways that few were socialized for. No longer subordinated to husbands, if they are to survive they need to take themselves seriously, make decisions, provide for their children, and do what needs to be done. Although women certainly do not give up valuing relationships and often turn to others for aid, in an essential way they discover that they must depend on themselves.

As women describe it, this transition to greater psychological separateness is hardly free of conflict, for they struggle to maintain a balance between independence and intimacy in their lives. The woman who is recently separated and an unemployed musician with two children says:

> Trying to be my own person, well, it's scary. It's very scary, you know, to take myself seriously in that sense. I think I had this cushion being part of this couple and I didn't have these expectations for myself (N008)

Divorce means losing the "cushion," and though it is "scary" there are also other feelings:

> There's a certain kind of exhilaration in taking yourself seriously, thinking about yourself as an entity, trying to be whole unto yourself. (N008)

Among other things, husbands can no longer be used as justifications for why women felt "trapped" in marriage:

> It wasn't ever true that it was his fault for everything, and yet I couldn't see that. Now I can really see that my life is my responsibility. (N031)

As women construct positive meaning out of loss, these transformations in understanding help them create and present to others a self that is growing and learning rather than a self that is beaten down by the difficulties of separation.

The greater self-reliance that women speak of goes hand in hand with increased self-confidence—another transformation that more than half the women describe. A waitress, separated less than a year, talks of "being more me," which means "knowing what I want" and "not being so wishy-washy with people" (N028). Lynn, who led the hospital strike, speaks forcefully about how getting a job and learning to be assertive at work spilled over:

> One big thing I've learned . . . was that when you believe you are right, you stand up for what you believe in, no matter what . . . and it didn't pertain just to the strike. (C022)

She goes on, "I'm a much better person today than I was when I was married"—a sentiment echoed by many other women, from a variety of class backgrounds:

> I feel much better . . . as a total person, more as a competent person. (C010, physician)

> I don't walk around feeling apologetic for myself all the time. I feel like more self-confident. (N029, bookkeeper)

I feel a lot more positive about myself as a person now than I did when I was married. (L004, teacher)

I guess [a benefit is] a stronger sense of myself, more security from within. (L002, teacher)

To describe this aspect of their new identities, these women are drawing on the language and categories of major movements of the 1970s—consciousness-raising groups of the women's movement, the human potential movement, and the associated culture of psychotherapy—whose messages are well suited to making positive sense of loss. Psychological understandings are especially prominent (more so than understandings from the women's liberation movement), perhaps because two-thirds of the women interviewed had been in some form of counseling at some point.

Divorcing women do implicate marriage in the genesis of their previous, less-than-confident, selves. But they stop short of a critique of marital roles and of associated power differences between women and men. In making sense of their new-found self-esteem, they blame particular husbands who prevented them from becoming full and developed people. In their minds, the problem is private and individualized, involving their particular situation—not social, involving power inequalities in the institution of marriage itself and the larger system of roles based on gender. Yet much of what many women contribute in marriage, such as housework and the raising of children, is not socially valued and does not have an audience, and consequently it is difficult for women to develop self-esteem on the basis of these activities—regardless of the appreciation individual wives might get from individual husbands. Upon divorce, women see that they feel better about themselves as they get out from under their husbands' control. What they fail to see is that they also feel affirmed because they are accomplishing things that are visible and held in greater esteem by their culture, such as managing money, holding down jobs, gaining education, and building independent lives.

At first glance, it is difficult to reconcile women's new-found positive sense of self with their high rates of depressive symptoms. Self-derogatory thoughts of feelings, after all, are usually thought of as a

defining feature of depression. Are women merely denying the negative and, as Weiss states, is their new confidence in themselves "inherently fragile"?[22] For some women, of course, it is. For most,
however, the picture is more complicated and even contradictory.
Clearly, clinical depression and enhanced self-esteem cannot coexist,
but as noted in Chapter 4, the CES-D scale does not necessarily measure clinical depression. It is possible, even likely, that women's positive views of self alternate with mood fluctuations and periods of
sadness.

Women's talk about their divorces reveals they experience a variety
of states of feeling. As they attempt to construct positive changes out
of loss, they reach for the "bright" side, the good outcomes that exist
alongside the difficulties, and they vacillate between these two realities, sometimes even in the same day. The unemployed musician
speaks of "exhilaration" at her new accomplishments, but then adds:

> At the same time, it's a hard struggle. I remember somebody asked me
> what my wish was for the New Year, and I said that my wish was that I
> could get to the point where I would always feel good about being my-
> self and having my own life. (N008)

Always feeling good about themselves is more difficult to achieve,
particularly with increased demands and financial hardship. For
women, especially, divorce is a "blessing and a burden."

The exigencies of women's lives force them to take on new activities and roles that in turn, women define as benefiting their development. As they transform their public identities, their private
selves change. The findings from the larger sample here are quite
consistent with smaller studies of the positive outcomes of divorce for
women.[23]

MEN AND DIVORCE: WHY THE DIFFERENCE?

Men as a group tend to interpret their divorces less positively than
women do, and 15 percent of men see no benefits to divorce whatsoever. And a number of men, though they construct a positive sense
of divorce, define it as a personal failure. It is striking that divorcing
women, though marriage has been viewed as the ultimate achievement for a woman, do not tend to define divorce as a failure in

achievement and, in fact, talk of their achievements *after* marriage. But typically, though marriage is not viewed as the ultimate achievement for men, many men feel like failures because they did not succeed in marriage. Previous investigators, in emphasizing work as men's primary arena for achievement, have ignored this point and thereby reinforced ideologies about the breadwinner role.[24]

Some men in this study make clear that, in their minds, divorce is public proof that they have not succeeded in a major way in their private lives. They speak of their "dreams going down the drain," losing everything they have "worked for" (C044). Success in U.S. culture, as they define it, means having "a family and a house and all that sort of thing" (C046). For a pharmacist, marriage and his associated place in the community had been an important source of personal power:

> I had a power base, I felt very good about myself. Now, you know, I'm different now. I just came out of a broken marriage. I don't have any real power base. (N019)

A truck driver said he feels "kind of less [of] a person . . . I mean like I couldn't keep my marriage together" (N039).

Another major reason some men feel diminished is that their private troubles become common knowledge. Their secrets are exposed, often for the first time, as this man says:

> I think everybody hates to have anybody know that they have problems . . . you always try and keep your problems to yourself. . . . I really didn't have any personal problems and then just like bingo. (N039)

A teacher separated almost two years describes how hard it is to say to others, "I'm divorced," adding, "It makes me feel like I'm almost a failure, in that kind of relationship anyway" (C023). As private problems become public and as they lose an important seat of power, some men feel that core features of their identities as competent and achieving people are thrown into question.

Yet despite this crisis, most men do manage to find positives in divorce. Like women, they define it as a "growth process," and they reveal a heterogeneity of responses as they innovate and develop new competencies in a wide range of areas.[25] As for women, men's under-standings of the constraints of marriage shape the areas of development they see in themselves upon divorce.

FREEDOM FROM OBLIGATION

As men make sense of divorce, 40 percent say it brings them "freedom," but by this they mean something different from what women, 55 percent of whom emphasize freedom as a benefit, mean. Independence and autonomy, which so dominate women's discourse, are not prominent in men's definition of their changes. As a store manager says, "I always felt independent and I guess it's just more so now" (N038). Instead men say they feel "less confined" (C040), or have "a sense of space where I felt really claustrophobic before" (N012). Freedom means "fewer responsibilities" (N041), "not being responsible to anyone" (C018), "not being responsible for anything except what I want to do" (N044). Money is a central concern, though differently than for women. An attorney who says spending his salary was a "joint decision" in his marriage describes his pleasure at using money in new ways:

> Just the freedom to be able to take trips and to do what I want to do. I could go into debt if I wanted to, or I could save if I wanted to, or I could buy something if I wanted to. That's fantastic . . . that's a real benefit. (N035)

Men also feel free of the scrutiny of their wives. Freedom from the disapproval of a wife—being able to come and go as they please, to be messy or clean, to pursue solitary hobbies—is echoed in the statements of nearly one-quarter of the men, exemplified by Al's remark:

> I am finally liberated from the two women in my life. My mother and my wife, who acted that way, who were judgmental, very judgmental. (C032)

Although some men's statements are reminiscent of those of women quoted earlier, there is a subtle difference. By invoking the vocabulary of freedom, men are saying they have been restricted in marriage by the role of breadwinner and confined by wives' expectations of domesticity. In this culture, men are measured by how well they provide materially for their families—how "responsible" they are as providers. Divorce releases them from this obligation, an external yardstick of their worth. As their standard of living improves, men can spend discretionary income on pursuits that might have been questioned in marriage.[26] Men also say that their wives "confined" them in homes and, like mothers, had exerted control by evaluating them on women's criteria of intimacy and responsibility. Divorce liberates men from "having to get permission" from women to be men. It frees them from passivity: no longer needing to "go along" with wives' plans and wishes, they are free to discover and do what gives them pleasure.

COMPETENCE IN THE MANAGEMENT OF DAILY LIFE

Divorce brings major changes to men's daily lives, as it does to women's, but in very different ways. All of a sudden, much more free time is available for men, and many of the changes that men define as positive follow from that. Faced with time on their hands, men have one of two choices, one man says: "Either to sit in front of the TV and get fat and ugly and depressed or do things that interest you" (N043). Most men do the latter. Marriage had routinized their lives—often in onerous ways, as they reconstruct it later—and now a major issue is to "occupy" time in new ways.

Jobs: Structure, Stabilization, and Success

Jobs are the primary arena in which divorced men find meaning. Careers become a central preoccupation for men with middle-class jobs. Especially those without custody of children speak of pouring energy into the job, "filling time" and bringing extra work home because they have "plenty of time." Because they work longer hours and also because they willingly accept travel assignments, their work life "flourishes," as one says (N042)—a clear benefit to their employers. Divorce frees men in middle-class jobs to work with an intensity that would have been difficult had they been married, as this store manager states:

[When I was married] I felt obligated to be home certain times. Now, I spend the 70 hours a week at work that I wanted to all along. . . . I don't have to worry about feeling obligated to anybody. (N038)

For men in working-class jobs, this outlet is not always available, though for a few, like this hospital x-ray technician on a rotating-shift schedule, a benefit of divorce is reduced conflict between work and family:[27]

Just the freedom to do as I please. My work schedule . . . my hours change from day to day. One day I might be working a 4 o'clock [shift], and one day I may be working at 8 o'clock, tonight I'm working at midnight . . . whereas before I felt restricted, almost felt guilty for working those hours. (N034)

As other men understand it, divorce gives them the chance to reassess the place of work in their lives. Having to "settle" for certain jobs while they were married because there was a family to support, they now have the freedom to consider other jobs. A man without children who was in the process of making a major career change spoke of "only having to worry about myself now" (C009). He planned to leave his tenured position at a university and work in the theater. Work, typically tied to fulfilling family responsibilities for men, becomes freed from these constraints.[28]

Single fathers have a different set of issues. An impending separation stimulated one man to get a better job:

The first thing I did was get another job, I got a better paying job . . . so that when she left . . . I was already in my new position and making new friends, I was doing new work. (C007)

As it does for women with children, divorce pushes men in similar circumstances to take jobs and careers more seriously.

Psychologists have argued that paid work, and achievement more generally, are core elements in men's psychology, primary definers of how many middle-class men, particularly, feel about themselves.[29] With divorce, middle-class jobs become a place where they can make a major time commitment, invest their energies, make friends, and feel in charge. Some have trouble concentrating at first, as we saw in the last chapter, but at the same time work provides an absorbing activity and structures time as men forge identities apart from those of husband and father. A new commitment to work, coupled with prior long histories of employment, sets the stage for career advancement, improved financial status, and consequently, heightens self-esteem—clear benefits of divorce for men.

Household Routines

Just as women talk of developing competence in fixing things, men describe how they learn to manage households, another activity that structures time for them and, in a different way from paid work, creates a sense of efficacy. As men think back to their marriages, they remember that wives typically planned menus, prepared meals, and made aesthetic decisions about how the home, and even how they themselves, should look.

Upon divorce, men revel in the discovery that they can develop competence in these areas. A factory foreman, who says he is "a different person," speaks to this issue:

I don't need anybody. I mean, I do need somebody, but I'm completely self-sufficient. I go grocery shopping, I do everything, I buy my own clothes, nobody does anything for me, nothing. (N027)

As women learn how to grow beyond dependence on a spouse and to survive, so do men, and often in very concrete ways:

I wash my dishes after I eat, I make my bed up in the morning when I leave, I sweep my floor and I, you know, keep things in a fair semblance of order and I like that. (L009)

One man who stresses learning to "survive," epitomized by doing his laundry, pokes fun at another:

I met some guy at the laundromat yesterday, he had been separated for five or six days, and already he was looking for a wife to do his laundry, he couldn't handle that. (N036)

A significant number of men are initially prevented from becoming self-reliant in household management, because chores like laundry and meals are handled by others—usually women—who step in to help men out. Especially right after separation, kin rally around men more than around women, thus delaying the development of men's mastery of these areas. As time passes, however, men reroutinize their lives. They fill some of the time when they are not at their jobs with household jobs, and they often get satisfaction from them, perhaps because of the novelty of the role. Sometimes mundane and repetitive activities become ritualized, bringing order to men's domestic lives and giving meaning to the ordinary.[30] One working-class man, separated almost two years, describes a weekly ritual:

> There is a routine that I have developed on Sunday morning of cleaning my house, getting it really clean. . . . I have four rooms spotlessly taken apart and cleaned. . . . There is a radio program on Sunday mornings, my favorite radio program, and I listen to that and I clean the house. No one calls me and I'm all alone . . . but instead of being unhappy where I am . . . it is a time that I really like a lot. (C028)

A businessman also experiences pleasure in learning to keep house for himself, and he draws an interesting analogy:

> I didn't really clean the house before [when I was married]. It was always done, somebody did it, kids, wife, whatever. . . . I didn't even know how to run the washing machine, so I can tell you, the first time I ever ran a washing machine, it was great fun to do, and Gee, the clothes came out clean. Wasn't so hard. Learning to vacuum clean, it's like mowing the lawn. (N044).

As men understand it, they find housecleaning particularly satisfying, as opposed to cooking, for example, because it yields tangible rewards—"when you get done, you can see the difference" (N042).

In emphasizing the management of households by themselves in their talk, men are making several important points. As women also find, it is comforting to become more self-sufficient at a time of heightened emotional vulnerability. But for the men who feel they "failed" in marriage, housework represents a tangible form of achievement, however private and unrewarded. Even more significant, in the companionate marriage men develop childlike dependency on women for daily care just as women depend on men for economic care. In separation, in breaking dependency on wives, the symbols of self-reliance men choose are the domains in which wives have expertise. Just as some women delight in displaying competence in managing money, some men delight in making a home. For both there is a connection between what marriage was like, and what divorce is like, and the seeming absence of gender roles when marriage ends.

Leisure and the Management of Time

Unlike women, men talk a good deal about leisure, which helps them fill time. They speak of tennis, running, racquetball, lifting weights—activities they remember not doing while married or doing with less intensity. A middle-class man without custody of his children defines sports as a major benefit of divorce:

> Because of time I've been able to get back in sports, and I love sports . . . go out and just throw a baseball around for a little while, or ride my bike, play hockey—a lot of sports, emphasis on sports. (N009).

These activities serve a number of purposes. They get men out of the house on weekends and provide new routines that can take the place of activities done with a family. Men make casual friends through sports, and they reconnect with a primary source of their identities as youths. Sports help men get away from difficult emotions, and they serve to "burn out frustrations and anxieties" (N009). As one said about running, a daily activity the first year of his separation: "It takes a lot of energy, it doesn't leave you so much energy for feeling angry" (C007). Simultaneously, sports are the locus for the legitimate expression of strong emotions of another sort, as men experience a sense of public glory in athletics.[31]

A large number of men, and not only those with middle-class jobs, take up hobbies that involve a considerable expenditure of time and money—flying airplanes, joining gun clubs, riding motorcycles— activities that vivify breaking away from the confines of domesticity and the breadwinner role. A factory worker who took up hang-gliding comments: "I want to push that as far as I can." Asked why he did not pursue this interest when married, he says:

> I wouldn't have done it then because it is kind of dangerous. Plus I couldn't afford it then, and it does occupy a lot of my time. (C044).

A businessman uses the same justifications to explain motorcycling:

> I took Wendy [former wife] off my insurance policy, generated cash value, I put all this [money] in this pool and I decided I was either going to go to Florida or buy a motorcycle. . . . I ended up buying a motorcycle . . . when I was married, I had absolutely no thoughts seriously of it because of the fact of the danger, it was a dangerous thing. Now I bought it and I love it. (C025)

More discretionary income and freedom from responsibility for others enables men to take more risks—a phrase many used. Released from the obligations and constraints of family, they enact masculinity with behaviors usually dampened in marriage, as Durkheim pointed out long ago.[32] The very danger of the activity seems to aid in regaining a sense of power and mastery for some. The pharmacist, who toyed with the idea of skydiving and white-water rafting, interprets their meaning for him: "Stuff that would be twenty years below my age . . . trying to be youthful again, and exciting again" (N019). Impulses that had been constrained by age and by responsibilities are released, as these men seek new forms of excitement and action.

Others turn to pursuits that are less dangerous but time-consuming, such as music and photography. Again, these are often activities that had been put away during the years of the marriage. Whether they write songs or play an instrument, men understand these as forms of emotional expression. As Al describes, he is "making a lot more time" for his music, adding, "I'm making time for things that move me" (C032).

Using Money in New Ways: Working on the Self

As a way of healing from the divorcing process, a small group of men with disposable incomes actively reconstruct themselves, using money for self-improvement. Men do not derive pleasure from getting their own checking accounts, their own credit, or bills in their name, because they have always had these symbols of financial independence. Instead, they experience greater control over money in a different way. They buy things that make them feel good, that they believe their wives prevented them from buying. As do some women, some men after separation feel free to buy something they always

wanted, without explanation to anyone. One man—a teacher—
says he had dreamed about having a leather reclining chair, but was
"talked out of it," and describes with pleasure how he "just got a re-
cliner" (C023). Charles made a purchase that had special meaning for
him, saying, "I always wanted a pair of cowboy boots, ever since I
was a kid" (C021). Several say they went "hog wild" with money after separation. The schoolteacher interprets his increased spending:

> Well, I just saved a lot of money and one day I went out and bought
> three coats for $300 and a lot of other clothes, you know, over a period
> of about three or four months. . . . I bought a brand new car. I don't
> know if you would call it an image change or not . . . but I spent a lot
> of money (C023).

The "image change" often involves going shopping—an activity
that is stereotypically associated with women—and buying sprees
seem to be part of an effort to shore up a sagging self-image. As men
explain it, in marriage they internalized their wives' views—about
how they should look, about how the house should be furnished—
which recalls wives' perceptions that they had gone along with their
husbands' views on other issues. Divorcing men, like their female
counterparts, break away from these patterns. Because they have
more income at their disposal, men can buy symbolic items such as
recliners and cowboy boots, that make them feel in control of who
they are again.

Others work more overtly to change their appearance—not surprisingly, in that the body plays a central role in men's self-esteem.[33]
The pharmacist, recently separated, got a hair transplant and spent
$4,000 on dental work, replacing teeth that had been "missing for
five years." He describes another expenditure:

> And then electrolysis. I have a lot of hair on my back and I'm cutting all
> that stuff off. I want to look better. I take better care of myself, let's put
> it that way. (N019)

Admitting that he is not very sure of himself because his marriage fell
apart, he justifies spending money on his appearance in order to do
better next time:

You have to compete out there again. You have to win a relationship all over again. (N019)

Although he is more direct than others, this man articulates an underlying motive for self-improvement. Because he defines himself as a personal failure because his marriage failed, spending money boosts his confidence so he can "compete" again. Money is a continuing symbol of men's power, and some use it to build themselves up.

CHANGES IN SOCIAL RELATIONSHIPS: DATING, KIDS, AND NEW FRIENDS

Both women and men emphasize the new ways in which they reach out to others upon divorce. Men diversify their social worlds in some ways that women do not, however, and this benefit of divorce, as they define it, takes a variety of forms. "Winning a relationship all over again" becomes a central concern of a number of men, who fill time, develop relationships, and construct identities as single men through dating. Michael Kimmel notes that sexual performance is one of the crucial arenas in which masculinity is enacted in this culture; regaining sexual freedom is a major benefit of divorce in the minds of a number of men.[34]

When asked about the greatest benefits of his separation, Bill, a maintenance supervisor, says, "I don't cheat on my wife anymore," adding that it "bugged" him to "sneak around" (C046). For some, it is freedom only to look at women, as this man states:

Just the relief, if I see a female on the street I can turn around and look and don't have to worry about it, about anybody screaming at me. I feel like I can live again. (L006)

This recently separated single father has not begun dating, because his children absorb all his time and, as another single father said about dating, "You have to put a lot of time into it" (C030). But time is not scarce for most men, most of whom do not have custody, and nearly three-quarters of men in the sample date (compared with slightly more than half the women). Men are also more than twice as likely as women to be dating more than one person. Without responsibility for children, and with considerable time on their hands, they turn to women to socialize with, to be their confidantes, and to have sex with. [35]

Although dating is a positive outcome of divorce in many men's minds, eventually some come to see these relationships as wanting. A machinist without custody of his children, who cites "freedom" as a benefit of divorce, looks back on the three years he's been separated and tries to explain this aspect of male culture to the woman interviewer:

> The relationships are shallow, let's put it that way. They're not long-range. I don't know how to put it to you. If you just get into bed with someone [names women], I suppose it satisfies your basic needs, let's put it that way. But it's not meaningful. That's the best way to explain it. So, in a sense you have your freedom. You can play the field, you're on the circuit, on the tour, as we call it. But I find that they're basically shallow. So I guess your freedom is basically shallow, as far as that goes. (N021)

Another man says:

> I'm dissatisfied not because I'm not having sex with somebody, but because I don't have a relationship with somebody. (N036)

Relationships: Old and New

A more enduring relationship for some men is with their children, whose presence preserves the emotional bonds of kinship after separation. [36] Although noncustodial fathers have limited access to their children, quite a few, especially recently separated men, say greater closeness with them is a positive outcome of divorce. A case in point is this accountant, father of two:

> I consider myself a weekend daddy and I can't stand that. . . . But it has benefited the core of our relationship in that I do feel closer to them, and love them more openly. (N032)

Why do men feel "closer" when they are around their children less of the time? Such statements could be thought of as a kind of justification, a rationalization for not being with them more. Men's own interpretations suggest other explanations, however. Visitation forces them to spend a different kind of time with children, to put "work" into the relationship. Saying that he now spends more "quality" time with his children, a factory worker explains, "When I am with them it's for them and only them," whereas in marriage it was "just intermittent, a few minutes here and there . . . in between chores or something" (C044). As fathers plan activities and get to know their children in a deeper way, and as they lean on them emotionally as well, relationships become more involving and, hence, more intimate. Men can also relate to children directly, without the mother as intermediary or buffer. With the loss of the symbols of family that men so prize, attachments to children mean they have not lost family altogether.

Single fathers—the fourteen men in the sample (27 percent of total men) who either have sole responsibility for their children or who care for them for half the week—are a special case in point. These men are especially likely to see increased closeness to their children as a major benefit of divorce. Their lives are harried, like those of their female counterparts, and yet despite all the difficulties, children give their lives structure and purpose and bind them to kin and community. Relationships become more solid as fathers reach out emotionally to children. As a machinist put it, "We draw from each other" (L006). An academic whose children live with him half the week is especially articulate about how his feelings toward his daughter have changed:

> Our relationship has definitely become a lot more solid and basically I think it has a lot to do with the fact that I was so in awe. I don't think I've ever seen it like this before, actually. . . . I was so in awe of the closeness, the umbilical-seeming . . . closeness that she had with Linda [his former wife] that seemed a lot to exclude me. (C041)

These men, no longer in contexts where they can feel excluded or where they can exclude themselves, discover emotional caregiving.[37] Men's greater closeness to children is paralleled by changes in relationships with friends, which some men also see as "closer." This group comprises primarily middle-class men without custody, separated one to two years. They express a need for "something to take the place of the marriage, for the time of being involved in the marriage" (N043). Because the maintenance of kinship ties is generally the province of women, kin relations dissipate over time for men after separation, particularly for men without children. In their place, some men fill up the "big vacuum" in their lives with new friend-ships, "a kind of home base to come back to" (L009). As for women, friendships enable socializing, taking the place "of the companion-ship that I had in my marriage," as one man says (C007). But unlike women's friendships, these relationships are casual, loose ties rather than close intense ones.[38]

Because men have to make an effort to form friendships, group membership often provides a context for these instant networks. More than women (who are confined to home because of children and limited incomes), men join organizations—from broader politi-cal groups, to self-help groups and advocacy groups concerned with fathers' rights, to gourmet clubs and service organizations in their communities—and they often comment that they have "never done this before" (C018). This financial analyst reflects:

> I've found that I've made myself available to other people much more than I ever did, a hockey organization, director of sailing [for the town] . . . three years ago I didn't even sail. That was a hell of an ex-perience, it was rewarding, just being able to give them my time. (N043)

In trying to create meaningful personal networks upon divorce, middle-class men are somewhat at a disadvantage, for wives often do the work of sustaining networks in marriage.[39] An attorney discov-ered that creating a social network is work:

> I never learned during anytime being married to her or prior to that how to develop relationships with people . . . sometimes I'm not very good at it and I'm amazed at the amount of effort and energy it takes. (N035)

Managing Aloneness

Ultimately, no matter how good men are at filling time with ac-tivities and people, divorce confronts them with being alone. Women generally relish time alone, but men are split on the issue. Some see it as a benefit of divorce, especially if they have easy access to or joint custody of their children, or if they feel that their wives put pressure on them for emotional intimacy. Divorce gives men permission to move away from intense relationships and to construct lives in more solitary ways:

> I really treasure coming home now and no one's around and I'm not sharing anything with anybody. (N042)

An extreme manifestation of seeking time alone is described by an academic, who decided to travel by himself to Bali right after his separation:

> To me there's some kind of strength . . . in getting off the plane in [foreign city] with no reservations, and finding a place to stay to sleep that night for $1.50, you know, and dealing with bureaucrats, getting permits and then walking through the . . . valley, completely alone with no other white people within twenty miles of you. And walking into a grass hut and [communicating] kind of with sign language—just the whole mystique of it that I discovered I could do . . . I never would have discovered any of those things [if I'd stayed married]. (C009)

Although this experience is more dramatic than most, a few others chose similar "wilderness tests" to prove their strength—the capacity to survive totally without others. Feeling that they have been ruled by the exigencies of domestic life, men dramatically break with constraining routines and commitments in order to search for who they are.

But not all men feel positively about being alone. Almost one-quarter, usually men without custody of their children or without children altogether, emphasize the negative aspects. For them, being alone often means being lonely. Bill uses a telling image to describe his loneliness:

> I just feel, you know, like I'm not in any continuum. You know, like the kids aren't with me. (C046)

Another man, who says being alone is one of the "greatest difficulties" of divorce, uses another metaphor:

It's just being alone, not being with someone. It's tough . . . a feeling of emptiness, not being whole and then you have to rebuild yourself and get whole again. (C005)

These statements about not being whole are in sharp contrast to many women's statements about feeling more whole after divorce. Some men, without wives to provide emotional connection and to sustain ties with kin and old friends and without children to give their lives structure and meaning, feel rootless and acutely lonely. Their talk suggests that there is some truth for men to one of the myths of the companionate ideal—they are whole in marriage and half a self without it.

Men are often surprised when they discover how hard it is to be alone. The x-ray technician, recently separated and without custody, speaks about the difference between the fantasy and the reality of living alone:

Just the quiet, the peace and quiet, you think when you get away from it [living with others] you'll like it, but when you do, you don't. (N034)

Several men, who at first enjoyed being alone, discover its limitations. Joe, the corrections counselor quoted in Chapter 2 who believed his ex-wife had too many obligations to others and who lamented the loss of privacy he experienced when his wife's brother lived with them, comments:

I actually liked the solitude a little bit at first. It was nice just to be by myself. I'll preface that when I was growing up, I grew up in an apartment in the city, in a triple decker. Six brothers and sisters, and I shared a nine by twelve room with three brothers for eighteen years. And it was really nice to have, for the first time in my life, to have a room to myself . . . I never even had a room to myself until I got divorced . . . it was a really nice change. After a while it became tiresome, I mean I like people a lot . . . I've been isolated and sequestered from other people. (N012)

Marriage does not easily allow for "a room of one's own." Such a haven, as this man makes clear, is something that not only women but some men also want. At the same time, for this man and

197

for others, a contradiction arises: being alone makes them more aware of the value of relationships.

TRANSFORMATIONS IN IDENTITY

Divorce stimulates men to begin to reexamine the most intimate aspects of themselves. The loss of what some define as key symbols of success, coupled with the profound changes in the organization of their daily lives, precipitates for many a crisis of identity. Although other research suggests that men are not accustomed to extensive introspection because this is seen as women's work, some men begin to do more of it, in large part because they define divorce as a failure.[40] They reason that divorce "forces you to analyze yourself" because "you don't want to make the same mistake twice" (N019). The process of self-examination is not always pleasant, as Charles, the production supervisor, intimates:

> I find myself sitting and doing a lot of thinking. . . . I should be out working and not thinking but, you know, I think too much. (C021)

Thinking opens the floodgates and shakes up some men's emotional worlds in profound ways. As one man says, "I was defining myself a lot in roles" and when that "all got taken away" it "forced me upon myself" (C041). Although at first this "felt mostly negative" (feeling "emotionally rawer" was how Al [C032] expressed it), it initiated "a real thinking process," out of which some men gain an expanded sense of who they are. This academic, separated between two and three years, looks back on the process:

> I started creating, or re-creating myself, to this place where the shambles was . . . defining myself in some ways for the first time that has really allowed for some exciting exploration. (C041)

About this process, he says:

> It ain't always been easy. It certainly hasn't always been fun. But it's been a really exciting adventure most of the time. (C041)

The "adventure" of self-discovery is primarily, though not exclusively, an outcome of divorce in the minds of middle-class men, and the experience is shaped in important ways by the values of psychotherapy—a major resource in this culture for reconstructing a self. Despite the fact that women and men in the sample seek out counseling in almost equal numbers, men talk about its effects differently from the way that women do.[41] It seems to play a major role in the development of greater interpersonal competence for men, as they learn to talk about feelings and to experience a wider range of them. As one says bluntly, "This personal development shit is good stuff" (C032).

For a few, the result is greater understanding of their desire *not* to connect, as Al states:

> I think back on the marriage, I think maybe she is right. Maybe what I really wanted, maybe the reasons she wanted to leave was because what I really wanted was to be left alone sometimes. I couldn't do it. You couldn't be left alone. . . . It was illegitimate or felt illegitimate to just lie down or listen to a piece of music. . . . If you weren't working, what was right was to be spending time being together. . . . We didn't have that mechanism which you could be by yourself. (C032)

Discovering the Value of Talk

More typically, men seem to discover the value of connectedness. They find that something important is missing from their lives, even as they reach out in new ways to friends, dates, and children. A physical therapist expresses it this way:

> The big thing about being separated, being on your own, is you don't have somebody around to share your life with. There are other things that you can compensate with or whatever, but there still is that fact, that you don't have somebody to share yourself and your feelings, your reflections and your time with. (N036)

Unlike women, who tend to create networks that contain a variety of "confiding" relationships, men realize they have lost their primary confidante with divorce.[42] Although sexual partners may be plentiful, some men see that a deeper bond is often absent from their lives, as noted earlier. Men miss the institution of marriage; they miss not having someone there to reconstitute family for them. In the absence of a close relationship, men discover the value of relationships, and this explains why some divorced men find spending time alone so difficult. Their previous sense of themselves as self-reliant is thrown into question. Many women become more autonomous through the crisis of divorce, but it appears that some men become more relational.

As men understand it, their identities are transformed as they try to develop parts of themselves that, in the words of one construction worker, had been "shut down as a child" (C028) as they were socialized into masculinity. Joseph Pleck and Jack Sawyer have said that core imperatives of the male role involve not only seeking achievement—"getting ahead"—but suppressing emotion—"staying cool."[43] Marriage further reinforces these patterns, if wives are charged with managing the feeling life of the family. Al makes a connection between what he was like before and what he's like now:

> I was much more of a traditional male . . . didn't ask myself those questions about whether I was happy or unhappy. . . . I didn't have much of a sense of what was going on inside of me. (C032)

Divorce, at least as a number of men understand it, seems to change these patterns. Sometimes a woman friend becomes a "tutor in communication," as one man put it, helping them locate and give voice to thoughts instead of "closing off" (C025). Other times it is a counselor or a minister who encourages them to explore some of the most private aspects of their lives. The construction worker talks about his therapy:

> I would let be known thoughts I had. . . . It was more of me coming out that I kept suppressed for years and years. (C028)

Whatever the source, men begin "talking about things more" (C025), expressing "a broader range of feelings as I came to know them" (C041), becoming "more open . . . more communicative . . . less defensive" (N040). Bob even cites his participation in the interview as evidence of his greater openness:

Just being able to sit here and let you have the tape recorder without worrying about it is a change. Two years ago . . . I never would have talked about anything. I found it difficult to talk about things with my wife three years ago. (N006)

As men construct the meanings of these changes, some note that they develop greater empathy for others. Neil, a man with a working-class job, cites self-understanding as the major benefit of his divorce, saying he is "more open-minded, more willing to listen to the other person, not so demanding" (C011). Rick, an academic, says he is "a whole lot more tolerant, having seen what intolerance has gotten me" (C035). Ironically, men learn from divorce to do some of what women had wanted from them in marriage.

This contradiction is not overlooked by men themselves. Although divorce brings them freedom from responsibility, it also helps some to accept responsibility, particularly for their role in the divorce. A factory worker says, "If I had to do it all over again I would have taken more time as a family with my wife . . . would have devoted more individual time to her than I did" (C044). Others echo this refrain, saying they would be less "goal-oriented" and would not need to "have things lined up" (C035). A typical case is Charles, who is thirty-six:

I always had the belief that if I worked hard, made enough money, then everything would be alright. I was, at one time, Mr. Respectability. You know, I had a beautiful wife, a beautiful home, a fine family. I always thought my daughter would always be saying Mommy and Daddy in the same house. You know, I ran for sheriff two years ago, I was first vice-president of the Elks Club, I was the clerk of the Democratic Party, I was on the planning board, I was going to run for selectman this year. So, you know, I was Mr. Respectability. But I took my wife for granted. I was in some ways a man on a golden pedestal who didn't listen to his wife when she was talking. (C021)

Embedded in his account is a story:

You know, like for example, well, I can remember last fall. We had just had our living room set done over, and she came to me one night and says, "let's just sit on the couch and kiss and talk." And I says, "Well,

Nancy, I can't, I've got to pay for the living room set. I've got to keep working, I've gotta get these reports done." And another time she came and she said, "Let's renew our wedding vows." Our anniversary was the first of September. I said, "No, Nancy, let's do it on the tenth, not the first. We'll do it in two years." So she was trying to give me a message and I didn't hear.

Int.: What do you think that message was?

Charles: She wanted more love and understanding, communication. (C021)

In reinterpreting themselves and their actions in these ways, men imply that they would be different in intimate relationships next time.

"There's Nothing Good about Divorce except for Therapy"

Although most men eventually make positive sense of divorce, some do not. No woman had difficulty responding to the interview question concerning the "greatest benefits" of divorce, but 15 percent of men did. Interestingly, these men are by and large not recently separated; they have been living apart for two to three years. They are also more likely to believe that they had little control over the decision to separate.[44] A laborer whose wife left him and his two children for another man says, "I don't see no benefits. Ain't no benefits in being alone" (C030). Even some men who admit using the experience to examine themselves and reorder their priorities deny any positives, such as this lawyer:

I don't see any benefits. One could say that you get to learn to know yourself better, but now I see I should have done that in the first place, so it's not a benefit to do something that you should have done in the first place. No, I don't see anything positive. (C005)

Men whose wives have left them and who see nothing positive in their separation often enter therapy, which they say does have some benefits. They discover that "talking helps" and, particularly those who have never been in counseling before, become strong advocates for it:

I'm convinced that everybody needs psychotherapy . . . my advice for people, if they're having problems, is to seek therapy, instantaneously. (C005, attorney)

I would recommend that anybody who goes through a separation, divorce, you know, even if you don't think you need one [a psychologist], just go. They can help you straighten out a lot of problems and all the different feelings you have. (N020, highway foreman)

I went through quite a bit of counseling, which the average person should go through. Anyway, I think that's the best thing to do. If I got any friend that has a problem, I'll just say, "Hey, go to counseling." As a joke, but it's not a joke. I truly have faith in it. A person cannot work his problems himself. (C030, laborer)

These converts to psychotherapy are not only middle-class.[45] The general laborer just quoted describes how significant a therapist was to him:

Mrs. Leslie, she was such a wonderful person that it was like she made it feel like I'm going to see my friend, Mrs. Leslie. (C030)

The lawyer goes so far as to say that getting into psychotherapy is the only positive thing to come out of his separation:

It's a terrible situation, divorce and separation, and there are no benefits except from psychotherapy . . . it's just bad news. (C005)

Therapy is thus another means through which some men discover how to talk about feelings and emotions—an activity that, as we have seen, they admit they resisted in marriage and that had been a major issue for their wives.

GENDER AND ADAPTATION

As the divorced themselves define it, divorce is not unremittingly negative, associated only with distress and symptoms—despite the perspective that previous investigators have tended to adopt. Nor are positive and negative feelings necessarily bipolar. Alongside the strains are opportunities for considerable personal growth and identity transformation. Indeed, it is the very frustrations that seem to drive the divorced toward innovation, as they "make sense of what has happened and assimilate it to their present circumstances in a purposeful way."[46]

Adaptation is the process by which individuals engage in environmental mastery—not only meeting situational requirements but making active efforts to create environments suited to their new psychological states. The divorced experience pleasure as they exercise competence—as they find they can *cause* changes in their environments rather than simply respond to them. It might be argued that relationship loss is an experience that is especially conducive to stabilizing a differentiated identity, because it turns on "becoming more aware of personal preference, and of the things for which one really wants one's life to stand."[47]

But this psychological process cannot be understood without close attention to the social contexts in which divorce occurs. Women and men face different social environments after divorce, and this is consequential for adaptation. Social circumstances are much more than "scenes" or "settings" for growth: they exert a force that strongly influences women and men in particular directions. In making sense of separation, moreover, the divorced use ideological categories that come out of a social context. Central to American consciousness is a vocabulary that emphasizes freedom, self-determination, and personal control. These categories of explanation help divorced individuals to manage their deviance and minimize the stigma of divorce, which in turn enables them to project a positive self-image and convince others that they are better people because of the experience. Although U.S. culture does not necessarily condone the act of divorce, it provides its members with a general psychological language and a set of values that constitute a powerful resource for transforming difficult experiences into growth-producing ones. That individuals use understandings from the human potential movement should not surprise us. As Marris notes, new constructions of meaning after loss are always socially grounded: they "represent the history, understanding, and relationships of a culture, as well as the individual organization of experience."[48]

In making sense of loss, both women and men single out missing pieces in their married lives that divorce enables them to fill in. Stated differently, they see benefits to divorce in the context of their particular experiences of marriage. At the same time that psychological explanations dominate their accounts and they thus seem "private," a closer analysis reveals the seeds of a social problem—one that the individual participants often miss, because the culture does not provide an easy language for it. Both women and men portray marriages that are steeped in gender and authority relations, as we saw in Chapter 2. With divorce, both women and men say that separation brings them "freedom," but in very different ways. Women get out from under their husbands' dominance (both latent and manifest forms), whereas men get out from under wives' expectations of responsibility. Freed from the asymmetry and inequality that are built into the structure and the ideology of the companionate marriage, women and men begin to construct new lives around different principles, and their identities change in the process. Men become more relational through self-examination; they discover their inner lives and the value of connectedness. As Daniel Levinson and his colleagues note, in transitional periods men often reintegrate polarities and become "less illusioned" about themselves.[49] Women's sense of themselves becomes more differentiated and autonomous out of the challenges of their social circumstances. For both sexes, greater innovation takes the place of the rigid social script of marriage.

Both women and men construct positive meanings out of the challenges of divorce, albeit quite differently, but women tend to do more of this than men. My findings in this regard concur with those of Weiss, who noted that women, particularly, "emerge with enhanced self-esteem," and those of Wallerstein and Kelly, who note that more women than men appeared "more content with life" in clinical interviews five years after separation. Survey data also show recently separated women to be happier on average than comparable men. Analysis of the talk of women and men in this book suggests some of the reasons why this finding might be true. Although marital dissolution is associated with economic and psychological distress for women, all the women interviewed could note specific ways in which their lives were better and most indicated corresponding improvements in self-confidence and esteem. These women's perceptions are in sharp contrast to the often negative view of social scientists, epitomized in a statement by Angus Campbell, Phillip Converse, and Willard Rodgers: "The picture of the divorced woman is unrelievedly negative . . . whatever the psychological costs of marriage, the costs of being [divorced] are greater."[50]

Why should women see divorce more positively than men, even in the face of economic hardship, role strain, and considerable personal trauma? Let me sketch out the beginnings of an interpretation for this seeming contradiction.

It is possible that women may emphasize the benefits of divorce because of methodological factors. Very simply, they may be more willing than men to express their positive feelings, just as they are more willing than men to talk about negative symptoms and distress. Because women are more responsive to feelings and expressive about emotions than men tend to be, women may disclose more about both the "bad" and the "good" in their lives when marriage ends.[51]

In the interview context, individuals may have reacted differently to the interviewers, two of whom were women. For women interviewees, the interview may have been an occasion to celebrate independence and to express solidarity and identification with the interviewers. For men, the interview may have been an occasion to elicit sympathy, to use the women interviewers as confidantes and comforters. Further, men may have been reluctant to report fully to women some of the areas that constitute positives for them, such as the freedom to pursue women sexually, for example. The Appendix contains a fuller discussion of the interview context.

Although this explanation cannot be entirely ruled out, one piece of information argues against the interview context as the only source of the gender difference. Women and men who were interviewed by a man (13 percent of total) did not appear markedly different from the sample as a whole in the benefits they cited. Thus, though the interview situation is an important context in this as in all studies, available evidence does not justify dismissing as simply an "interviewer effect" the finding that women interpret divorce more positively than men do.

The issue of gender and the experience of marriage sheds light on this finding in at least four ways. First, research consistently shows that men are more satisfied with their marriages than women are. There is further evidence, though it is not altogether consistent, that men's roles in marriage benefit their mental health more than women's roles do, and that married women feel more stress in their family roles than married men do. It is important to note that marriage benefits the health of *both* women and men, but it may well be that in certain socioemotional respects "his" marriage is better than "hers," because marriage is the key axis of social integration and support for men. With divorce, men lose family roles that recent research suggests may be far more important for most men's well-being than paid work roles, and that may be especially consequential for men's confidence and self-esteem, as well. Some men, too, define divorce as a failure in achievement, and thus the loss of wife and children may have a particularly negative import for them.[52]

Women have a very different experience of marriage than do men, and they may have more to gain, in some respects, in divorce. In many ways, modern marriage is a "greedy" institution, especially for women. In the words of Lewis Coser, institutions are greedy "insofar as they seek exclusive and undivided loyalty," and if this is the case, the demands on women in marriage are omnivorous indeed. True, modern marriage creates a kind of social isolation for both spouses, who are expected to turn to one another for strong emotional commitment. Socializing is subordinated to marriage, except when the interaction involves couples, and social ties outside of marriage have to be fitted into "down" times. But wives, especially if they are unemployed, have limited opportunities to meet a variety of people for possible friendships. If there are children, constraints on women's friendships are even greater, because of the degree of allegiance and energy children require, typically from women. The companionate ideal does not encourage the development or maintenance of close outside relationships. Its defining characteristics—emotional intimacy, companionship, and sexual expression—require attention, and therefore spouses have limited availability to others. The marital bond is expected to be the primary bond, and men in particular expect this to be true for women. Marriage imposes constraints on friendship for women that divorce eases.[53]

Second, a number of the women in this study reported domination and devaluation in marriage and told of their experiences of sexual, physical and psychological abuse by their husbands. Given these memories of marriage, it stands to reason that these women would view divorce in a positive light. Not only does divorce lessen this source of vulnerability, it also sets the stage for women to move into roles that bring external valuation and recognition, such as schooling and employment. Although few divorcing women interpret their experiences in political terms, I would argue that the inequality of marriage takes a toll on women. Divorce hardly offers women equality with men, but it does begin a process that gets women out from under one kind of male authority.

Third, and related to the difference in the power white women and men have in marriage, women often experience greater control over significant aspects of their lives with divorce. Research suggests that a sense of control is associated with positive states of mind. Rosalind Barnett, Lois Biener, and Grace Baruch argue that low control is a dominant motif in women's lives:

> The female gender role prescribes dependency, non-assertiveness and subordination of one's needs to others. Neither the perception that one has control over one's life nor the ability to take control is part of the standard to which most women are socialized. Indeed, the price of being a fully socialized female in our culture may be a predisposition to feelings of lack of control and ultimately to depression. [54]

Although women themselves do not necessarily define it this way, the structure of traditional marriage further places white women in a situation of high demands and low control, a condition that investigators of stress find is associated with conflict and dissatisfaction. By contrast, white men have high levels of control in marriage. By virtue of their status as primary economic providers, husbands typically have considerable authority over wives, children, and households. [55]

With divorce, men experience a decline in their spheres of control and women experience an increase in theirs. Divorce provides opportunities for women to take charge of areas such as finances, children, and the household or, at the very least, stimulates effort in that direction. Women talk about how much this means to them. Divorce can in some sense be viewed as a kind of training ground in competence for women, where they can explore who they are, develop their instrumental sides, and stand on their own. To use the metaphor of Robert White, women may construct divorce into a "backbone incident" that produces an "astonishing transformation in development." Precisely because of the exigencies of their lives, white women have the potential for developing a sense of their own efficacy, what Jean Baker Miller describes as "a belief in their own ability to generate action and gratification" rather than waiting "for others to provide solutions and satisfactions." Miller argues further that the very situation of oppression "can foster the development of a form of creativity" that is "unavailable to the dominant group"— white married men.[56]

Fourth, divorced women can more easily than men replace, or cope with the absence of, the benefits marriage provided for their mental health. Marriage provides white women with a material base—income—whereas men benefit more from the socioemotional features of marriage—a confidante and other social ties.[57] Although divorced women certainly do not live at the same standard that they did when married, most do survive economically with a combination of welfare benefits, jobs, and help from kin. Women with education and careers do much better, of course. Men have much more difficulty replacing what a wife and family provided. Divorce creates expressive hardships for men that it does not create for women.

CHAPTER 6

Divorce Is Here to Stay

What Can We Learn from It?

. . . human kind
Cannot bear very much reality.

—T. S. ELIOT, "Burnt Norton"

It is customary to bemoan the prevalence of divorce. Some argue we no longer value the family—commitment has died. Others cite the large number of divorces as proof that American individualism has gone too far. All agree that the welfare of large numbers of children is thrown into question, because as a society we have not made provisions for the care and rearing of children outside of the two-parent family (and even in that context it is assumed that mothers stay home to care for them).

Can divorce, however, transform marriage in some positive ways, that is, do individuals who remarry have a different experience the second time around? Do individuals carry into remarriage the skills and understandings they learned from divorce, and if they do, can this make the institution of marriage more equal? For those who do not remarry, are there alternative structures that might allow for intimate connection and community without "greediness"?

DIVORCE IN CONTEXT

This study has been guided by the assumption that individuals act on the basis of a definition of a situation. Those who divorce leave marriages that do not live up to their definition of what marriage should provide—the vision of the companionate ideal. Using culturally shared vocabularies and structures, they construct narrative accounts to explain and persuade listeners that their definitions of their divorcing situations are correct. They also explain their turbulent emotions, both depressed and elated, after divorce by using a vocabulary of motives that is available through their culture. In the words of Kenneth Burke, their motives are not "some fixed thing, like a table, which one can go look at."[1] Instead, they are personal interpretations that make sense to listeners to the extent that they are situated in a shared worldview. The divorced are not passive creatures; they constantly interpret what the perceive to be true about their marriages and their separations.

Collectively, members of a culture also interpret what goes on around them, assign motives, and develop shared understandings of social life. In the case of divorce, the collective definition is typically negative and is reflected in language: divorce is seen as a social "problem," evidenced by "broken" families that are in sharp contrast to "intact" families we are taught to prize; "whole" families have a husband and a wife, those headed by women are "broken." Collective definitions not only reflect a cultural understanding but perpetuate it, for the way a problem is defined dictates the solutions that are applied. Particular social policies develop out of our views of marriage and divorce.[2]

Divorcing individuals in this study challenge some of our collective wisdom, both popular and scholarly, by suggesting that divorce isn't all bad. The prevailing view that marital dissolution is one of the major social problems of our time, unremittingly negative in its consequences, might also be challenged.

It is important to remember that marital dissolution is not a new phenomenon in U.S. society, though what is currently bringing it about—divorce—*is* quite new, on any widespread basis. As I noted at the beginning of this book, marriage ended abruptly in the funeral parlor throughout the nineteenth century, usually after a sudden and painful illness in a young spouse, leaving the surviving partner, typically the wife, to care for many growing children. Remarriage was frequently her only recourse, as it was for husbands when their wives died (often in childbirth). Reconstituted families—in which the family unit includes children from several marriages—are not particular to our age, but have a permanent place in the history of the family. Desertion, too, was common in the nineteenth century, as men left their wives to go to the frontier or join the army. The work force in many early factories was composed of women and children who had been abandoned, and the settlement house movement was, in part, an effort to deal with this problem.

There were thus different ways of getting "divorced" in earlier times. Legal divorce, at least in terms of the number of people it affects, is the modern-day equivalent of death and desertion for the American family. It is a new cultural form that limits the length of time spent in any one marital relationship.[3]

Divorce talk tells us a great deal about marriage today. In individuals' accounts, in which they express, directly or indirectly, their romantic visions of marriage, we see how pervasive the expectations are for emotional intimacy, primacy and companionship, and sexual fulfillment—all to be realized with one person, in a long life together. These expectations are inevitably disappointed by the "rough reality of married life, with its critical in-laws, cranky children, disabling sickness, and the frustrating day-to-day grind of intimate cohabitation."[4]

Unlike previous generations, couples are now taking the ending of marriages into their own hands. Like previous generations, the contemporary form of marital dissolution typically leaves women to raise children alone.

REMARRIAGE: A TEST CASE

Although marriage did not work the first time around, most try again. Remarriage is a way to heal the pain, for various reasons. In U.S. culture marriage is defined as the primary medium for achieving a deep and abiding human connection with another adult. This may be especially true because other meaningful forms of connection—church, community, neighborhood—have broken down in this secularized and individualized society. It is difficult to find *communitas* in the modern world, and in this context the romantic image of the traditional family is very seductive—the myth is that marriage will fill the void. In the companionate ideal, all needs are thrown onto another person. There are few other formalized ways of fully sharing our lives.

We come to an essential paradox. On the one hand, individuals find much to praise in the divorced state. Women in the sample, especially, spoke at length of the freedom and personal growth of their newly constructed lives as single people, of regaining aspects of life that they never knew they had lost. On the other hand, within five years most of them will have remarried. Although those interviewed were not recontacted for this information, there is no reason to expect this group, chosen with care to represent the divorced at large, to be any different than the population generally. According to demographers, about three-quarters of the divorced can be expected to eventually remarry (interestingly, this is a somewhat lower proportion than in previous generations).[5]

Individuals remarry for security, which comes in many forms and guises and means different things to different people. For women, in particular, financial security is pivotal—remarriage ensures greater economic well-being for them and their children than does divorce. In the context of financial strain and worry about support (and in the absence of social policies that could ameliorate these problems), divorced women experience many symptoms of emotional depression, as we have seen. Under conditions of economic inequality between women and men, remarriage is a rational choice, as it was in previous generations for the widowed and deserted—a way out of poverty and, for many women, a way out of depression, as well. Women with college educations can achieve a measure of financial security on their own and, they tend to delay remarriage or postpone it altogether. Even for these women, however, the standard of living improves upon remarriage, because two households are pooled and resources can go further.

A second and critical dimension, of course, is emotional security— a spouse is "someone to come home to," "someone to be there to help." Many of the problems the divorced, especially women, face are linked to the absence of emotional and practical help. Both women and men look to remarriage as a stable source of affection, emotional support, and help with daily life even after first marriages that were disappointing in this regard. Remarriage also promises sexual security—the availability of a stable partner (increasingly important, one might expect, for divorced women and men in the age of AIDS).

Finally and most important, remarriage ensures normative security; remarriage is a way of legitimating oneself and one's children. The divorced can again live within the social script that American society so highly prizes—conjugal family. Marriage brings privilege, and few would walk away from that.[6]

But there is another side, as well. Marris argues that individuals are guided by a "conservative impulse": at the same time that they adapt to change they are led to protect the particular forms with which they are familiar. Most people depend on families, and one important aspect of becoming a couple is that it is a way to form a legitimate family. Societies, too, depend on families or, as Rayna Rapp corrects, on households: "the family is the normative, correct way in which people get recruited into households." In addition, divorce is a normless status and, some argue, this creates pressures toward remarriage, which in turn sustains the kinship structures necessary for the survival of society. Yet, as Ann Goetting asks, why is it that we as a society do not create clear norms for the divorced? Structures could be created, through social welfare policy and other initiatives, to ensure the well-being of individuals, including children, outside of marriage. Alternative household arrangements could also be legitimated—a point I will take up shortly.[7]

Given that most remarry, the crucial question is whether and how it is different the second time. We have seen that divorced individuals learn new skills and gain new competencies. They develop aspects of themselves that they had put away in marriage. Women learn labor market skills, for example, and men learn domestic skills. Do these new competencies get brought into new marriages, or do individuals go back to the gender-based division of labor characteristic of traditional marriage?

Research on the remarried suggests that subtle changes occur. In one of the few extensive studies, Frank Furstenberg and Graham

Spanier resurveyed nearly two hundred individuals who had been studied previously while divorced, and interviewed in depth a sub-sample of twenty-five couples.[8] They found that the balance of power is different in first and second marriages, shifting toward greater equality. Although more process-oriented studies are needed to see how marital power actually gets negotiated the second time around, Furstenberg and Spanier's findings suggest that something important occurs. Husbands have greater involvement in domestic roles than in their previous marriages, and wives have greater participation in important decisions. The authors conclude that there is a "shake-up effect" and some restructuring of traditional gender roles for these families. Not surprisingly, they also note that husbands and wives do not always agree on how decisions are made and domestic tasks performed. It is significant, in any case, that individuals viewed their second marriages as more egalitarian than their first ones—they did not take the traditional division of labor in marriage for granted—which suggests that an attitudinal shift may take place with remarriage, even if concrete behaviors do not always follow along.

In the absence of economic equality between husbands and wives, the "shake-up effect" may not persist over time. Rosanna Hertz found with dual-career couples that the division of labor in the home was transformed because husbands and wives had similar salaries and faced equal work demands, not because of an ideological commitment to equality. In more traditional marriages, wives' economic dependency on their husbands effectively keeps women in subordinate position, and there are no economic incentives to reward couples who challenge the status quo.[9] Without job parity, equality between women and men in marriage is difficult to sustain, despite the best efforts of individual couples. Ideology is not enough; structural change is necessary, too. There is no reason to expect remarriage to be any different from marriage in this regard, though more investigation of the "shake-up effect" is needed.

There is further evidence that divorce may be transforming remarriage, in ways that are not easy to interpret. Although we are only beginning to understand how remarriage differs from marriage, it is clear that individuals are even less inclined to stay in unhappy second marriages than they were in first marriages. Conventional wisdom suggests that second marriages will be more successful than first marriages—after all, people should make a better choice, negotiate the stresses and strains better, be able to compromise better—but the facts do not bear out this prediction. There is now convincing evidence that there exists a greater risk of divorce among the remarried than among those married for the first time: 39 percent of all remarriages begun in 1975 are expected to end in divorce within ten years, compared with 30 percent of first marriages begun at the same time. Although the high rate of failure in second marriages can be attributed to character flaws in the partners and to the unique stresses and strains of these unions (particularly the complex family structures and norm ambiguity that partners must negotiate), there is also an alternative explanation: individuals may simply refuse to stay in negative relationships. Having survived divorce once before, and perhaps remembering some of its positive aspects, they are willing to strike out on their own again, if need be. Furstenberg and Spanier report that the remarried they interviewed in depth said they "were unwilling to be miserable again simply for the sake of preserving the union."[10]

There is thus some limited evidence from others' research that divorced women and men transfer some of the attitudes and skills they developed as independent people into their new marital unions. Although a significant number of these marriages ultimately do not survive, divorce may exert various kinds of subtle pressure. It may shape the process within remarriage in progressive directions, and it may enable individuals to leave these new relationships when they are not satisfactory. There is pressure on partners to change the traditional rules when conjugal change is a viable option.

Once again, however, women and men differ in the extent to which remarriage is a viable option, and women differ among themselves as well. Demographic studies of divorce after remarriage show that it is men, more than women, who are more likely to get divorced again. And yet, paradoxically, women tend to be less happy in second marriages than are men. In the absence of an economic alternative, women may stay in unhappy second marriages. Paul Glick estimates that 61 percent of white men in their thirties in 1980 will eventually redivorce, compared with 53 percent of white women. Blacks have the opposite pattern, with more women than men redivorcing. One reason for this may be that black women as a group have greater economic equality with black men; marriage is not the source of financial security to nearly the same degree that it is for white women. Whatever complex processes may be involved, it is clear that remarriage and redivorce do not have a universal meaning but that there are gender-based and culturally diverse pathways to it.[11]

CONNECTION AND COMMUNITY WITHOUT REMARRIAGE

Although most of the divorced remarry, not all do, and there are important gender, age, and class variations in the likelihood of remarriage. In the United States today, many individuals are constructing lives outside of marital arrangements (not always by choice, of course). Marriage is not the only game in town.

Unrelated adults who live together constitute the fastest-growing form of household, though they still remain a small percentage of the total. Not all of these households are composed of the formerly married, and these households differ widely in intensity of interaction and interdependence. But it is true nevertheless that there are many ways to build caring ties and commitments to others into the fabric of life. To name only a few, individuals in U.S. society can live intimately with another unmarried person, that is, without the benefit of marriage, though this is tolerated only in some communities. Alternatively, the divorced can live alone with an intimate other closeby. They can live communally with a number of others, sharing residence, responsibilities, and pooling resources in a variety of ways. All of these arrangements provide for the establishment of important relationships, albeit in quite different ways. Society, however, makes it difficult to develop and sustain these kinds of households.

Little is known about these alternatives and about how individuals achieve connection and community in ways that are not supported by the dominant culture. In general, single life has been studied not as an alternative to marriage but as a way station, a transitory marital status.[12] Yet we know that women are more likely than men to stay single after divorce, and because women live longer than men and because they marry men older than themselves, the majority of women ultimately live outside of marriage, whether they want to or not.

A closer look at the remarriage rates of different groups of women reveals that social class and age have important influences. A significant percentage of educationally advantaged women who divorce do not remarry right away; in 1980 only 46 percent of women in their thirties with some graduate education had remarried, compared with 64 percent of comparable men. Though some might define these women as the "casualties" of divorce and of the "marriage squeeze," the findings here suggest that women who have a choice (that is, those with careers who can be self-supporting) fear that traditional marriage will be constraining. Having found positive aspects of themselves through the process of divorce and through subsequently living alone, they may be reluctant to enter traditional marital arrangements again. We do not know how many of these women have dependents. Constructing a life outside of marriage may mean something quite different when no children are involved. With respect to social class, however, the findings are quite clear. Glick argues that the more education a woman has, the more likely she is to enter remarriage "more deliberately or decide to remain unmarried." He observes that in contrast, women without college educations tend to remarry rather quickly. Even these women have lower remarriage rates than their male counterparts, however; in fact, at every educational level women are less likely than men to remarry (though the gender differences are most pronounced for the highly educated). Taken together, these findings suggest that the benefits of divorce, as defined by women, may be influencing some women's attitudes about marrying again.[13] At the very least, it can be said that women are reentering legal unions more cautiously.

Women over forty are much more likely to stay single than are younger women. Older women may constitute a vanguard in some ways, devising imaginative household arrangements in lieu of remarriage. Perhaps they feel they have little to lose, and because they no longer have small children in the home, alternatives to traditional families are possible in ways they would not have been before. Not all remain single voluntarily. Older women come up against the fact that older men tend to remarry younger women, while the option of marrying a younger man is not as culturally acceptable or available for older women. But for some divorced women in their fifties and sixties, there is a reluctance to risk another divorce, to live through a husband's illness, even his death, if remarriage means giving up the independence they worked hard to achieve.

In society's collective definition of the situation, these women are often portrayed as victims. Many, of course, live on a limited income, and there is no denying their economic disadvantage; social concern ought to extend to working to correct that imbalance. But older women, whether poor or not, are especially likely to be pitied when they live in institutional contexts such as retirement colonies and nursing homes. This pity may be misplaced and unrealistic, however, if it dismisses the possibility that these women are constructing lives outside of traditional marriage, banding together with others (usually women) to establish caring relationships and community in nontraditional ways.

The pockets of women living together—not great in number but significant nonetheless—warrant detailed study. In some respects these women are "ghettoized," isolated from mainstream society— an experience that is common to minority groups. While a ghetto has many negative features, within the context of a hostile or unsupportive environment it can serve as a source of security and comfort— "a haven," William Chafe says, "in which to seek support and sustenance for the next encounter with the outside world." He points out that unlike other minority groups, women have not been segregated but have lived "in greater intimacy with their 'oppressors' than with each other." After divorce and to survive economically, some women are choosing to live with each other. Others are doing so because they have no choice: their lives are getting longer and longer, and men predecease them.[14]

There is much to be learned from these communities. What ideologies about marriage do women hold? Do they build into their lives what companionate marriage promises but does not usually deliver—emotional intimacy, primacy and companionship, and sexual expression? Do they constitute their lives around completely different organizing principles? How do they provide for themselves financially, and how do they negotiate money with each other? How, collectively, do they devise solutions to the problems of loneliness? Do they develop intimate bonds that are less greedy, more generous than marriage? What supports are available from the larger culture, and what is lacking?

It is appropriate to end a book about divorce with a series of questions. The individuals interviewed for this study say that ending a marriage is an open-ended process. Divorce does not close a life but opens up a new one, they repeatedly tell us. The observations and interpretations I have offered about remarriage and its alternatives suggest that scholars and social critics cannot "close" the subject of divorce by focusing only on what is lost. For all of us, interpreting the past can open up questions and possibilities for the future. We have the opportunity to explore the myriad ways we can maintain connection to others and feel part of communities, at the same time that we deal—inevitably—with loss and change.

A *Narrative about Methods*

This study was originally designed to fall within the sociological tradition of survey research, to apply quantitative methods to an investigation of adaptation after divorce. The design, sampling procedures, and interview schedule were indeed based on the logic and strengths of survey research, but the final result is quite different from what I originally envisioned. Critical incidents changed the course of the project and my analysis of it, and hence any discussion of research methods or approach must include some account of this transformation.[1]

ORIGINAL CONCEPTUALIZATION

At the outset this study was intended to examine the postseparation adaptation of women compared with men, and Naomi Gerstel and I designed it together. Because of our concern with generalizability, we put considerable effort into finding a sample that was representative of the population of individuals going through the process of marital dissolution and into developing an interview schedule that tapped the major domains of life that divorce alters.

Sample Design and Selection

Women and men who are divorcing form a very mobile population, and for a variety of reasons, individuals are often extremely reticent. In addition, there is no systematic way to locate those who are only informally separated—individuals who have not yet taken legal action.

To deal with these problems, we decided to generate a sample from two sources: public documents and referrals to the study. Sixty-one percent of those we ultimately interviewed were located through probate court records of those filing for divorce in two counties in the Northeast. We sent letters inviting participation in a study about "family life" and followed up with phone calls to all those who met our criteria, detailed below. The remainder of the sample of 104 was located through a modified "snowball" procedure. This approach became necessary because we wanted to include the recently separated, who tend to be under-represented in the courts (most couples who file for divorce have already been living apart for at least a year). Those who heard about the study told us about people who had just separated, but more typically, the referral cases were identified by individuals from the probate court sample. At the end of each interview with someone we had located through the courts, we asked for the names of people they knew who had been separated less than one year. We interviewed no more than one person named by each interviewee. All those contacted through this referral method agreed to participate. The response rate for the court sample was 55 percent (calculated as the proportion who agreed to be interviewed over the total who met sampling criteria and could be located). Although the latter rate is somewhat lower than is typical for surveys in general, it is comparable to other studies of the divorced that rely on public records.[2] There were no significant differences in statistical comparisons between the two sources of interviewees on a set of demographic characteristics (such as years of education, gender, presence of children, years married, and other variables).

Because we wanted to study the effects of divorce on women compared with men, the sample included equal numbers of each (fifty-two). Given that marital dissolution is a process rather than a static life event, and because we were interested in adaptation during various parts of the divorcing process, we stratified the sample by time: one-third of each gender group had been separated less than one year, one-third had been separated one to two years, and one-third had been separated two to three years. With these sources of variability built into the sampling design, we tried to minimize other sources of variation. Consequently, we limited eligible cases to those who were between the ages of twenty-five and forty-eight; had been married for at least a year; had lived apart from the spouse (our operational definition of "separation") for no more than three years; and were not full-time students.

These procedures yielded a very heterogeneous sample, unlike those of many of the classic studies of divorce that have relied on individuals who choose to participate in a clinical or self-help program. The sample here includes both working-class and middle-class individuals, with a wide range of annual income—from $4,000 to over $50,000, with a median of $18,000.

Levels of education also varied widely: about one-fourth had not finished high school and roughly the same number had four or more years of college. The sample includes some interviewees whose primary source of income came from public assistance, and significant numbers of individuals who had manual, clerical, and professional jobs. Only 11 percent were not employed and another 9 percent were working part-time. Although not a deliberate sampling strategy, 97 percent were white and 3 percent were Hispanic. (The two counties that we sampled have very few black residents.) The median age of the interviewees was thirty-three years and the mean number of years married was nine; all but a handful had been married only once. Twenty individuals (ten couples), out of 104, had been married to someone else in the sample. This was unintentional. These cases were not analyzed separately or differently from the rest, because there were too few to represent a reliable cross-section of the total sample. Thirty percent of the sample had no children, 19 percent had one child, and the remaining 51 percent had more than one child.

Interview Schedule
Survey research, like all interview studies (and much of social life as well), is organized around the asking and answering of questions. In keeping with the original plan of the study, the interview schedule was one in which everyone was presented with the same set of questions in a preordered sequence—identical stimuli that promised to yield variability in response that could be analyzed.[3]

We constructed an interview schedule composed of more than one hundred questions with fixed response categories, and a few broad open-ended questions. The structured portion of the schedule included items (some adapted from the work of others) about social networks, changes in habits and routines, worries and pressures, contact with children, financial situation, as well as routine sociodemographic information. As our measure of psychological distress, we used the Center for Epidemiological Studies Depression (CES-D) scale—a twenty-item scale that is widely used in studies of mental health in the general population. The scale was tested for internal consistency, and the alpha was .93.[4]

The open-ended (or unstructured) parts of the interview included fewer than ten questions, which were interspersed with the fixed-response items. The unstructured items asked about several broad areas, including loneliness, changes in relationships, and phases of the separation process. Three of the questions—grouped together in the middle of the interview schedule—proved to be especially valuable for this book: "Would you state, in your own words, what were the main causes of your separation?"; "What are the greatest difficulties you have experienced in the process of separating?"; "What are the greatest benefits that have resulted from your separation?"

Three of us did all the interviewing for the study. Naomi Gerstel and I conducted 87 percent of the interviews, and Larry O'Brien, a graduate student, did the remaining 13 percent. (The three interviewers, N, C, and L, are identified by the first letter in each interviewee's identification number, found after each quotation from an interview.) Most of the interviews took place in the interviewees' home, although at the request of several individuals, a few were interviewed in our offices and, in one case, in my home. We used a tape recorder in order to pick up answers to the open-ended questions. Originally, we planned to switch it on only at these points in the interview. This proved distracting, however, and we decided to tape the entire interview, although only the qualitative responses were transcribed. As it turned out, interviewees spoke spontaneously and at some length at many places in the interview, not only in response to open-ended questions. Not unlike the field worker who goes into the field and writes up everything, not knowing what will turn out to be important, we had a valuable source of data in the tapes unknown to us when we began the study.

THE TRANSFORMATION: INTERVIEWING

A series of incidents critical for the course of the research occurred during the interviewing phase. The first clue that something unexpected was happening was that many of the interviews took much longer than we had planned. In our pretest interviews, it had been possible to complete the interview schedule in less than two hours. Once in the field, however, we found that some interviews took as long as six hours (and we needed to return once and even twice to complete them). Interviewees often departed from the structure of the interview schedule as we had constructed it and elaborated their answers even to the fixed-response items in lengthy asides. Occasionally they took issue with the response categories they were allowed, but more typically they simply seized every opportunity in the conversation to tell about their lives. Another unexpected occurrence was that as interviewers, we felt a tension arising between getting through the interview schedule, that is, covering all the questions we had decided on, and letting people talk about what was important to them.

I felt this tension vividly in one of the earliest interviews in the study, with an artist who had two small children and who had been separated for only a few weeks. She seemed to become less and less forthcoming as the interview progressed and looked drained by the end. As I was leaving, I asked her in a standard question to evaluate the interview. She said it made her feel "depersonalized," adding it "wasn't an opportunity to really talk." An academic interviewed a bit later in the study commented in response to the same question that "there was this switching between the number of questions which weren't particularly interesting and the thought questions," the "more reflective stuff." A sales representative, also one of the early interviewees, said he felt "too much of the interview was canned." Although not everyone was critical, we decided to cut several sections of fixed-response questions in order to give people more time to "really talk." Still, our training as social scientists often led us in the interview to try to stick to the schedule and thereby obtain uniform data on everyone. Rather than letting our informants lead us down *their* trails, we persisted in seeking answers to *our* questions. We would each return from our interviews and describe to each other how the interviewee had "gone on and on."[5]

I remember an interview with a single father, who made brownies while I interviewed him in his kitchen. He said the interview "felt like therapy." As I began to understand what he meant, I heard others, even people who had never been in counseling, say the same thing. The interviews caused one woman "to reflect on aspects of my life, kind of an inventory-taking," stimulated another "to think of things in ways that I hadn't thought about before," and was a "catharsis" for another as it "brought out many feelings I didn't know I had." It was not uncommon for interviewees—both women and men—to cry during the interview as they recalled their marriages and tried to put aspects of their new lives together with their old ones. A clerical worker said she had benefited from the "level of the conversation," adding "I enjoy getting into my mind and heart."

Not only did the interviewing process have an effect on them, it also strongly affected me. I was divorced, as my mother and grandmother had been before me, and though I was aware that this personal history had stimulated my choice of the topic, I was not entirely prepared for my response. Listening to people's painful accounts of their marriages and trying to probe sensitively for their understandings of what had happened was sometimes difficult. It was difficult, too, when a few male interviewees asked for dates (this happened to both women interviewers) and when one threatened me when I refused. During the coding and analysis process, I had more trouble empathically interpreting men's experience than I did women's.

Yet it was also the case that because I was a divorced single parent, rapport was often easily established. A number of interviewees (both women and men) asked me during the course of the interview if I "had been through it," and when I responded affirmatively (I always answered such questions matter-of-factly), several said, "Then you understand." Yet I wanted their, not my, understandings, and in some ways I had to work harder and probe more than I would have if I had not been seen as a veteran of the experience.[6] At the same time, the fact that I was divorced placed me in a more egalitarian relationship with those I was studying and created a greater reciprocity than is customary in research interviews. Being a survivor of the experience also helped me attend to subtle but very important cues.

One woman, for example, sensitized me to a manifestation of self-reliance in women that I had previously taken for granted. She was recently separated and, at her request, was interviewed in my home. As she left it she observed that "a woman alone can make a nest for herself, not for a man," adding that she had never realized this before. In another case, a man wanted to know about my children and whether "they ever see their father"—an issue in his own divorce. For a few interviewees the issue was not so much my marital but my class status. One man, who described himself as "just a flunky, trying to get by in this world," said his job was "menial" and then added "I'm not fortunate like you to have a good education, to be down at Smith College." It was impossible for me, as it was for my colleagues in other ways, to stand in a neutral relationship to the data. Like all investigators, we were not "robots, programmed to collect pure information."[7]

We had entered into a relationship with those we were studying. The interviewees had become participants, or informants—resident experts on the topic of divorce—rather than "respondents" to our questionnaire (a word I have avoided here because of its passive connotations). The structured interviews had become in-depth interviews, as we increasingly allowed people to talk about their experiences in marriage, even though the original intent of the study had been to focus on the postseparation phase. Rather than suppressing this process, we saw it as an opportunity to broaden our research design and be responsive to our informants. Although we still asked every question on the final interview schedule of every person in the sample, it became clear that those we were studying were doing something with the interview other than what we had intended. They were deviating from the fixed design by telling about their marital lives and their interpretations of them. Narratives were not always a response to open-ended items, nor were they always told in response to a question that manifestly elicited them. As interviewing progressed, we got better and better at listening for them (though I was not aware that these *were* narratives until midway through the study). Because the interviews were taped, a text was being created even as we persisted in administering the interview schedule.

Appendix

CODING AND DATA ANALYSIS: DIFFERENT REPRESENTATIONS
OF THE DIVORCE EXPERIENCE

More discoveries were made during the coding and analysis process. It became clear that we had generated several kinds of data—quantitative counts and at least two kinds of qualitative data—each requiring a different approach. Grouping fixed-response items into scales and testing internal consistency was a straightforward procedure, but grouping responses to the qualitative data (responses to the open-ended items, spontaneous "asides," and lengthy narratives) was not nearly so straightforward.

I had difficulty categorizing responses into the code categories we had initially developed, such as "reasons for separation." Although many interviewees mentioned a similar set of marital events (which other divorce researchers have coded into discrete complaints), these events seemed to mean very different things and to constitute very different experiences. For some, for example, marital infidelity—either the interviewee's or the spouse's—was interpreted as causal; it was a sufficient condition to end the marriage. For many others, an affair was only part of the story—the catalyst, as it were. For still others, an extramarital affair had existed for some time but another event brought the decision to separate to a head. How could we put these very different events, or these same events with different meanings, into the same coding category?

My thinking shifted in the interviewing and coding process because I could no longer view the interviewees as objects, from whom data could be extracted and analyzed separate from the contexts in which they were created.[8] I saw active, imaginative subjects, women and men who reflected on themselves and on the gendered world of marriage. Although we had designed the study so that we could analyze and compare women and men's adaptation over time, through the stages of divorce, I began to see divorce as an interpretive process, not as a series of stages. I became intrigued with the imaginative enterprise itself—how individuals, through talk, construct meaning out of loss, and how gender is meaningful in this interpretive work. The subjects had changed the investigator and, thus, the research. It was close to this point that Naomi Gerstel and I decided to pursue independent lines of inquiry, though we continued to do some work together.

I began to search for methods of analysis that could better capture this aspect of what I was hearing and seeing. Grounded theory provided an approach to some of the qualitative materials, particularly the themes manifested in the open-ended responses.[9] I applied this approach systematically in a series of steps. I read (and read and read again) the transcripts, and out of these rereadings developed a set of broad codes that I then noted in the margins, "saturating" (to use Anselm Strauss's term) the transcripts with these preliminary categories. Out of this process, I discovered concepts that had not been fully a part of the original coding scheme, such as an American vocabulary of "freedom," "liberation," and "independence" that eventually proved significant in analyzing the positive aspects of divorce. I then went back to the transcripts I had coded earlier and recoded them in light of these new concepts. This recursive process was repeated several times until the coding categories accounted for every interview. The next step was to examine each broad analytic category more closely, to uncover the dimensions and parameters for the emergent category and to uncover meaning of the category for women compared with men. As I systematically proceeded through the interviews using each category, I drew up tables enumerating the frequency that women and men mentioned a topic and then took apart these summations to see how individual people and subgroups in the sample talked about the theme (for example, single parents versus individuals without children or without custody; those with working-class compared to middle-class jobs).

These procedures may be seen in the process used to generate the analysis of divorce accounts in Chapter 2 (the same general approach was used to study the psychological distress and positive outcomes of divorce, the themes of Chapters 4 and 5). After discovering that interviewees were developing accounts to explain their divorces in the light of taken-for-granted expectations about marriage (which I have called the companionate ideal), I searched within this broad category for its dimensions, which I named emotional intimacy, primacy and companionship, and sexual expression. I defined each dimension, or construct, on the basis of the interviewees' description. Emotional intimacy, for example, was coded positively or negatively whenever an interviewee mentioned communication about feelings and/or daily events with a spouse as either present or absent. The absence of primacy was coded whenever an interviewee complained about the spouse's (nonsexual) relationship to others. Companionship was coded as present or absent whenever joint activities with the spouse were mentioned. Sexual issues were coded whenever interviewees talked about infidelity (actual or suspected) and/or sexual problems in the marriage, such as complaints about frequency or quality of sex life. Similar procedures noted the frequency of devaluation and domination in marriage. Devaluation was coded whenever there was mention of being "insulted," "humiliated," or treated with "lack of respect," and psychological domination was defined with key words that interviewees used, such as "demand," "bullying," or "authoritarian." An instance of physical abuse was counted whenever individuals reported that either they or the spouse had "pushed," "hit," "beaten," or thrown a knife or other object at a spouse or child. The two cases of marital rape were also coded as physical abuse. I then classified each topic by gender, noting its frequency, and looked more closely within each category at its meaning and significance for individual women and men. I closely analyzed the individual texts that had been classified in the category, and moved them to other categories or developed other codes when necessary. In selecting interview excerpts to exemplify each theme in the book, I tried to portray the variability and range of expression in each category.

Out of this lengthy process of analysis I developed the set of ideas that form the basis for Chapter 2—the taken-for-granted assumptions about a companionate marriage that women and men draw upon to explain why they divorced. The conceptualizations are "grounded" because they unfolded during the course of data analysis, though I would be the first to say that they were also informed by preexisting perspectives and the theoretical orientations I find most useful. In keeping with grounded theory, however, the conceptualizations did not exist in some "full-blown" form prior to the interview or coding process, with the data fitted into them. Nor were there a set of preexisting hypotheses that were formally tested in the course of the study.

Although the approach of grounded theory proved helpful in making sense of themes, it was not always sufficient. The method necessitates fragmenting the interview text into codable chunks that share a common content area or topic. In the words of Strauss, the analyst "fractures the data in the service of their interpretation."[10] While coding, however, I noticed sections in which interviewees stitched several themes together into long narratives, providing context for interpretation along the way through the structure of their accounts. As I became more interested in the actors' viewpoints, their definitions of their divorcing situations, I wanted to respect the way interviewees organized their replies in the analysis and find an alternative to fracturing their texts.

As I coded one interview, an interviewee suggested a solution to the problem. When asked to state in his own words the main causes of his separation, he said, "Well, you know, that's a real long story (laughs), but maybe I can sum it up by saying . . . ," and gave a list of complaints. In coding other interviews, I again saw that individuals tried to tell long stories and other forms of narrative about their experiences in marriage and after. Some even succeeded, despite the interviewer's impatience with talk that went "on and on."

As I explain more fully in Chapter 3, narrative theory and methods, especially the work of Elliot Mishler and Susan Bell, provided a way into these texts.[11] Not everything was narrative, however broadly defined, but some of it was, as individuals used the classic form of storytelling to recapitulate and reinterpret their lives. I noted these passages in the transcripts and selected a number to retranscribe in fuller detail and to analyze as case studies. The major findings of Chapter 3 come out of the close textual analysis of these transcripts. As detailed there, narrativizing is a major way that individuals make sense of their past marriages and heal biographical discontinuities. There are different genres of narrative, and each form helps narrators solve the "teller's problem" (convincing the listener of the justification for the teller's perspective and actions) somewhat differently. Narratives allow for the elaboration of the actor's definition of the situation—the reality as he or she understands it at that moment.

In keeping with the constructionist approach that ultimately guided the research, I wanted to avoid the usual transformation of "data" into a written report that disembodied the subject and represented the results as a set of "findings." The solution that I adopted was to devote considerable space to excerpts from the interviews, which show how individuals themselves constructed their accounts.[12] This was consistent with my interest in giving prominence to the ways in which the actors made sense of their marriages and divorces rather than using interviewees' responses to elucidate prior sociological categories. As I wrote I felt a tension between the sociologist's interpretive voice and letting people's own understandings speak for themselves, and when I had to choose, I sought to allow those I interviewed to speak on their own behalf. Quoting extensively from narratives and other qualitative replies allows the reader to see how individuals themselves make meaning out of loss—a problem that the methodology of survey research cannot address.

Lengthy quotations from individual texts do not substitute for analysis of them, of course. I have shown that women and men construct marriage differently and that consequently they experience divorce in contrasting ways. In describing patterns across the interviews, I too have constructed a text and also a context—a big picture—in which I situate and interpret individuals.

Interviewees' texts are thus available to the reader both as evidence for my generalizations and because other readings of them are possible. Paul Rabinow and William Sullivan speak to this last point: "The text is plurivocal, open to several readings and to several constructions. But it is not infinite. Human action and interpretation are subject to many but not indefinitely many constructions. Any closure of the process through an external means is violence and often occurs. But just as interpretive social science is not subjectivism, neither is it simply intuitionism."[13] It is a testimony to the power of the texts that women and men created in this study that they are open to different readings, and I hope that the lengthy interview excerpts in this book will invite close analysis by others.

1. Making Sense of Divorce

1. Lawrence Stone argues that in the nineteenth century, divorce became a functional substitute for death and provided a way out when, as death rates declined, marriages were lasting longer and longer. Only after 1960 did divorce rates rise independently of death rates. For a discussion of divorce set in the historical perspective of mortality, see Lawrence Stone, *The Family, Sex, and Marriage: England 1500–1800* (New York: Harper & Row, 1977). For a comprehensive history of divorce in the Western world from the Reformation to the present, see Roderick Phillips, *Putting Asunder: A History of Divorce in Western Society* (New York: Cambridge University Press, 1988).

2. Peter Marris, *Loss and Change* (London: Routledge & Kegan Paul, 1974). The revised edition (1987) includes a new introduction, which expands and clarifies Marris's theoretical framework. See also Peter Marris, *Meaning and Action: Community Planning and Conceptions of Change* (London: Routledge & Kegan Paul, 1987).

3. C. Wright Mills, *The Sociological Imagination* (New York: Oxford University Press, 1959), 8. Unlike Mills, I am differentiating between "social" and "public," reserving the latter term for political affairs, relations with strangers, the state, and social policy issues, that is, life outside the "private" realm of family and friends. See Richard Sennett, *The Fall of Public Man* (New York: Vintage, 1974), 3–27. Feminists have argued that the distinction between public and private is, in fact, a deceptive one. See Barrie Thorne, "Feminist Rethinking of the Family: An Overview," in *Rethinking the Family: Some Feminist Questions*, ed. Barrie Thorne with Marilyn Yalom (New York: Longman, 1982), 1–24.

4. Andrew Cherlin, as quoted in Robert E. Tomasson, "A Lower Divorce Rate is Reported," *New York Times*, January 9, 1985. There is evidence that

both world wars and the Vietnam War had strong effects on the divorce rate, in each instance raising it to a new level. For a discussion of U.S. divorce trends over time and how demographers interpret them, see Teresa Castro and Larry Bumpass, "Recent Trends and Differentials in Marital Disruption," working paper 87-20, Center for Demography and Ecology, University of Wisconsin, Madison, June 1987. See Phillips, *Putting Asunder*, for a more general review of divorce trends, historical and cultural analysis of divorce, and comparisons across countries. Phillips notes that the official divorce rate bears little relationship to the frequency of private separations—a customary method in the past for resolving marital difficulties. Historically, the ability to obtain a divorce (or an annulment, in Catholic countries) was tied to social class and was typically available only to the rich and powerful. The poor could not afford divorces until legal aid became available around 1920. On divorce rates in England, see Lawrence Stone, "The Road to Polygamy," *New York Review of Books*, vol. 36, no. 3 (March 2, 1989), 12.

5. Stone, "The Road to Polygamy," 12.

6. Naomi Gerstel, "Divorce and Stigma," *Social Problems* 34 (1987): 172–186.

7. Lillian Rubin found this in the 1970s. See her *Worlds of Pain: Life in the Working-Class Family* (New York: Basic Books, 1976), 171–184. The trend toward greater participation in the labor force by women is not unrelated to divorce. As women enter the labor market, particularly at its upper end, where they have a chance to become self-supporting, they are more likely to divorce. See Andrew J. Cherlin, *Marriage, Divorce, Remarriage* (Cambridge: Harvard University Press, 1981).

8. Arlie Hochschild, with Anne Machung, *The Second Shift: Working Parents and the Revolution at Home* (New York: Viking, 1989).

9. U.S. Bureau of the Census, *Statistical Abstracts of the United States, 1985: National Data Book and Guide to Sources* (Washington, D.C.: U.S. Government Printing Office), 455. There is a large literature on the topic of women, divorce, and poverty. See Irwin Garfinkel and Sara S. McLanahan, *Single Mothers and Their Children: A New American Dilemma* (Washington, D.C.: Urban Institute, 1986); Ruth Sidel, *Women and Children Last: The Plight of Poor Women in Affluent America* (New York: Penguin, 1987); Lenore Weitzman, *The Divorce Revolution* (New York: Free Press, 1985).

10. For a review of the data on divorce and illness and a discussion of the complex issues of interpretation and causal order, see Catherine Kohler Riessman and Naomi Gerstel, "Marital Dissolution and Health: Do Males or Females Have Greater Risk?" *Social Science and Medicine* 20 (1985): 627–635. It may also be true that divorced women go to doctors more, and di-

vorced men go to hospitals more, for reasons other than increased illness and depression (e.g., in marriage individuals may look to spouses for a remedy for the same symptoms). On the flight from marriage, see Bryce J. Christensen, "The Costly Retreat from Marriage," *Public Interest* 91 (1988): 59–66.

11. Major works on the stress paradigm are: Leonard I. Pearlin, Morton A. Lieberman, Elizabeth G. Menaghan, and Joseph T. Mullan, "The Stress Process," *Journal of Health and Social Behavior* 22 (1981): 337–356; Leonard I. Pearlin and Carol S. Aneshensel, "Coping and Social Supports: Their Functions and Applications," in *Applications of Social Science to Clinical Medicine and Health Policy,* ed. L. H. Aiken and D. Mechanic (New Brunswick: Rutgers University Press, 1986), 417–437. For a review of the complex gender issues in stress research, see Susan Gore and Mary Ellen Colten, "Gender, Stress, and Distress: Social Relational Influences," in *The Social Context of Coping,* ed. J. Eckenrode (New York: Plenum, forthcoming).

12. For examples of these measurement approaches, see Leonard I. Pearlin and Carmi Schooler, "The Structure of Coping," *Journal of Health and Social Behavior* 19 (1978): 2–21; Richard S. Lazarus and Susan Folkman, *Stress, Appraisal, and Coping* (New York: Springer, 1984). On Aaron Antonovsky's approach, see his *Unraveling the Mystery of Health: How People Manage Stress and Stay Well* (San Francisco: Jossey-Bass, 1987). George Brown and colleagues also bypass the question of the personal meaning of life events in their otherwise contextual approach. For a discussion of this issue and a critique of stress research on the question of personal meaning, see Catherine Kohler Riessman, "Life Events, Meaning, and Narrative: The Case of Infidelity and Divorce," *Social Science and Medicine* 29 (1989): 743–751.

13. Antonovsky, *Unraveling the Mystery.* For examples of early work on stress physiology, see Walter B. Cannon, "Stresses and Strains and Homeostasis," *American Journal of Medical Science* 189 (1935): 1–14; Hans Selye, *The Stress of Life* (New York: McGraw Hill, 1956).

14. Robert S. Weiss, *Marital Separation* (New York: Basic Books, 1975), 55; idem, *Going It Alone: The Family Life and Social Situation of the Single Parent* (New York: Basic Books, 1979), 263. For examples of research that links divorce to political and economic issues, see Terry Arendell, *Mothers and Divorce: Legal, Economic, and Social Dilemmas* (Berkeley: University of California Press, 1986); Weitzman, *Divorce Revolution.* The two positive studies are Janet A. Kohen, Carol A. Brown, and Roslyn Feldberg, "Divorced Mothers: The Costs and Benefits of Female Family Control," in *Single Life: Unmarried Adults in Social Context,* ed. P. Stein (New York: St. Martin's Press, 1981); Jean Baker Miller, "Psychological Recovery in Low-Income

Single Parents," *American Journal of Orthopsychiatry* 52 (1982): 346–352. Although their study does not analyze in any detail the positive outcomes of divorce, Spanier and Thompson used the affect balance scale and found that positive and negative affects coexisted in their sample. See Graham B. Spanier and Linda Thompson, *Parting: The Aftermath of Separation and Divorce* (Beverly Hills: Sage, 1984), 213–216.

15. See Judith S. Wallerstein and Sandra Blakeslee, *Second Chances: Men, Women, and Children a Decade after Divorce* (New York: Ticknor & Fields, 1989). There are a number of problems with this study. Like others in the divorce literature, it uses a sample of convenience, drawn from volunteers participating in a preventive intervention program. In the case of Wallerstein and Blakeslee's follow-up study, the authors go to great pains to argue that this is not a clinical sample and, consequently, represents "divorce under the best of circumstances" (p. xiii), especially given that the respondents are from a white, middle-class community that borders on San Francisco. Yet the sample was recruited from referrals from schools and attorneys, the families participated in a "planning program for children" run by professional psychologists and clinical social workers, and perhaps most significantly, the respondents in the study are sometimes referred to as "clients" (p. xiii) and the interviews as "sessions" (p. 312). Moreover, because there is no comparison group of similar-aged children whose parents have not divorced, it is by no means clear that these children's difficulties were "caused" by divorce. For a critical review of the book that discusses some of these problems, see Carol Tavris, "A Remedy But Not a Cure," *New York Times*, book review section, February 26, 1989, 13–14.

16. See William J. Goode, *Women in Divorce* (New York: Free Press, 1956); Mary J. Bane, *Here To Stay: American Families in the Twentieth Century* (New York: Basic Books, 1976); George Gilder, *Wealth and Poverty* (New York: Basic Books, 1981), chap. 6.

17. Weiss, *Marital Separation*, 14. Weiss suggests, but does not develop, the idea that accounts have a narrative form. He draws an analogy to a story, "a plot structure with a beginning, middle and end" (p. 15). Ironically, however, despite this seeming awareness of narrative structure, he uses traditional content analysis to analyze his data, bypassing the meanings encoded in the form of talk. On attribution theory, see John H. Harvey, Ann L. Weber, Kerry L. Yarkin, and Bonnie E. Stewart, "An Attributional Approach to Relationship Breakdown and Dissolution," in *Personal Relationships*, vol. 4, *Dissolving Personal Relationships*, ed. S. Duck (New York: Academic Press, 1982), 107–128.

18. Research in the "complaint tradition" includes Bernard L. Bloom, Robert L. Niles, and Anna M. Tatcher, "Sources of Marital Dissatisfaction among Newly Separated Persons," *Journal of Family Issues* 6 (1985): 359–373;

Frank F. Furstenberg and Graham B. Spanier, *Recycling the Family: Remarriage after Divorce* (Beverly Hills: Sage, 1984); Goode, *Women in Divorce;* Gay C. Kitson, "Marital Discord and Marital Separation: A County Survey," *Journal of Marriage and the Family* 47 (1985): 693–700; Gay C. Kitson and Marvin B. Sussman, "Marital Complaints, Demographic Characteristics, and Symptoms of Mental Distress in Divorce," *Journal of Marriage and the Family* 44 (1982): 87–101; George Levinger, "Sources of Marital Dissatisfaction among Applications for Divorce," *American Journal of Orthopsychiatry* 36 (1966): 803–807; George J. McCall, "Becoming Unrelated: The Management of Bond Dissolution," in *Personal Relationships*, vol. 4, *Dissolving Personal Relationships*, ed. Duck; Spanier and Thompson, *Parting;* Majda Thurnher, Cathy Birtley Fenn, Joseph Melichar, and David A. Chiriboga, "Sociodemographics: Perspectives on Reasons for Divorce," *Journal of Divorce* 6 (1983): 25–35.

19. Marris, *Loss and Change*, 1987 ed., 7–8. Marris defines meaning as "a comprehensive, integrative structure of interpretations which each of us elaborates through experience and depends upon for confidence to act" (ibid., 6). This definition assumes that meanings reside in the teller and are relatively "fixed"—a perspective that Chapter 3 challenges.

20. Tamotsu Shibutani, *Social Processes: An Introduction to Sociology* (Berkeley: University of California Press, 1986), 11; see also Bertram J. Cohler, "Personal Narrative and Life Course," in *Life-Span Development and Behavior*, ed. P. B. Bales and O. G. Brim (New York: Academic Press, 1982), 228. On scientists, see Susan Leigh Star, "Simplification in Scientific Work," *Social Studies in Science* 13 (1983): 205–228. For classic treatments of the problem of social reality and action in problematic situations, see W. I. Thomas and Dorothy S. Thomas, *The Child in America: Behavior Problems and Programs* (New York: Knopf, 1978), 572; George H. Mead, *Mind, Self and Society* (Chicago: University of Chicago Press, 1934); Peter L. Berger and Thomas Luckmann, *The Social Construction of Reality* (New York: Doubleday, 1966).

21. On narratives as ways to achieve coherence, see Cohler, "Personal Narrative"; Roy Schafer, "Narration in the Psychoanalytic Dialogue," in *On Narrative*, ed. W. J. T. Mitchell (Chicago: University of Chicago Press, 1981), 25–49; Donald P. Spence, *Narrative Truth and Historical Truth: Meaning and Interpretation in Psychoanalysis* (New York: Norton, 1982). See also Elliot G. Mishler, "Meaning in Context: Is There Any Other Kind?" *Harvard Educational Review* 49 (1979): 1–19.

22. Marris, *Loss and Change*, 1987 ed., xii; Shibutani, *Social Processes*, 58.

23. Although I am treating the two traditions as distinct for heuristic purposes, sociologists in fact generally assume that personal meanings are rooted in both social and historical contexts. For classic writings on this

topic, see Mead, *Mind, Self and Society;* Anselm L. Strauss, *Mirrors and Masks: The Search for Identity* (Glencoe, Ill.: Free Press, 1959); Berger and Luckman, *Social Construction of Reality;* Herbert Blumer, *Symbolic Interaction: Perspective and Method* (Englewood Cliffs, N.J.: Prentice-Hall, 1969).

24. For a review of symbolic interactionists' views on this topic, see Shibutani, *Social Processes.* On the contextual basis of motives, see C. Wright Mills, "Situated Actions and Vocabularies of Motive," *American Sociological Review* 5 (1940): 904–913.

25. Erving Goffman, *The Presentation of Self in Everyday Life* (New York: Doubleday, 1959). For a case study that utilizes Goffman but also criticizes the framework for its Machiavellian views of the social actor, see Catherine Kohler Riessman, "Strategic Uses of Narrative in the Presentation of Self and Illness," *Social Science and Medicine,* forthcoming.

26. Melvin B. Scott and Stanford M. Lyman, "Accounts," *American Sociological Review* 46 (1968): 46–62; Erving Goffman, *Stigma: Notes on the Management of Spoiled Identity* (Englewood Cliffs, N.J.: Prentice-Hall, 1963); John P. Hewitt and Randall Stokes, "Disclaimers," *American Sociological Review* 40 (1975): 1–11.

27. Talcott Parsons and Robert F. Bales, *Family, Socialization, and the Interaction Process* (Glencoe, Ill.: Free Press, 1955). For a review of theories of the family and their problems, see Naomi Gerstel and Harriet Gross, *Commuter Marriage: A Study of Work and Family* (New York: Guilford Press, 1984), chap. 1. On inequality and marriage, see Rosanna Hertz, *More Equal Than Others: Women and Men in Dual-Career Marriages* (Berkeley: University of California Press, 1986). On power relations in the family, see Thorne, "Feminist Rethinking."

28. On "his" and "hers" marriage, see Jessie Bernard, *The Future of Marriage* (New York: Bantam, 1972). There is another tradition of feminist scholarship on the social construction of gender that is less central to this study, but nevertheless suggestive. Some sociologists argue that the world of two sexes, rather than being a product either of biology or of roles and socialization, is a result of socially shared, taken-for-granted methods used by everyone to construct reality. In other words, gender distinctions are socially accomplished in everyday life, achieved rather than ascribed, as people reproduce gendered relations in minute interactions with one another. This perspective alerts us to look for how divorcing women and men construct accounts of themselves and their spouses that reproduce both the social order and a gendered social order. For an analysis of gender as a socially constructed category, see Suzanne J. Kessler and Wendy McKenna, *Gender: An Ethnomethodological Approach* (Chicago: University of Chicago Press, 1978). For a discussion of different theoretical perspectives on gender, in-

cluding ethnomethodology, see Alexandra Todd and Sue Fisher, eds., *Gender and Discourse: The Power of Talk* (Norwood, N.J.: Ablex, 1988), 1–16.

29. Russell Jacoby, *Social Amnesia* (Boston: Beacon Press, 1975), 104.

30. On the historical context of motives, see Mills, "Situated Actions." The manner in which events are explained in society is a topic of central concern in symbolic interaction theory in sociology; for a review, see Shibutani, *Social Processes.*

31. Ira Shor and Paulo Friere, *Pedagogy for Liberation: Dialogues on Transforming Education* (South Hadley, Mass.: Bergin and Garvey, 1987); Arlie Russell Hochschild, "The Sociology of Feeling and Emotion: Selected Possibilities," in *Another Voice: Feminist Perspectives on Social Life and Social Science,* ed. M. Millman and R. M. Kanter (Garden City: Anchor/Doubleday, 1975), 280–307; Jeff Adams, *The Conspiracy of the Text: The Place of Narrative in the Development of Thought* (New York: Routledge & Kegan Paul, 1986), 5.

32. Elliot G. Mishler, *Research Interviewing: Context and Narrative* (Cambridge: Harvard University Press, 1986).

33. Mills, "Situated Actions," 910, emphasis added; Kenneth Burke, *Permanence and Change: An Anatomy of Purpose* (New York: New Republic, 1935), 32.

34. Gary Peller, "Reason and the Mob: The Politics of Representation," *Tikkun* 2, no. 3 (1987): 94; Clifford Geertz, *Works and Lives: The Anthropologist as Author* (Stanford: Stanford University Press, 1987).

35. Harold Garfinkel, "Studies of the Routine Grounds of Everyday Activities," *Studies in Ethnomethodology* (New York: Prentice-Hall, 1967), 36.

36. In the logical positivist tradition in social science, this problem has been formulated as how "interviewer effects" may "bias" findings. For an example of this approach, see Catherine Kohler Riessman, "Interviewer Effects in Psychiatric Epidemiology," *American Journal of Public Health* 69 (1979): 485–491. I thank Deborah Tannen for helping me with these formulations.

37. Arendell, *Mothers and Divorce;* Weitzman, *Divorce Revolution.*

38. For a critique of essentialism in women's studies, see Elizabeth V. Spelman, *Inessential Woman: Problems of Exclusion in Feminist Thought* (Boston: Beacon, 1988).

2. Mourning Different Dreams

1. Ann Swidler, "Love and Adulthood in American Culture," in *Themes of Work and Love in Adulthood,* ed. N. J. Smelser and E. H. Erikson (Cambridge: Harvard University Press, 1980), 120–147. For a somewhat different analysis of the history of love and gender differences, see Arlie Russell

Hochschild, "Attending to, Codifying, and Managing Feelings: Sex Differences in Love," in *Feminist Frontiers: Rethinking Sex, Gender, and Society*, ed. L. Richardson and V. Taylor (Reading, Mass.: Addison-Wesley, 1983), 250–262.

2. On the value of struggle, see Swidler, "Love and Adulthood." Others have also found similar assumptions about communication in women's talk about relationships. See Francesca Cancian, *Love in America: Gender and Self Development* (New York: Cambridge University Press, 1987); Lillian Rubin, *Intimate Strangers: Men and Women Together* (New York: Harper & Row, 1983).

3. David Halle, *America's Working Man: Work, Home, and Politics among Blue-Collar Property Owners* (Chicago: University of Chicago Press, 1984), 34–73.

4. Sara Ruddick, *Maternal Thinking: Toward a Politics of Peace* (Boston: Beacon Press, 1989).

5. For a fuller discussion of this Hispanic woman's account, especially the ways in which it is different in its organization from a white middle-class woman's account, see Catherine Kohler Riessman, "When Gender Is Not Enough," *Gender and Society* 1 (1987): 172–207.

6. Rubin, *Worlds of Pain*, 95.

7. This study's figure of active infidelity, 34 percent, is slightly lower than the incidence of self-reported extramarital sex in other studies of the divorced. Spanier and Thompson, in *Parting*, report that 38 percent of their sample (about equal percentages of women and men) reported engaging in extramarital coitus during the marriage. Differences between their findings and the findings here can be explained methodologically. I coded the frequency from qualitative data—its mention in the account; they specifically asked about affairs during the marriage.

8. For an analysis of how this belief operates in women's extramarital affairs, see Annette Lawson, *Adultery: An Analysis of Love and Betrayal* (New York: Basic Books, 1988); for more on women's tendency to link sex and love, see Cancian, *Love in America*; Rubin, *Intimate Strangers*.

9. Rubin, *Intimate Strangers*, 76.

10. See Scott and Lyman, "Accounts."

11. Deborah Belle, "Gender Differences in the Social Moderators of Stress," in *Gender and Stress*, ed. R. C. Barnett, L. Biener, and G. K. Baruch (New York: Free Press, 1987), 257–277.

12. For more on working-class couples' patterns of companionship and leisure in marriage, see Theodore Caplow and Howard M. Bahr, Bruce A. Chadwick, Reuben Hill, and Margaret Holmes Williamson, *Middletown Families: Fifty Years of Change and Continuity* (Minneapolis: University of Minnesota Press, 1982); Halle, *America's Working Man*; Mirra Komarovsky,

Blue-Collar Marriage (New York: Random House, 1967). On women as moral arbiters, see Carl N. Degler, *At Odds: Women and the Family in America from the Revolution to the Present* (New York: Oxford University Press, 1980), 26–27. Rubin (*Worlds of Pain*, 202) argues that working-class spouses do not go their separate ways in social activities: "Their leisure hours are more often spent together than in rigidly sex-segregated activities of earlier generations." The difference between the studies might be explained in a number of ways. Most obviously, the interviews here are with people from marriages that failed, whereas Rubin talked to couples who were still married. Sharing leisure may be an important dimension that in the working class differentiates those who stay married from those who divorce. Less obviously, interviewees here were engaged in developing accounts of their marital failures, and they were thus drawing on cultural themes of what a marriage "should" be like, including companionship in leisure. It may be that the working-class women and men in my sample seized upon this theme in reconstructing their experience to emphasize that their marriages were deviant and that they were justified in leaving them.

13. On men's dissatisfaction with sex in marriage, see Caplow et al., *Middletown Families*, 177. Lawrence Stone generalizes that in Western societies, "Men have tended to find it easier than women to separate the purely physical pleasures of sex from emotional commitment." He relates prostitution, and massage parlors in the modern period, to this male predilection. See Stone, "The Road to Polygamy," 12.

14. Phillips, *Putting Asunder*, 344–354; Lawson, *Adultery*, 35–62, 209–216.

15. For a full discussion of this case, see Riessman, "Strategic Uses of Narrative."

16. On gender roles in modern U.S. marriage and how these vary by class and race, see Hertz, *More Equal Than Others*; Hochschild, *Second Shift*; Carol Stack, *All Our Kin: Strategies for Survival in a Black Community* (New York: Harper & Row, 1974). For a critique of the public/private split in family research, see Thorne, *Rethinking the Family*.

17. This finding is consistent with previous research. Middle-class men may espouse expanded roles for women, but their behavior often belies these liberal beliefs; in Goode's words, "Educated men are likely to concede more rights ideologically than they in fact grant" (William J. Goode, "Why Men Resist," in *Rethinking the Family*, ed. Thorne, 20); see Hochschild, *Second Shift*.

18. Cherlin, *Marriage, Divorce, Remarriage*. Degler states that the "marriage least likely to disrupt is one in which the husband is the sole breadwinner" (*At Odds*, 454).

19. Rayna Rapp, "Family and Class in Contemporary America: Notes

toward an Understanding of Ideology," in *Rethinking the Family*, ed. Thorne, 168–187. For a review of research on the division of household tasks in marriage and some new data, see Hochschild, *Second Shift*, 1–10, 275–276.

20. On marriage as a joint enterprise, see Weitzman, *Divorce Revolution*. Given this relatively nonhierarchical emphasis, it is no accident that modern marriage evolved at the same time that democratic institutions of government were being forged in the United States. As Tocqueville observed on his visit to America in the early nineteenth century, "a species of equality prevails around the domestic hearth" (quoted in Degler, *At Odds*, 75). Even at that time the assumption was that although men and women differed in identity, and therefore differed in their "natural" roles, they were nevertheless equal. Whether separate can ever be equal has, of course, been a matter of considerable debate ever since. Nevertheless, an ideology of equality in marriage continues to dictate that marital partners should honor one another; further, the husband's and the wife's contributions to the marriage, however different, should both be valued.

21. On private and public patriarchy, see Carol Brown, "Mothers, Fathers and Children: From Private to Public Patriarchy," in *Women and Revolution*, ed. L. Sargent (Boston: South End Press, 1981). On invisible work, see Arlene Kaplan Daniels, "Invisible Work," *Social Problems* 34 (1987): 403–415; Martha Fowlkes, *Behind Every Successful Man* (New York: Columbia University Press, 1980).

22. The notion that violence is the ultimate act of inequality is from Letty Cottin Pogrebin, *Family Politics: Love and Power on the Intimate Frontier* (New York: McGraw-Hill, 1983). In the sample here, 16 percent of the cases where violence was mentioned, men were physically abusive by their own report (four cases, including one marital rape) or by women's reports (twelve cases, including one marital rape). In an additional 3 percent of the male cases, violence was strongly suspected, judging by the presence of restraining orders. In three cases, the wife initiated the physical violence, according to the men, and in five cases, the battering was reciprocal. These figures, based on the divorced, underestimate the incidence of physical violence in marriage. See Richard J. Gelles and Murray A. Straus, *Intimate Violence* (New York: Simon & Schuster, 1980); Murray A. Straus, Richard J. Gelles, and Susan Steinmetz, "A Marriage License Is a Hitting License," in *Family in Transition*, 5th ed., ed. S. Skolnick and J. H. Skolnick (Boston: Little, Brown, 1986), 290–303. Men in the sample generally have little to say about physical abuse of their wives, to either female or male interviewers. One exception is a man who tells a story to a woman interviewer about getting drunk and raping his wife on her birthday (he defines his actions as "rape"). Another exception is a narrative about physical violence told by a man to a woman interviewer. This account is analyzed in Chapter 3.

23. Thorne, *Rethinking the Family*, 18.

24. Leo Tolstoy, *Anna Karenina* (New York: Charles Scribner's, 1913), 1.

25. Clifford Geertz, "From the Native's Point of View: On the Nature of Anthropological Understanding," *Local Knowledge* (New York: Basic Books, 1983), 63.

26. As Dizard and Gadlin note, historian Lawrence Stone calls the emergent family arrangement that he observes among the late eighteenth-century English elite "companionate marriage," following a usage made popular by Ernest W. Burgess in his textbook written with Harvey J. Locke, *The Family: From Institution to Companionship* (New York: American Book Co., 1953). On this point, see Jan E. Dizard and Howard Gadlin, *Private Good/Public Good* (Amherst: University of Massachusetts Press, forthcoming).

27. Stone, "The Road to Polygamy," 12.

28. Nathaniel Branden, "A Vision of Romantic Love," in *The Psychology of Love*, ed. R. J. Sternberg and M. L. Barnes (New Haven: Yale University Press, 1988), 218–231.

29. Elaine Tyler May, *Great Expectations: Marriage and Divorce in Post-Victorian America* (Chicago: University of Chicago Press, 1980), 158. The material to follow is based primarily on Degler, *At Odds;* Edward Shorter, *The Making of the Modern Family* (New York: Basic Books, 1975); Stone, *The Family, Sex, and Marriage.* See these works for a more detailed analysis, and for other views, see Christopher Lasch, *Haven in a Heartless World: The Family Besieged* (New York: Basic Books, 1977); Eli Zaretsky, *Capitalism, the Family and Personal Life* (New York: Harper & Row, 1976).

30. Although there were important changes in nineteenth-century ideologies about women's sexuality (see Degler, *At Odds*), the evidence suggests that for women themselves sex existed not merely in the service of reproduction but became a source of pleasure in and of itself. On the redefinition of family in emotional terms, see Stone, *The Family, Sex, and Marriage*, chap. 6. There was a corresponding trend to treat children more kindly, as persons with feelings of their own. See Philip Ariès, *Centuries of Childhood: A Social History of Family Life* (New York: Random House, 1962). For more on marriage and divorce in the late nineteenth century, see May, *Great Expectations*. In this period many women were suspicious of divorce law reform: "They were fearful that it would enable their husbands to trade them in for younger wives, leaving them to end their days in loneliness and poverty. As it turned out, this prediction was not far from the truth" (Stone, "The Road to Polygamy," 13).

31. For more on what women gained and lost with the redefinition of femininity, see Nancy Cott, *The Bonds of Womanhood: Women's Sphere in New England, 1790–1835* (New Haven: Yale University Press, 1977). There is a

large literature on the class and ethnic variations in primacy and companionship in modern marriage. See Caplow et al., *Middletown Families;* Rubin, *World of Pain;* Stack, *All Our Kin;* Halle, *America's Working Man.*

32. On mutual reliance of spouses, see Caplow et al., *Middletown Families;* on the family as refuge, see Lasch, *Haven in a Heartless World;* on the self and love, see Robert N. Bellah, Richard Madsen, William M. Sullivan, Ann Swidler, and Steven M. Tipton, *Habits of the Heart: Individualism and Commitment in American Life* (New York: Harper & Row, 1985). For another perspective on the consequences of the retreat from public life into intimate relations, see Sennett, *Fall of Public Man.* On work on self, see Swidler, "Love and Adulthood."

33. On the companionate ideal as a middle-class phenomenon, see Rubin, *Worlds of Pain;* as infusing the working class as well, see Shorter, *Making of the Modern Family,* and Caplow et al., *Middletown Families.*

34. See Francis L. K. Hsu, as quoted in Sternberg and Barnes, *Psychology of Love,* 275–276.

35. See Nancy Chodorow, *The Reproduction of Mothering: Psychoanalysis and the Sociology of Gender* (Berkeley: University of California Press, 1978); Carol Gilligan, *In a Different Voice: Psychological Theory and Women's Development* (Cambridge: Harvard University Press, 1982); Jean Baker Miller, *Toward a New Psychology of Women* (Boston: Beacon Press, 1976).

36. Rubin, *Intimate Strangers,* 76; Canacian, *Love in America,* chap. 5.

37. Rapp, "Family and Class," 173.

38. Gilligan studies a "highly educated sample." Chodorow's evidence comes from psychoanalytic accounts that, in turn, are based on observations of middle- and upper middle-class patients. See Spelman, *Inessential Woman,* chap. 4, for a critique of Chodorow's formulations on this point and others.

39. For a classic theoretical analysis of work and alienation, see Harry Braverman, *Labor and Monopoly Capital* (New York: Monthly Review Press, 1974). For a vivid account, see Barbara Garson, *All the Livelong Day: The Meaning and Demeaning of Routine Work* (New York: Doubleday, 1975). On gender, class, and leisure, see Rubin, *Worlds of Pain;* Hochschild, *Second Shift.*

40. See Chodorow, *Reproduction of Mothering;* Nancy Julia Chodorow, "Divorce, Oedipal Asymmetries, and the Marital Age Gap," in *Toward a New Psychology of Men: Psychoanalytic and Social Perspectives,* ed. R. M. Friedman and L. Lerner (New York: Guilford, 1986). For more on the expectations for emotional exclusivity in marriage, and how this varies by class and gender, see Naomi Gerstel, "Divorce, Gender, and Social Integration," *Gender and Society* 2 (1988): 343–367.

41. On working-class kinship structures, see Elizabeth Bott, *Family and Social Network* (London: Tavistock Publications, 1957); Komarovsky, *Blue-Collar Marriage*.

42. May, *Great Expectations*.

43. Michael Moerman, *Talking Culture: Ethnography and Conversation Analysis* (Philadelphia: University of Pennsylvania Press, 1988). For a different theoretical perspective, see Aafke Komter, "Hidden Power in Marriage," *Gender and Society* 3 (1989): 187–216.

44. For an early analysis of this problem in the feminist literature, see Constantina Safilios-Rothchild, "Companionate Marriages and Sexual Equality: Are They Compatible?" in *Toward a Sociology of Women*, ed. C. Safilios-Rothchild (Lexington, Mass.: Xerox College Publishing, 1972), 63–70. For a more recent treatment of the issues, see Diane Ehrensaft, *Parenting Together: Women and Men Sharing the Care of Their Children* (New York: Free Press, 1987), 37–73.

45. Cancian, *Love in America*.

46. Mills, *Sociological Imagination*, 12. For more on the love myth as the resolution for contradictions, see Swidler, "Love and Adulthood."

3. The Teller's Problem

1. Goffman, *Presentation of Self in Everyday Life*, 9–10. This chapter may not contain enough attention to form for narrative analysts but may seem too technical to other readers. I have tried to strike a balance; some of the more technical material appears in the notes. There are a number of approaches to the structure of talk. The approach here was chosen to show important differences in how speakers construct narratives about stressful events to those who may not be specialists in narrative analysis.

2. For more on the question of "difference" in gender studies, see Spelman, *Inessential Woman*.

3. Katharine Young makes an important distinction between the "story-realm" (the realm of the narrative discourse and its intersubjective world of sociality and communication) and the "taleworld" (in which events the story recounts are understood to have transpired). Teller and listener create an enclave in the conversation so that the narrator can move into the story realm, and then move through that realm into the taleworld. Young draws on phenomenology and particularly on Schutz's notion of the existence of different realms of being, or multiple realities. See Katharine Galloway Young, *Taleworlds and Storyrealms* (The Netherlands: Martinus Nijhoff, 1987).

4. It is an empirical question whether speakers tend to use one type of

narrative or whether they use different types depending on context and strategic aims. From examining the narratives in this study, my sense is that the latter is true, but this issue warrants further research. Another topic needing more research is whether there are systematic differences in narrative genres between women and men—which I briefly looked for but did not find.

5. Dennie Wolf, pers. comm., May 10, 1988.

6. Kenneth Burke, *A Rhetoric of Motives* (New York: Prentice-Hall, 1952). For a synthesis and discussion of Burke's theory on the sociology of language, see Hugh Dalziel Duncan, *Communication and Social Order* (New York: Bedminster Press, 1962), 143–176. For a somewhat different view that emphasizes dramatistic roles and how they persuade audiences, see Theodore R. Sarbin, "Emotion and Act: Roles and Rhetoric," in *The Social Construction of Emotions*, ed. R. Harré (New York: Blackwell, 1986), 83–97.

7. Some use the term "story" synonymously with "narrative." I am distinguishing between the two; here "story" refers to a particular genre of narrative, as explained in the text. Not all interviewees used narrative forms to account for their divorces. Some used a "short form," an enumeration of marital complaints, perhaps expecting that this was what the research interviewer wanted to hear. Further research is needed to specify the characteristics of settings, tellers, and listeners that generate narrative as opposed to non-narrative accounts. For more on invited stories of divorce, see E. C. Cuff and D. W. Francis, "Some Features of 'Invited Stories' about Marital Breakdown," *International Journal of Sociology of Language* 18 (1978): 111–133.

8. Hayden White, "The Value of Narrativity in the Representation of Reality," in *On Narrative*, ed. W. J. T. Mitchell (Chicago: University of Chicago Press, 1980), 1; James P. Gee, "The Narrativization of Experience in the Oral Style," *Journal of Education* 167 (1985): 11. For more on meaning and narrative retelling, see Mishler, *Research Interviewing*, appendix; Harold Rosen, "The Autobiographic Impulse," in *Linguistics in Context: Connecting Observation and Understanding*, ed. D. Tannen (Norwood, N. J.: Ablex, 1988), 69–88. For an example of different theoretical approaches to narrative, see Mitchell, *On Narrative*; Dan P. McAdams and Richard L. Ochberg, eds., *Psychobiography and Life Narratives*, special issue of *Journal of Personality* 56, no. 1 (1988); Young, *Taleworlds and Storyrealms*.

9. For a beginning discussion of narrative genres, see Livia Polanyi, *Telling the American Story: A Structural and Cultural Analysis of Conversational Storytelling* (Norwood, N.J.: Ablex, 1985), 10–12; for a discussion of rhetorical devices, see pp. 12–16. Although temporality is usually seen as a defining characteristic of narrative, some have demonstrated that narratives can be

organized around associated topics rather than time. These forms of telling have been observed particularly among minority group members. See Sarah Michaels, "'Sharing Time': Children's Narrative Styles and Differential Access to Literacy," *Language and Society* 10 (1981): 423–442; Riessman, "When Gender Is Not Enough." For more on stories as a form of conversational discourse, see William Labov, "The Transformation of Experience in Narrative Syntax," in *Language in the Inner City: Studies in Black English Vernacular*, ed. W. Labov (Philadelphia: University of Pennsylvania Press, 1972); Livia Polanyi, "Conversational Storytelling," in *Handbook of Discourse Analysis: Discourse and Dialogue*, vol. 3, ed. T. A. Van Dijk (London: Academic Press, 1985), 189.

10. There are no universally agreed-upon rules for representing speech as written text. The effort here is to strike a balance between providing a readable transcript and including the detail necessary to do a narrative analysis. Because the emphasis is on narrative structure and interaction, there is less attention to intonation, volume, pacing, and other features of the quality of speech. Speakers are identified by name (of narrator) and by *Int.* (for interviewer); sometimes an abbreviation of the narrator's name is used. Punctuation marks are used when intonation clearly marks the end of an utterance, e.g., a full stop, a question mark, or quotation marks indicating someone else's voice. Italic indicates a marked increase in loudness and/or emphasis. A dash is used to indicate a break-off, interruption, or overlapping speech. Pauses are distinguished as (p) for a pause of 3 seconds or less and (P) for a pause of more than 3 seconds. Nonlexicals are interviewer utterances during narrator's speech, and are enclosed in parentheses and indicated by *I* (e.g., *I*: uh-huh).

11. For a discussion of the legal views of rape, see Susan Estrich, *Real Rape* (Cambridge: Harvard University Press, 1988), chap. 6; on the definition of rape as a crime, see David Margolick, "Rape in a Marriage Is No Longer within Law," *New York Times*, December 23, 1986; on women as sexual property and the law, see Diana E. H. Russell, *Rape in Marriage* (New York: Macmillan, 1982), chap. 2.

12. Paul Ricoeur, *Hermeneutics and the Human Sciences: Essays on Language, Action and Interpretation*, ed. and trans. J. B. Thompson (New York: Cambridge University Press, 1981), 278.

13. See Trudy Mills, "The Assault on the Self: Stages of Coping with Battering Husbands," *Qualitative Sociology* 8 (1985): 103–123.

14. Elaine Hilberman Carmen, "Overview: The 'Wife-Beater's Wife' Reconsidered," in *The Gender Gap in Psychotherapy: Social Realities and Psychological Processes*, ed. P. P. Rieker and E. H. Carmen (New York: Plenum, 1984), 225.

15. For a social analysis of rape, see Pauline B. Bart and Patricia H. O'Brien, *Stopping Rape* (Elmsford, N.Y.: Pergamon Press, 1985); Margaret T. Gordon and Stephanie Riger, *The Female Fear* (New York: Free Press, 1989).

16. I would like to thank G. Rosenwald and R. Ochberg for this observation.

17. See Mills, "The Assault on the Self." Elaine Hilberman Carmen makes this observation in her study of sixty clinical cases of abused wives: "The violent encounter with another person's loss of control of aggression precipitates great anxiety about one's own controls. . . . In the life experiences of battered women, there is little perceived or real difference between affect, fantasy, and action. Thus it is not surprising that fear of loss of control was a universal concern [in her sample]. These fears were often expressed in vague, abstract terms but were unmistakably linked to aggression" (Carmen, "Overview," 225). In Tessa's narrative, it is interesting to speculate why there is such a difference in relative elaboration in the three episodes of the narrative. I tend to think that the rape story is more central to the underlying theme of the episodic narrative—powerlessness—than the lack of food or even the punching stories (in the latter Tessa surmounts her powerlessness, albeit in a way that is unacceptable to her). Consequently, Tessa gives the first episode more detail, using great care in setting it up with a habitual narrative and telling the story with a thoroughness of evaluation. But it could also be that the latter two stories get briefer treatment because Tessa has, in some sense, already made her point; the latter two episodes, in this view, are merely flanking portraits. I thank Dennie Wolf for her insights about this narrative.

18. For more on linked stories, and the application of this structure to the narrative of a DES daughter, see Susan E. Bell, "Becoming a Political Woman: The Reconstruction and Interpretation of Experience through Stories," in *Gender and Discourse: The Power of Talk,* ed. Todd and Fisher, 97–123.

19. For more on societal conditions and their relation to a text, see Sara Lennox, "Feminist Scholarship and *Germanistik,*" *German Quarterly* 62 (1989): 158–170; for a critique of the essentialist view of women in feminist work, see Spelman, *Inessential Woman;* for a discussion of the implications of this case study for clinical research, see Catherine Kohler Riessman, "From Victim to Survivor: A Woman's Narrative Reconstruction of Marital Sexual Abuse," *Smith College Studies in Social Work* 59 (1989): 232–251.

20. For the full transcript and the analysis of synchrony between the interviewer and Susan, see Riessman, "When Gender Is Not Enough."

21. Although temporal sequencing may be the dominant form for recapitulating past experience in a narrative, it is not the only form. For an

analysis of an episodically structured narrative told by a working-class Puerto Rican woman that is misunderstood by a middle-class listener, see ibid.

22. I thank Deborah Tannen for bringing this last point to my attention.

23. Betty Friedan, *The Feminine Mystique* (New York: Dell, 1963), chap. 1.

24. Charlotte Linde, "Private Stories in Public Discourse," *Poetics* 15 (1986): 187.

25. On entrance and exit talk, see Gail Jefferson, "Sequential Aspects of Storytelling in Conversation," in *Studies in the Organization of Conversational Interaction*, ed. J. Schenkein (New York: Academic Press, 1979), 219–248. Jefferson synthesized this concept from the lecture notes of Harvey Sacks.

26. Sociolinguists make the point that an event must be "reportable" or "storyworthy" to warrant the teller's holding the floor for such a lengthy time. The narrator must counter the objection, "So what?" (On this point, see Labov, "The Transformation of Experience"; Linde, "Private Stories"; Polanyi, *Telling the American Story*.) In research interviews, of course, interviewees are expected to hold the floor, though typically not for very lengthy turns, and the telling of stories is usually not expected. (See Mishler, *Research Interviewing*.) More work is needed on how stories function in narrative accounts. The assumption has been that there is a correspondence between events in the world and how they get storified (though see Young, *Taleworlds and Storyrealms*). Although many stress that events must be reportable to warrant a story, the opposite is also true; tellers can make events reportable by storifying them. The point is that "reportability" does not exist independent of context. Presumably *anything* in an interview is reportable, or at least can be made so.

27. For more on marriage as work, see Swidler, "Love and Adulthood."

28. This speaks to the issue of when narratives emerge in research interviews; see the Appendix. Al's narrative would in all probability not have been recorded had traditional interview practice been followed. See also Mishler, *Research Interviewing*.

29. Marianne A. Paget, "Experience and Knowledge," *Human Studies* 6 (1983): 67–90.

30. These are state clauses in Polanyi's framework. See Polanyi, *Telling the American Story*.

31. Although line 27 is not in the simple past tense, it is nevertheless an event clause (Polanyi, *Telling the American Story*) in my reading, because it describes the narrator's affect at the discrete moment in the story and thus is not durative. This demonstrates that the verb tense is not always a sufficient indicator of the structural parts of a story, contrary to what Labov ("The Transformation of Experience") suggests. I interpret lines 28–29, in which Al describes listening to music, as state clauses, but they can also be seen as

an action. In my interpretation they are one more instance of a structural dynamic in this narrative: the speaker begins to tell the plot, backs off to orient, begins to tell again, and backs off, in repeated cycles. As I argue in the text, this structure builds tension, just as it re-creates the feeling tone of the storyworld.

32. For more on the recipient design of stories, as well as the broader issue of context-dependence of stories in conversation, see Jefferson, "Sequential Aspects," and her review of Harvey Sacks's work. For a summary of several of his lectures (compiled by Jefferson and published posthumously), see Harvey Sacks, "Some Considerations of a Story told in Ordinary Conversation," *Poetics* 15 (1986): 127–138. Note how Al steps out of the storyworld a little later on as well (see lines 46–57), controlling the listener's interpretation of his wife's and his mutual violence by the commentary he provides.

33. Linde, "Private Stories," 187. In this article Linde also discusses how an expert theory—like psychoanalysis—eventually becomes part of common knowledge and hence available to narrators.

34. For a vivid instance of this, see Elliot G. Mishler, "Work, Identity, and Narrative: An Artist-Craftsman's Story," in *Storied Lives*, ed. G. Rosenwald and R. Ochberg (New Haven: Yale University Press, forthcoming); Jerome Bruner, *Actual Minds, Possible Worlds* (Cambridge: Harvard University Press, 1986), 25.

35. Others have argued in a different way that accounts of difficult experiences are, at least in part, an interactional accomplishment, jointly constructed by interviewee and interviewer, and this can be seen in the talk between them. See Susan E. Bell, "Narratives of Health and Illness: DES Daughters Tell Stories," paper presented at annual meeting of Sociologists for Women in Society, Washington, D.C., August 1985; Mishler, *Research Interviewing*; Paget, "Experience and Knowledge."

36. As J. B. Thompson notes, Paul Ricoeur identifies two hermeneutic approaches. One (exemplified in Freud, Marx, and Nietzsche) involves the "demystification of a meaning . . . that is presented in the form of a disguise." There is a skepticism toward the given, a "distrust of the symbol as a dissimulation of the real." Thus the goal is to "transcend this falsity through reductive interpretation and critique." Another approach to hermeneutics (the one adopted here) involves restoring meaning "addressed to the interpreter in the form of a message. [It] is animated by faith, by a willingness to listen, and is characterized by a respect for the symbol as a revelation of the sacred." See Ricoeur, *Hermeneutics and the Human Sciences*, 6. I thank Elliot Mishler for bringing these distinctions to my attention.

37. This is the approach of story grammarians. For an example, see Jean M. Mandler and Nancy Johnson, "Remembrance of Things Parsed: Story

Structure and Recall," *Cognitive Psychology* 9 (1977): 111–151. For a critique of the tradition that reduces narrative to memory storage, see Allyssa McCabe, "Narrative Structure as a Way of Understanding," in *New Directions in Developing Narrative Structure*, ed. A. McCabe and C. Peterson (Hillsdale, N.J.: Erlbaum, forthcoming).

38. There is some disagreement in the literature about time and the ontological status of narratives, that is, the correspondence between event sequences and storied accounts of them. In contrast to Labov ("The Transformation of Experience"), Polanyi argues that the order of the events mirrors the order in which they are *to be interpreted* as having taken place (see "Conversational Storytelling"). Young goes further and argues that talk itself constructs the events—that all we have is the story (see *Taleworlds and Storyrealms*).

39. For an explication of the moral element in narratives, see Geoffrey Baruch, "Moral Tales: Parents' Stories of Encounters with the Health Professions," *Sociology of Health and Illness* 3 (1981): 275–295; Gareth Williams, "The Genesis of Chronic Illness: Narrative Reconstruction," *Sociology of Health and Illness* 6 (1984): 175–200.

4. Personal Trauma in Women and Men

1. Marris, *Loss and Change;* idem, *Meaning and Action*, preface.

2. Geertz, "From the Native's Point of View," 57. Geertz borrows the distinction between "experience-near" and "experience-distant" from the psychoanalyst Heinz Kohut.

3. Some investigators prefer the term "demoralization" to psychological distress or depression, because scales typically correlate highly with measures of low self-esteem, helplessness-hopelessness, sadness, and anxiety. For more on this issue, see Bruce Link and Bruce P. Dohrenwend, "Formulating Hypotheses about the True Prevalence of Demoralization in the United States," in *Mental Illness in the United States: Epidemiological Estimates*, ed. B. P. Dohrenwend, B. S. Dohrenwend, M. Schwartz-Gould, B. Link, R. Neugebauer, and R. Wunsch-Hitzig (New York: Praeger, 1980), 114–132. I use the terms "depressed," "distressed," "personal trauma," and "levels of symptoms" interchangeably in this text. It should be clear, however, that I am not necessarily referring to clinical states with these categories. See ibid. for a discussion of the difference between psychological disorder as clinicians understand and measure it and the summary scale approach used in surveys of the general population. Regarding the relationship between marital status and psychological distress, there are complex issues of causal order. Yet there is evidence from longitudinal research (a married

sample was followed prospectively) that depression among the divorced largely reflects negative life conditions, rather than preexisting deficits. See Elizabeth G. Menaghan and Morton A. Lieberman, "Changes in Depression Following Divorce: A Panel Study," *Journal of Marriage and the Family* 48 (1986): 319–328.

4. National Center for Health Statistics, *Basic Data on Depressive Symptomatology, United States, 1974–1975*, Vital and Health Statistics, series 11, number 216 (Washington, D.C.: U.S. Government Printing Office, 1980).

5. The *p* values are results of tests of significance using analysis of variance. Although the focus of this analysis is on the conditions of life after separation and their relationship to depression, I examined some other factors, including how the decision to separate was made (as defined by the interviewee). There was no relationship between this factor and depression, for women or for men. Regarding women's significantly higher rates, considerable research documents that, overall, women report more depression in general population surveys. For a review, see Myrna M. Weissman and Gerald Klerman, "Sex Differences in Depression," *Archives of General Psychiatry* 34 (1977): 98–111. There are exceptions to this trend, notably when women's status and responsibility in the family vary from traditional patterns. See Sarah Rosenfield, "Sex Differences in Depression: Do Women Always Have Higher Rates?: *Journal of Health and Social Behavior* 21 (1980): 33–42.

6. Some researchers have argued that women's greater exposure to stressors and enduring life strains is a major factor in explaining their higher rates of depression in community studies. See Paul Cleary and David Mechanic, "Sex Differences in Psychological Distress among Married People," *Journal of Health and Social Behavior* 22 (1983): 379–393; Walter R. Gove and Jeanette R. Tudor, "Adult Sex Roles and Mental Illness," *American Journal of Sociology* 78 (1973): 812–835; Leonard I. Pearlin, "Sex Roles and Depression," in *Proceedings of the Fourth Life-Span Developmental Psychology Conference*, ed. N. Datan and L. Ginsberg (New York: Academic Press, 1975). Other investigators have argued against the differential exposure hypothesis. See Barbara S. Dohrenwend, "Social Status and Stressful Life Events," *Journal of Personality and Social Psychology* 9 (1973): 203–214; Ronald C. Kessler, "Stress, Social Status, and Psychological Distress," *Journal of Health and Social Behavior* 20 (1979): 259–272. For a review of these and other issues in stress research, see Gore and Colten, "Gender, Stress, and Distress." For more on the empirical relationship between persistent life circumstances and psychological distress among the divorced, see Leonard I. Pearlin and Joyce S. Johnson, "Marital Status, Life Strains, and Depression," *American Sociological Review* 42 (1977): 704–715; Blair Wheaton,

"Where Work and Family Meet: Stress across Social Roles," in *Stress between Work and Family*, ed. J. Eckenrode and S. Gore (New York: Plenum, forthcoming); Gay C. Kitson, ed., issue devoted to adjustment to widowhood and divorce, *Journal of Family Issues* 10 (1989). For a review of research on parenting and psychological well-being, see Sara McLanahan and Julia Adams, "Parenthood and Psychological Well-Being," *Annual Review of Sociology* 5 (1987): 237–257.

7. Research on the mental health of custodial fathers (a small group in all studies) tends to be inconsistent. Pearlin and Johnson, "Marital Status, Life Strains," found single fathers to be similar to single mothers in depression levels. Regarding the effects of children for men in general after divorce, Spanier and Thompson found none of their child-related variables related to psychological well-being for men, though they were for women; see *Parting*, 222–223.

8. Financial strain was measured with a five-item summary scale, adapted from Pearlin and Johnson, "Marital Status, Life Strains." It asks how often the person does not have enough money to afford: (1) food; (2) medical care; (3) clothing; (4) leisure activities; and (5) furniture or household equipment that needs replacing. Response categories are never; once in a while; fairly often; and very often. Although a measure of perceived economic status, it is also significantly correlated with per capita income ($r = .58$). Spanier and Thompson, *Parting*, found that financial insecurity and strain, rather than actual income, was the critical circumstance that compromised psychological well-being in their sample.

9. Sixteen percent of the women said they were receiving alimony payments, and 82 percent of the women with children said they were receiving child-support payments (not all were receiving the full amount or receiving them regularly). These are somewhat higher figures than reported by others (e.g., Weitzman, *Divorce Revolution*), perhaps because my sample includes people who had been separated no more than three years. Recent Census Bureau figures indicate that 71 percent of white women were awarded child-support payments in 1985, but less than half actually got the full amount. See *A Call for Action* (Washington, D.C.: Children's Defense Fund, 1988), 11. Here, the measure of worry about support payments taps a specific worry, not a generalized tendency to worry. Its pattern of correlation with the CES-D scale was different (and significantly greater) than the other items about worries (about job, time pressures, housework). Thus it is conceptually and empirically distinct from depression. Also, worry about support payments is sufficiently independent of perceived financial strain to suggest that it is measuring a separate dimension of money worry (r of financial strain and worry about support is .24 for women). There is a trend

for the small group of single and joint-custody fathers to be more depressed if they also worry about making support payments, though this association is not statistically significant. For most of the men, worry about financial responsibility to their families is not related to depression.

10. The measure of help is based on the work of Claude Fisher (*To Dwell among Friends*, Chicago: University of Chicago Press, 1982) and consists of the total number of people named by interviewees who had helped them in the last month with one or more of nine specific tasks, which included both practical and personal types of aid. For a full description of the measure, see Naomi Gerstel, "Divorce and Kin Ties: The Importance of Gender," *Journal of Marriage and the Family* 50 (1988): 209–219.

11. The square of the multiple correlation coefficient tells us the percent of variance in the dependent variable (depression) that is predicted on the basis of the combined effects of the independent variables (children, financial strain, worry about support payments, help, and years of education). Given the sample size, the results should be viewed with caution.

12. Mills, *Sociological Imagination*. There is considerable debate in the literature about the extent of emotional difficulties that children from divorced families have, and to what degree this is attributable to economic as opposed to psychological factors. For a discussion of this issue, see Arendell, *Mothers and Divorce*, 86–87.

13. Jean Baker Miller, "Women and Power," Works in Progress Series, Stone Center for Developmental Services and Studies, Wellesley College, 1982. For a commentary on self-in-relation theory and a critique of its lack of attention to the variety of women's experiences, see M. Brinton Lykes, "Gender and Individualistic vs. Collectivist Bases for Notions about the Self," *Journal of Personality* 53 (1985): 356–383.

14. Daniels, "Invisible Work."

15. The classic works on the value in women's orientation toward others are Gilligan, *In a Different Voice*, and Miller, *Toward a New Psychology of Women*. For the original work on the contagion of stress and its effect on women's mental health, see Vivian Parker Makosky, "Stress and the Mental Health of Women: A Discussion of Research and Issues," in *The Mental Health of Women*, ed. M. Guttentag, S. Salasin, and D. Belle (New York: Academic Press, 1980), 117; W. Wilkins, "Social Stress and Illness in Industrial Society," in *Life Stress and Illness*, ed. E. Gunderson and R. Raye (Springfield, Ill.: Thomas, 1974), 250. The first investigator to use the concept of the costs of caring was Deborah Belle; see her "The Stress of Caring: Women as Providers of Social Support," in *Handbook of Stress: Theoretical and Clinical Aspects*, ed. L. Goldberger and S. Breznitz (New York: Free Press, 1982), 496–505. For a subsequent treatment of the issue, see Ronald C. Kes-

sler and Jane D. McLeod, "Sex Differences in Vulnerability to Undesirable Life Events," *American Sociological Review* 49 (1984): 620–631.

16. My approach here is different from that used in the narrative analysis in Chapter 3 and is adapted from the work of James Gee; see his "Units in the Production of Narrative Discourse," *Discourse Processes* 9 (1986): 391–422. Transcripts 1 and 2 are "ideal realizations" of the text, because the false starts and narrator's nonlexical utterances have been deleted to make the poetic structures more apparent. The interviewer's nonlexical utterances are also excluded, because the focus here, unlike in Chapter 3, is not on the interaction.

17. See ibid. and James Gee, lecture to MIDAS (Multi-disciplinary Discourse Analysis Seminar), Massachusetts Institute of Technology, May 13, 1987. For a classic treatment of the poetic structures in speech, see Dell Hymes, *"In vain I tried to tell you": Essays in Native American Ethnopoetics* (Philadelphia: University of Pennsylvania Press, 1981). For an analysis of how role strain in married women leads to psychological symptoms, see Catherine E. Ross and John Mirowsky, "Child Care and Emotional Adjustment to Wives' Employment," *Journal of Health and Social Behavior* 29 (1988): 127–138.

18. If Cindy's full text is compared with Transcript 1, it can be seen that the text's discourse markers, which include connectives (well, and, so) and nonlexical expressions (uh), set off the portions I have organized as episodes and stanzas in the transcript (where the connectives remain but the nonlexical expressions have been omitted).

Narratives in interviews are jointly accomplished, as discussed in Chapter 3. In this instance, the interviewer asks a question ("What happened?") that requires narrative retelling. The structure of Cindy's narrative episode about financial strain is different from the narratives in Chapter 3. Though it moves through time and contains considerable elaboration, there are only two narrative clauses (lines 37 and 66) that encode a sequence of events or "plot," in the traditional sense. Although it is true that the narrator finally resolves the conflict between welfare eligibility, job, and school with an event clause in the simple past tense ("I just quit welfare"), much of the forward movement in the story is achieved not by consequential events but by unfolding internal dilemmas. The narrative is full of verbs that encode states and processes ("my choice was," "I was worried that," "I didn't want to take a chance of"), rather than verbs that encode events that physically happened. She also uses passive verbs at key points ("I got cut way down," "being forced out of school"), conveying her sense of lack of control over the institution responsible for her dilemma—the welfare department. Because much of the action is still ongoing, she does not rely only on the past tense but uses the present tense as well ("I don't have anything to fall back on," "I really need to be looking for a new job"). She moves the action forward by coupling statements about precipitating circumstances with statements about her reactions ("number one they [welfare] cut me a whole lot / . . . so my choice at that point was . . ."). She also builds tension by repetitions, underscoring the conflict at the core of the narrative in couplet-like structures ("but um financially I just couldn't do it / there was no way I could do it"). This narrative episode is different in its structure from those in Chapter 3 precisely because it is as much about affective "events," things that the narrator feels and says to herself, as it is about "what happened" in a more objective sense. Telling about subjective experiences and events that unfold over time and even extend into the present requires a different narrative form. As I noted in Chapter 3, Labov's theory (see Labov, "The Transformation of Experience") and the relatively simple stories he analyzes do not provide an adequate model for many of the narratives told in interviews.

19. Dennie Wolf and Deborah Hicks, "The Voices within Narrative: The Development of Intertextuality in Young Children's Stories," *Discourse Processes* 12 (1989): 329–351.

20. On the tape immediately after this utterance there is a long pause, broken by what sounds like sniffling, followed by joint laughing, as if to acknowledge the emotional moment between the women.

21. Note that stanzas 1 and 7 in Transcript 1 have a similar *a b a b* structure.

22. Lines 3–29 and lines 102–106 represent enduring conditions that form the context for the two narrative episodes. Enduring portions of the discourse are *not* narrative; they last and have an ongoing quality that testifies to the durative, the progressive, the nonspecific. It is within these enduring states, which begin and end the discourse, that the two narrative episodes, the first a story about a specific past-time event involving welfare and workfare (lines 35–79), and the second a hypothetical narrative about a dream of being nurtured (lines 92–101), are embedded. Although there are episodes in between, these two narratives are counterposed and this structure attests to the essential dilemma. The tension is between the actual and the possible, the real and the wished-for. Just as Cindy's explanation pivots on thematic contrasts, so too does its form—juxtaposing the non-narrative and the narrative, the story and the dream. I am grateful to Dennie Wolf for this scheme and for her insights about the structure of Cindy's narrative generally.

23. Clifford Geertz, "Thick Description: Toward an Interpretative Theory of Culture," in *The Interpretation of Cultures* (New York: Basic Books, 1973), 3–30.

24. For more on this point, see Joy Perkins Newmann, "Gender Differ-

ences in Vulnerability to Depression," *Social Service Review* 61 (1987): 447–468.

25. See "Women, Families and Poverty: An Alternative Policy Agenda for the Nineties," Working Seminar on Employment, Welfare and Poverty, Institute for Policy Studies, 1987. For other analyses of the problem and some similar recommendations, see Garfinkel and McLanahan, *Single Mothers and Their Children;* Sidel, *Women and Children Last,* chap. 10.

26. Some scholars have argued that the CES-D items scale differently for women and men, which may partially account for these results. See Virginia A. Clark, Carol S. Aneshensel, Ralph R. Frerichs, and Timothy M. Morgan, "Analysis of Effects of Sex and Age in Response to Items on the CES-D Scale," *Psychiatry Research* 5 (1981): 171–181. Also, the measure may be tapping dysphoric mood states rather than a depressive syndrome. One investigator found that when item in a scale similar to the CES-D are disaggregated, women have more sadness (dysphoric mood) and men have more worthlessness, guilt, and suicidal thoughts (depressive syndrome). See Newmann, "Gender Differences in Vulnerability."

27. Rick is in a very different social class position from Cindy, an important distinction if we were directly comparing their symptom profiles, since social class is the most important predictor of distress. The focus here is on how women and men express distress through language, however, and Rick and Cindy are emblematic cases for this more general point.

28. Dennie Wolf, pers. comm., 1988.

29. Ibid. The listener's question asks about a feeling state, and the teller's response is to tell about this state. It would be difficult to tell a story in this context, though Rick could have moved from a general description of feelings to an illustration of a particular instance when they were particularly intense, as Al did, for example (see Chapter 3). But Rick's point is not that feelings turned the tide, so this strategy would not have been appropriate.

30. It could be argued that an anxiety scale might have better picked up men's modes, though previous research in psychiatric epidemiology suggests that anxiety and depression are difficult to discriminate in general population samples. See Link and Dohrenwend, "Formulating Hypotheses."

31. The estimate for heavy drinkers in the sample is probably conservative, because it counts only those who brought drinking up spontaneously (the interview schedule did not include a direct question about it). The finding that divorced men are more likely than divorced women to be problem drinkers and risk-takers has been demonstrated in large-scale surveys. See Debra Umberson, "Family Status and Health Behaviors: Social Control as a Dimension of Social Integration," *Journal of Health and Social Behavior* 28 (1987): 306–319.

32. On alcohol mitigating depression, see Weissman and Klerman, "Sex

Differences in Depression." For a review of depression as a cause of drinking, see Harold M. Schmeck, "Depression and Anxiety Seen as Cause of Much Addiction," *New York Times*, November 15, 1988.

33. For more on this point, see E. M. Hetherington, M. Cox, and R. Cox, "Divorced Fathers," *Family Coordinator* 25 (1976): 417–428; Gay C. Kitson and H. Raschke, "Divorce Research: What We Know, What We Need to Know," *Journal of Divorce* 4 (1981): 1–38; Weiss, *Going It Alone*.

34. Frank F. Furstenberg, Christine Winquist Nord, James L. Patterson, Nicholas Zill, "The Life Course of Children of Divorce: Marital Disruption and Parental Contact," *American Sociological Review* 48 (1983): 656–668.

35. For more on this point, see Naomi Gerstel, Catherine Kohler Riessman, and Sarah Rosenfield, "Explaining the Symptomatology of Separated and Divorced Women and Men: The Role of Material Conditions and Social Networks," *Social Forces* 64 (1985): 84–101; Beth E. Vanfossen, "Sex Differences in the Mental Health Effects of Spouse Support and Equity," *Journal of Health and Social Behavior* 22 (1981): 130–143.

36. Others have also found that men experience depression over job issues. See Pearlin, "Sex Roles and Depression"; Lenore S. Radloff and Donald S. Rae, "Susceptibility and Precipitating Factors in Depression: Sex Differences and Similarities," *Journal of Abnormal Psychology* 88 (1979): 174–181. The finding suggests that women and men experience depression in different contexts. For more on this point, see Eve S. Chevron, Donald M. Quinlan, and Sidney J. Blatt, "Sex Roles and Gender Differences in the Experience of Depression," *Journal of Abnormal Psychology* 87 (1978): 680–683; Allan F. Chino and Dean Funabiki, "A Cross-Validation of Sex Differences in the Expression of Depression," *Sex Roles* 11 (1984): 175–187; Lynda W. Warren, "Male Intolerance of Depression: A Review with Implications for Psychotherapy," *Clinical Psychology Review* 3 (1983): 147–156. For more on the general question of the effects of divorce on work life, see Faye Crosby, "Divorce and Work Life among Women Managers," in *The Experience and Meaning of Work in Women's Lives*, ed. N. L. Chester and H. Grossman (Hillsdale, N.J.: Erlbaum, 1990), 121–142.

37. Robert May argues that the theme of destructiveness in men's psychology is the "kernel of a character style involving the denial of hurt, the compensatory assertion of power, and an aversion to the 'feminine' qualities of attachment and tenderness." This originates in the boy's turn away from the mother, because he cannot *be* a mother (or, as other psychoanalysts have formulated, from the boy's resolution of the oedipal crisis). See Robert May, "Concerning a Psychoanalytic View of Maleness," in *Toward a New Psychology of Men*, ed. Friedman and Lerner, 189. For another viewpoint that emphasizes how men's ambivalence toward women affects adult heterosexual

relationships and divorce, see Chodorow, *Reproduction of Mothering;* idem, "Divorce, Oedipal Asymmetries."

38. Arthur Kleinman and Joan Kleinman, "Somatization: The Interconnections in Chinese Society among Culture, Depressive Experiences, and the Meaning of Pain," in *Culture and Depression*, ed. A. Kleinman and B. Good (Berkeley: University of California Press, 1985), 429–490. Regarding gender and physical illness after separation, research by psychoimmunologists suggests that divorced men's immunological systems do not function as well as married men's, making them more vulnerable to a range of infectious diseases. Women appear to do better. See Janice K. Kiecolt-Glaser, Susan Kennedy, Susan Malkoff, Laura Fisher, Carl E. Speicher, and Ronald Glaser, "Marital Discord and Immunity in Males," *Psychosomatic Medicine* 50 (1988): 213–229.

39. For more on the general topic, see *The Social Construction of Emotions*, ed. Harré. For more on men's patterns of displaying emotions, and the infrequency of crying, see Jack W. Sattel, "The Inexpressive Male: Tragedy or Sexual Politics," *Social Problems* 23 (1976): 469–477; Catherine E. Ross and John Mirowsky, "Men Who Cry," *Social Psychology Quarterly* 47 (1984): 138–146.

40. This point is made in passing by Kitson and Raschke, "Divorce Research."

41. For more on the gender bias in rating scales of psychological distress, see Clark et al., "Analysis of Effects of Sex"; Newmann, "Gender Differences in Vulnerability." Another problem with the quantitative measures of emotional distress used in epidemiological research is that they are acontextual. The typical format includes a series of declarative statements (such as "I felt lonely" or "I had crying spells") that the interviewee is asked to rate in frequency in the last week. Yet I found that when women and men talk spontaneously about their feeling states, feelings seemed to be evoked by particular events and situations, such as seeing the spouse with someone else or (for men) memories of helping children with homework or putting them to bed. For interviewees, the relevant unit is the situational context, whereas the unit of analysis for the quantitative mental health researcher is the frequency that the symptom was experienced, irrespective of what provoked it or whether the last week was at all typical. This disparity in the meaning of a "symptom" for the researcher and the researched is a major source of bias that has received little attention. For alternative approaches that build on people's own understandings of their distress, see Byron J. Good and Mary-Jo Delvecchio Good, "The Meaning of Symptoms: A Cultural Hermeneutic Model for Clinical Practice," in *The Relevance of Social Science for Medicine*, ed. L. Eisenberg and A. Kleinman (Boston: D. Reidel,

1981), 165–196; George A. Kelley, *The Psychology of Personal Constructs*, vols. 1 and 2 (New York: Norton, 1955); Arthur Kleinman, *Patients and Healers in the Context of Culture* (Berkeley: University of California Press, 1980); Williams, "The Genesis of Chronic Illness."

42. Bruce P. Dohrenwend and Barbara S. Dohrenwend, "Sex Differences in Psychiatric Disorders," *American Journal of Sociology* 81 (1976): 1447–1454.

43. Research on the CES-D scale documents that the largest female to male ratio is found on negative affect items, including crying and feeling sad. See Clark et al., "Analysis of Effects of Sex." On valuing affective experience, see Stephen Hansell and David Mechanic, "Introspectiveness and Adolescent Symptom Reporting," *Journal of Human Stress* 11 (1985): 165–176.

44. Gerald Gurin, Joseph V. Veroff, and Sheila Feld, *Americans View Their Mental Health* (New York: Basic Books, 1960), 210.

45. Warren, "Male Intolerance of Depression," 151.

46. On gender and emotions, see Arlie Russell Hochschild, *The Managed Heart* (Berkeley: University of California Press, 1983); idem, "Attending to, Codifying, and Managing Feelings: Sex Differences in Love," *Feminist Frontiers: Rethinking Sex, Gender, and Society*, ed. L. Richardson and V. Taylor (Reading, Mass.: Addison-Wesley, 1983), 250–262.

47. Riessman and Gerstel, "Marital Dissolution and Health."

48. Joy P. Newmann, "Gender, Life Strains, and Depression," *Journal of Health and Social Behavior* 27 (1986): 163.

5. Starting a New Life

1. Marris, *Loss and Change*, 1987 ed., xi.

2. Irving Zola suggests that we all carry around "missing pieces," though some types, such as disabilities, may be more visible. We often construct our lives in a way that hides them, making them invisible to others' view. See Irving K. Zola, *Missing Pieces: A Chronicle of Living with a Disability* (Philadelphia: Temple University Press, 1982).

3. Antonovsky, *Unraveling the Mystery of Health*, 12.

4. This point, intuitively obvious, is supported by surveys of mental health. See Morton Beiser, "Components and Correlates of Mental Well-Being," *Journal of Health and Social Behavior* 15 (1974): 320–327; Gurin, Veroff, and Feld, *Americans View Their Mental Health*; Daniel Offer and Melvin Sabshin, *Normality: Theoretical and Clinical Concepts of Mental Health*, rev. ed. (New York: Basic Books, 1974).

5. For a discussion of women's psychological dependency, see Irene P. Stiver, "The Meanings of 'Dependency' in Female-Male Relationships,"

Works in Progress Series, Stone Center for Developmental Services and Studies, Wellesley College, 1984. For a discussion of the myth of self-sufficiency in dual-career couples, see Hertz, *More Equal Than Others;* Rosanna Hertz, "Dual-Career Couples and the American Dream: Self-Sufficiency and Achievement," *Journal of Comparative Family Studies*, forthcoming.

6. For more on this aspect of American culture, see Bellah et al., *Habits of the Heart*.

7. Ibid., 93.

8. Robert W. White, "Motivation Reconsidered: The Concept of Competence," *Psychological Review* 66 (1959): 297–333.

9. See ibid. for a review of Piaget's research on this topic.

10. Philip Blumstein and Pepper Schwartz, *American Couples* (New York: Morrow, 1983); Jan Pahl, "The Allocation of Money and the Structuring of Inequality within Marriage," *Sociological Review* 31 (1983): 237–262; Constantina Safilios-Rothschild, "The Study of Family Power Structure: A Review of 1960–69," *Journal of Marriage and the Family* 32 (1970): 539–551.

11. For an empirical study just on this topic, see Crosby, "Divorce and Work Life."

12. For more on the changes in women's and men's social networks after divorce, see Gerstel, "Divorce and Kin Ties"; idem, "Divorce, Gender, and Social Integration."

13. Previous research suggests that in middle-class marriages, especially, couple friendships originate in husbands' interests and work. See Nicholas Babchuk, "Primary Friends and Kin: The Associations of Middle-Class Couples," *Social Forces* 43 (1965): 483–493; Nicholas Babchuk and Alan P. Bates, "The Primary Relations of Middle-Class Couples: A Study of Male Dominance," *American Sociological Review* 28 (1963): 377–384; Robert R. Bell, *Worlds of Friendship* (Beverly Hills: Sage, 1981).

14. For a classic sociological treatment of secrets in social life, see Georg Simmel, *Sociology of Georg Simmel*, ed. K. H. Wolf (New York: Free Press, 1950), 330–338.

15. White women receive powerful socialization for dependency, and consequently the "fear of being alone" is often an impediment to a decision to end a marriage.

16. For more on women and ritual in families, see Joan Laird, "Women and Ritual in Family Therapy," in *Rituals and Family Therapy*, ed. E. Imber-Black, J. Roberts, and R. Whiting (New York: W. W. Norton, 1988), 331–362.

17. Miller, "Psychological Recovery."

18. The classic text on this topic is Erik H. Erikson, *Identity: Youth and Crisis* (New York: Norton, 1968). For a study of relationship disillusion and identity change in women, with types of response, see Julianne Baker,

"Women's Identity and Relationship Breakdown: A Phenomenological Study" (honors thesis, Department of Psychology and Education, Mount Holyoke College, 1985).

19. Gilligan, *In a Different Voice;* Judith Jordan, "Empathy and Self Boundaries," Works in Progress Series, Stone Center for Developmental Services and Studies, Wellesley College, 1984; Alexandra Kaplan, "The 'Self-in-Relation': Implications for Depression in Women," Works in Progress Series, Stone Center, Wellesley College, 1984; Janet Surrey, "Self-in-Relation: A Theory of Women's Development," Works in Progress Series, Stone Center, Wellesley College, 1985.

20. The exaggeration of gender differences and the blurring of class and race distinctions are a consequence of feminist theories that posit affiliation as a characteristic of women. For more on alpha bias in gender typifications, see Rachel T. Hare-Mustin and Jeanne Marecek, "The Meaning of Difference: Gender Theory, Postmodernism, and Psychology," *American Psychologist* 43 (1988): 455–464. On adaptation to subordination, see Miller, *Toward a New Psychology of Women*, 9–12. On "learned helplessness," see Lenore Radloff and Megan K. Monroe, "Sex Differences in Helplessness—With Implications for Depression," in *Career Development and Counseling of Women*, ed. L. S. Hansen and R. S. Rapoza (Springfield, Ill.: Charles Thomas, 1978), 199–221; M. E. P. Seligman, *Helplessness: On Depression, Development and Death* (San Francisco: Freeman, 1975).

21. Sandra S. Tangri, "Implied Demand Character of the Wife's Future and Role Innovation: Patterns of Achievement among College Women," in *Women and Achievement*, ed. M. Mednick, S. Tangri, and L. Hoffman (Washington, D.C.: Hemisphere, 1975), 239–254; Elizabeth Douvan, "Sex Differences in Adolescent Character Process," *Merrill Palmer Quarterly* 6 (1960): 203–211.

22. Weiss, *Marital Separation*, 55.

23. Kohen, Brown, and Feldberg, "Divorced Mothers"; Miller, "Psychological Recovery."

24. Levinson and his colleagues argue that men have a "dream" of the kind of life they want to live, which centers on achievement at work. Although he emphasizes occupational goals, my data suggest that marriage and children are central to the realization of "the dream," as well. See Daniel J. Levinson, with Charlotte N. Darrow, Edward B. Klein, Maria H. Levinson, and Braxton McKee, *The Seasons of a Man's Life* (New York: Ballantine, 1978). For a critique of the class bias in Levinson's analysis on this point, see Rosalind Barnett and Grace K. Baruch, "Social Roles, Gender, and Psychological Distress," in *Gender and Stress*, ed. Barnett, Biener, and Baruch, 122–143.

25. On the heterogeneity of masculinities, see Tim Carrigan, Bob Connell, and John Lee, "Towards a New Sociology of Masculinity," *Theory and Society* 14 (1985): 551–604.

26. Weitzman, *Divorce Revolution*.

27. On the structural strains in marriage that shift work produces and the solutions that wives devise to ameliorate them, see Rosanna Hertz and Joy Charlton, "Making Family under a Shiftwork Schedule: Air Force Security Guards and Their Spouses," *Social Problems* 36 (1989): 491–506.

28. Robert S. Weiss, "Men and the Family," *Family Process* 24 (1975): 49–58.

29. For classic works on this topic, see Erik H. Erikson, "Identity and the Life Cycle," *Psychological Issues* 1 (1959): 1–171; Levinson et al., *Seasons of a Man's Life;* George E. Vaillant, *Adaptation to Life* (New York: Little, Brown, 1977).

30. On kin rallying, see Gerstel, "Divorce and Kin Ties"; for a classic study on how ritual brings order and meaning, see Barbara Myerhoff, *Number Our Days* (New York: Simon & Schuster, 1978).

31. For a somewhat different perspective on men's leisure and spending, see Barbara Ehrenreich, *The Hearts of Men: American Dreams and the Flight from Commitment* (New York: Anchor/Doubleday, 1983). On the significance of sports for men, see Michael Messner, "The Life of a Man's Seasons: Male Identity in the Life Course of the Jock," in *Changing Men: New Directions in Research on Men and Masculinity*, ed. M. S. Kimmel (Beverly Hills: Sage, 1987), 53–67.

32. Emile Durkheim, *Suicide: A Study in Sociology* (1897; New York: Free Press, 1951). For a more contemporary treatment of the problem, including data on how marriage and the presence of children in the home deter behaviors that carry health risks for men, see Umberson, "Family Status and Health Behaviors."

33. Marc E. Mishkind, Judith Rodin, Lisa R. Silberstein, and Ruth H. Striegel-Moore, "The Embodiment of Masculinity: Cultural, Psychological, and Behavioral Dimensions," in *Changing Men*, ed. Kimmel, 37–52. On the presentation of a new self through bodily change after leaving a role (including divorce), see Helen Rose Fuchs Ebaugh, *Becoming an Ex: The Process of Role Exit* (Chicago: University of Chicago Press, 1988), 154.

34. Michael S. Kimmel, "Rethinking 'Masculinity': New Directions in Research," in *Changing Men*, ed. Kimmel, 9–24.

35. There is a large literature that documents that women serve as confidantes for men, just as they do for other women—another form of "invisible work." See Daniels, "Invisible Work." See also Sattel, "Inexpressive Male"; Pamela M. Fishman, "Interaction: The Work Women Do," in *Women*

and Work, ed. R. Kahn-Hut, A. Daniels, And R. Colvard (New York: Oxford University Press, 1982), 170–180. For more on divorced men's patterns of dating compared to women's, see Spanier and Thompson, *Parting*.

36. For more on this point, see Gerstel, "Divorce and Kin Ties."

37. For more on fathers' relationships with children after divorce, see Kristine M. Rosenthal and Harry F. Keshet, *Fathers without Partners: A Study of Fathers and the Family after Marital Separation* (Totowa, N.J.: Rowman & Littlefield, 1981); Spanier and Thompson, *Parting;* Weiss, *Marital Separation;* idem, *Going It Alone.*

38. On maintenance of social ties, see Alan Booth, "Sex and Social Participation," *American Sociological Review* 37 (1972): 183–192; Alice Rossi, "Life Span Theories and Women's Lives," *Signs* 6 (1980): 4–32; Micaela di Leonardo, "The Female World of Cards and Holidays: Women, Families, and the Work of Kinship," *Signs* 12 (1987): 440–453. For a more detailed analysis of the social networks of men in this sample, see Gerstel, "Divorce and Kin Ties"; idem, "Divorce, Gender, and Social Integration."

39. Ibid.; Bell, *Worlds of Friendship.*

40. On gender and introspection, see Hansell and Mechanic, "Introspectiveness."

41. Those interviewed were not directly asked about counseling, but it was coded when it was spontaneously mentioned. Nearly two-thirds (slightly more women than men) indicated that they had sought help from a mental health professional or a member of the clergy at some point in the separation process. Although this is a remarkably high proportion (this may be because the sample is from the Northeast), it is similar to other studies of the divorced. For example, see Robert A. Caldwell, Bernard L. Bloom, and William F. Hodges, "Sex Differences in Separation and Divorce," in *Social and Psychological Problems of Women: Prevention and Crisis Intervention*, ed. A. U. Rickel, M. Gerrard, I. Iscoe (New York: Hemisphere Publishing Corp, 1984).

42. On women's "confiding," see Deborah Belle, "Gender Differences in the Social Moderators of Stress," in *Gender and Stress*, ed. Barnett, Biener, and Baruch, 257–277; Fisher, *To Dwell among Friends.*

43. Joseph H. Pleck and Jack Sawyer, *Men and Masculinity* (Englewood Cliffs, N.J.: Prentice-Hall, 1974).

44. Vaughn argues that the effects of divorce vary, depending on whether the person initiated the break-up or not. See Diane Vaughn, *Uncoupling: Turning Points in Intimate Relationships* (New York: Oxford University Press, 1986). I did not find a relationship between who made the decision and level of depression. Determining who took the initiative is difficult, because it involves interviewees' interpretations and may bear only a small relationship to what "really" happened.

45. Traditionally, more members of the middle class than the working class seek psychotherapy. For a review, see Bruce Link, "Reward Systems of Psychotherapy: Implication for Inequities in Service Delivery," *Journal of Health and Social Behavior* 24 (1983): 61–69. For another discussion of the culture of psychotherapy and its class bias, see Anne Parsons, "Cultural Barriers to Insight and the Structural Reality of Transference," idem, *Belief, Magic and Anomie* (New York: Free Press, 1951).

46. Marris, *Loss and Change*, 1987 ed., xiii.

47. Robert W. White, *Lives in Progress*, 2d ed. (New York: Holt, Rinehart and Winston, 1966), 380. For classic work on adaptation, see H. Hartmann, *Ego Psychology and the Problem of Adaptation* (New York: International Universities Press, 1958); for a review, see Marie Jahoda, *Current Concepts of Positive Mental Health* (New York: Basic Books, 1958). Robert White refers to the infant's process of discovering and exercising competence as the discovery of "joy in being a cause"; see White, "Ego and Reality in Psychoanalytic Theory," *Psychological Issues* 3, monograph 11 (1963): 185. See also idem, "Motivation Reconsidered."

48. Marris, *Loss and Change*, 1987 ed., xii. For a sociological discussion of adult psychological development, see Dale Dannefer, "Adult Development and Social Theory: A Paradigmatic Reappraisal," *American Sociological Review* 49 (1984): 100–116. On contemporary U.S. ideological categories about the self, see Bellah et al., *Habits of the Heart*; Herbert J. Gans, *Middle American Individualism: The Future of Liberal Democracy* (New York: Free Press, 1988); Edward E. Sampson, "The Debate on Individualism," *American Psychologist* 43 (1988): 15–22.

49. Levinson et al., *Seasons of a Man's Life*, 245–249.

50. Weiss, *Going It Alone*, 263; Judith Wallerstein and Joan Berlin Kelly, *Surviving the Breakup* (New York: Basic Books, 1980), and for a follow-up of the cases in Wallerstein and Kelly, see Wallerstein and Blakeslee, *Second Chances*; for survey data showing separated women to be happier than separated men, see David A. Chiriboga, John Roberts, and Judith A. Stein, "Psychological Well-Being during Marital Separation," *Journal of Divorce* 2 (1978): 91–96; Angus Campbell, Phillip Converse, and Willard Rodgers, *The Quality of American Life* (New York: Russell Sage, 1976), 438.

51. Monica Briscoe, "Sex Differences in Psychological Well-Being," *Psychological Medicine*, monograph supplement 1 (1982).

52. On gender and satisfaction in marriage, see Campbell, Converse, and Rodgers, *Quality of American Life*. On gender roles and mental health, see Walter R. Gove, "Sex, Marital Status, and Mental Illness," *Social Forces* 51 (1972): 34–55; Walter R. Gove and Jeanette R. Tudor, "Adult Sex Roles and Mental Illness," *American Journal of Sociology* 78 (1973): 812–835; for a different analysis, see Constance A. Nathanson, "Illness and the Feminine Role:

A Theoretical Review," *Social Science and Medicine* 9 (1975): 57–72, and Constance A. Nathanson, "Social Roles and Health Status among Women: The Significance of Employment," *Social Science and Medicine* 14A (1980): 463–471; Mary Clare Lennon, "Sex Differences in Distress: The Impact of Gender and Work Roles," *Journal of Health and Social Behavior* 28 (1987): 290–305. On health benefits of marriage, see Riessman and Gerstel, "Marital Dissolution and Health." On "his" versus "her" marriage, see Bernard, *Future of Marriage*. On importance of family roles to men, see Joseph H. Pleck, *Working Wives/Working Husbands* (Beverly Hills: Sage, 1985); Joseph Veroff, Elizabeth Douvan, and Richard A. Kulka, *The Inner American* (New York: Basic Books, 1981).

53. On the concept of "greedy institutions" in general, see Lewis Coser with Rose Coser, *Greedy Institutions* (New York: Free Press, 1974), 4. For evidence of social class differences and friendship, see Bell, *Worlds of Friendship;* Caplow et al., *Middletown Families;* Rubin, *Worlds of Pain.* On constraints posed to friendship by children, see Fisher, *To Dwell among Friends.* For an analysis very similar to mine, see Gerstel, "Divorce, Gender, and Social Integration."

54. Barnett, Biener, and Baruch, *Gender and Stress*, 358. The authors do not distinguish between the socialization of black and white women. The former are encouraged from an early age to be self-sufficient and not to give over control to men. See Jacqueline Jones, *Labor of Love, Labor of Sorrow: Black Women, Work, and the Family from Slavery to the Present* (New York: Basic Books, 1985). On control and positive states of mind, see Judith Rodin, "Aging and Health: Effects of the Sense of Control," *Science* 233 (1986): 1271–1276.

55. Barnett and Baruch, "Social Roles, Gender, and Psychological Distress."

56. White, "Motivation Reconsidered," 391; Miller, "Psychological Recovery," 351, 352. On divorce as training ground in competence for women, see Kristen Walsh Haggman Mitchell, "Sense of Competence and Well-Being in Suburban Divorced and Remarried Mothers" (Ph.D dissertation, Graduate School of Education, Harvard University, 1979).

57. Gerstel, Riessman, and Rosenfield, "Explaining the Symptomatology."

6. Divorce Is Here to Stay

1. Burke, *Permanence and Change*, 38.

2. Joseph R. Gusfield, *The Culture of Public Problems* (Chicago: University of Chicago Press, 1981).

3. Lawrence Stone argues that "untrammeled individualism" and the weakening of formal religion are the principal causes of the escalation in di-

vorce rates over the last century. Yet he also makes the point that divorce is the functional equivalent of death (see Stone, *The Family, Sex, and Marriage*, 46). An alternative argument could be made for serial polygamy as an essential feature of social life, which is realized either through death of a spouse or divorce, depending on historical and cultural circumstances.

4. Stone, "The Road to Polygamy," 15.

5. For a demographic analysis of remarriage, see Cherlin, *Marriage, Divorce, Remarriage*; Paul C. Glick, "Marriage, Divorce, and Living Arrangements: Prospective Changes," *Journal of Family Issues* 5 (1984): 7–26; Paul C. Glick and Sung-Ling Lin, "Recent Changes in Divorce and Remarriage," *Journal of Marriage and the Family* 48 (1986): 737–747.

6. The idea that individuals remarry for "security," in all its guises, was the response given to me recently when I posed the question to some women social scientists, who shall remain nameless. I thank them for their insights about why they married when other options were clearly available.

7. Marris, *Loss and Change*; Rapp, "Family and Class in Contemporary America," 170; Goode, *Women in Divorce*; Ann Goetting, "The Six Stations of Remarriage: Developmental Tasks of Remarriage after Divorce," *Family Relations* 31 (1982): 213–222.

8. Furstenberg and Spanier, *Recycling the Family*.

9. Hertz, *More Equal than Others*. On the consequences of the conflict between employment and family for women, see Hochschild, *Second Shift*. On the more general issues, see Naomi Gerstel and Harriet Gross, eds., *Families and Work* (Philadelphia: Temple University Press, 1987).

10. Furstenberg and Spanier, *Recycling the Family*, 192. On rate of divorce in second marriages, see U.S. National Center for Health Statistics, Vital and Health Statistics, "National Estimates of Marital Dissolution and Survivorship," series 3, no. 19 (Washington, D.C.: U.S. Government Printing Office, 1980). Another view of remarriage is that it is an incomplete institution. Andrew Cherlin argues that there is institutional ambiguity in remarriage—that is, there are no common guidelines for coping with problems, including kin relations (see Cherlin, "Remarriage as an Incomplete Institution," *American Journal of Sociology* 84 [1978]: 634–650). In many ways, the situation is like that of remarried families in the nineteenth century; the death of a young spouse and the remarriage of the surviving one resulted in complex kin ties. Yet with divorce, because the former spouse has a continuing presence in the family, the process is different (and often tension-filled), even though the structure is similar.

11. On gender and happiness in second marriages, see Norval D. Glenn, "The Well-Being of Persons Remarried after Divorce," *Journal of Family Issues* 2 (1981): 61–75; Lynn K. White, "Sex Differentials in the Effects of Remarriage on Global Happiness," *Journal of Marriage and the Family* 41

(1979): 869–876. On redivorce rates of women and men, see Glick, "Marriage, Divorce, and Living Arrangements," 97–99.

12. Although remarriage is not taken into account, Blumstein and Schwartz studied cohabiting heterosexual couples and gay and lesbian couples, and noted many points of contrast with the married. See *American Couples*. On single life as a transitory status, see Peter Stein, ed., *Single Life: Unmarried Adults in Social Context* (New York: St. Martin's Press, 1981).

13. On remarriage of educationally advantaged women, see Glick, "Marriage, Divorce, and Living Arrangements"; quotation at 96.

14. William Chafe, *Women and Equality: Changing Patterns in American Culture* (New York: Oxford University Press, 1977), 5, 3. Although they do not focus particularly on divorced women, there are studies of communities of women. See Arlie Russell Hochschild, *The Unexpected Community: Portrait of an Old Age Subculture* (Berkeley: University of California Press, 1973); Susan Krieger, *The Mirror Dance: Identity in a Women's Community* (Philadelphia: Temple University Press, 1983).

Appendix: A Narrative about Methods

1. Although this dual focus may be somewhat unusual in a discussion of methods, there is a long tradition in sociology that focuses on the process of doing research and the transformation of the researcher. For examples, see William Foote Whyte, *Street Corner Society*, enlarged ed. (Chicago: University of Chicago Press, 1955), appendix; Phillip E. Hammond, ed., *Sociologists at Work: Essays on the Craft of Social Research* (New York: Basic Books, 1964); John Van Maanen, *Tales of the Field: On Writing Ethnography* (Chicago: Univeristy of Chicago Press, 1988); Robin Williams, "A Neglected Form of Symbolic Interactionism in Sociological Work: Book Talks Back to Author," *American Sociologist* 11 (1976): 94–103; Zola, *Missing Pieces*, prologue, 2–7.

2. For example, see Spanier and Thompson, *Parting*.

3. For more on behavioral bias in the standard approach to interviewing, see Mishler, *Research Interviewing*, chap. 1; he notes that questions are not always asked as written in survey interviews, even though the assumption is that everyone receives the same "stimulus."

4. For more on the CES-D scale, including a list of its items, see Lenore Radloff, "Sex Differences in Depression: The Effects of Occupation and Marital Status," *Sex Roles* 1 (1975): 249–265. To test the internal consistency of the scale, we used Cronbach's alpha. See Lee Cronbach, *Essentials of Psychological Testing*, 2d ed. (New York: Harper & Row, 1960).

5. As Mishler notes in *Research Interviewing*, traditional interviewing prac-

tice teaches respondents to restrict their answers. The interviewer controls meaning by determining what is considered a relevant or "correct" response to a question. When respondents qualify their answers, these elaborations may not be considered relevant and thus may not be recorded by the interviewer or taken into account when coding. If there is a problem, it is usually defined as the respondent's—he or she "misunderstood" the question. In addition, investigators assume that all respondents understand a question in the same way. If not, the problem is defined as measurement "error." In all these ways, the voice of the researcher dominates the voice of the subject. Others have noted that respondents can talk at length about topics that are important to them. For a discussion that emphasizes how the interviewer can maintain "objectivity and nonintrusiveness" by adapting clinical interviewing techniques, see Ebaugh, *Becoming an Ex*, Appendix B (p. 218). The assumptions of her approach contrast sharply with Mishler's.

6. For more on the advantages and disadvantages of the insider role in interaction, see Robert K. Merton, "Insiders and Outsiders: A Chapter in the Sociology of Knowledge," *American Journal of Sociology* 78 (1972): 9–47.

7. Stephen J. Gould, *The Mismeasure of Man* (New York: Norton, 1981), 21. For a discussion of the process of engagement in field work and what happens to the researcher in the course of conducting a study, see Arlene Kaplan Daniels, "Engagement and Ethical Responsibility in Field Work," *Newsletter*, Society for the Study of Social Problems, vol. 16, no. 3 (1985). For a detailed account of how one investigator transformed analytic distance and estrangement from her data to empathy with and connection to those she studied, see Susan Krieger, "Beyond 'Subjectivity': The Use of the Self in Social Science," *Qualitative Sociology* 8 (1985): 309–324.

8. Feminist critics have taken issue with the detached model of doing science. See Evelyn Fox Keller, *Reflections on Gender and Science* (New Haven: Yale University Press, 1985); Ann Oakley, "Interviewing Women: A Contradiction in Terms," in *Doing Feminist Research*, ed. Helen Roberts (Boston: Routledge & Kegan Paul, 1981), 30–61. Others who do not identify themselves as feminists also argue for a more engaged and even emancipatory model of research. See Yvonna S. Lincoln and Egon G. Guba, *Naturalistic Inquiry* (Beverly Hills: Sage, 1985); Patti Lather, "Issues of Validity in Openly Ideological Research: Between a Rock and a Soft Place," *Interchange* 17 (1986): 63–84.

9. For a summary, see Kathy Charmaz, "The Grounded Theory Method: An Explication and Interpretation," in *Contemporary Field Research: A Collection of Readings*, ed. Robert M. Emerson (Boston: Little, Brown, 1983), 109–126. For more detail, see Barney G. Glaser and Anselm L. Strauss, *The Discovery of Grounded Theory: Strategies for Qualitative Research* (New York:

Aldine, 1967); Anselm L. Strauss, *Qualitative Analysis for Social Scientists* (New York: Cambridge University Press, 1987).

10. Anselm Strauss, "Codes and Coding," paper given at Eleventh World Congress of Sociology, New Delhi, India, August 1986.

11. Mishler, *Research Interviewing*.

12. For a rare discussion of the writing-up process, including various narrative conventions for presenting findings and their epistomological assumptions, see John Van Maanen, *Tales of the Field: On Writing Ethnography* (Chicago: University of Chicago Press, 1988). For an analysis of scientific writing as a form of rhetoric, see Joseph Gusfield, "The Literary Rhetoric of Science: Comedy and Pathos in Drinking Driving Research," *American Sociological Review* 41 (1976): 16–34. For a feminist analysis of the meaning and use of qualitative data, see Marjorie L. DeVault, "Talking and Listening from Women's Standpoint: Feminist Strategies for Analyzing Interview Data," paper presented at a meeting of the Society for the Study of Symbolic Interaction, New York, August 1986; Marianne A. Paget, "Unlearning to Not Speak," *Human Studies*, forthcoming.

13. Paul Rabinow and William W. Sullivan, "The Interpretive Turn: Emergence of an Approach," in *Interpretive Social Science: A Reader*, ed. P. Rabinow and W. M. Sullivan (Berkeley: University of California Press, 1979), 12.

Index